Charles H. Haeseler

Across the Atlantic

Charles H. Haeseler

Across the Atlantic

ISBN/EAN: 9783337256593

Printed in Europe, USA, Canada, Australia, Japan

Cover: Foto ©Andreas Hilbeck / pixelio.de

More available books at **www.hansebooks.com**

ACROSS

THE ATLANTIC.

LETTERS FROM

FRANCE, SWITZERLAND, GERMANY, ITALY,
AND ENGLAND.

BY

CHARLES H. HAESELER, M.D.

PHILADELPHIA:
T. B. PETERSON & BROTHERS;
306 CHESTNUT STREET.

Entered according to Act of Congress, in the year 1868, by
CHARLES H. HAESELER, M.D.,
In the Clerk's Office of the District Court of the United States, in and for the Eastern District of Pennsylvania.

FROM THE MINER'S JOURNAL.

"ACROSS THE ATLANTIC."—This is the title of a book of four hundred pages, just issued from the press of Messrs. T. B. Peterson & Brothers, Philadelphia. It contains a series of letters from France, Switzerland, Germany, Italy, and England, written by Dr. Charles H. Haeseler, of this place, during a tour of Europe made by him last year. Nearly all of the letters appeared originally in the "MINER'S JOURNAL," but they have been rewritten and enlarged materially, so that the form in which they appear in the book, is more complete and interesting than that in which they were originally published. Of the great merit of these letters of Dr. Haeseler, it would be superfluous for us to speak in this community, where they were read with so much interest by all classes during their first publication. Their freshness and originality, combined with the varied information they contained, were themes of constant commendation, and there was but one opinion, that these letters were decidedly the best which had appeared for years. It will be a source of gratification, we are sure, to many who have read and admired Dr. Haeseler's letters, to know that they are now preserved in the enduring form of a neat, well-printed book, and we do not doubt that the work will have an extended circulation, not only in this county, but in Boston, New York, Philadelphia, and all the other cities of the Union, when it shall become known; and, in fact, everywhere where the "JOURNAL" is taken, and where the letters published in its columns have been read and admired. We feel great pleasure in announcing the appearance of "Across the Atlantic." It is published in a beautiful duodecimo volume, printed on the finest paper, and bound in cloth, in the best and strongest manner, with gilt back and side, and is sold at the low price of Two Dollars a copy.

TO

CHARLES WITTIG, M.D.,

OF PHILADELPHIA,

THE FRIEND AND COMPATRIOT OF MY FATHER, AND ONE OF
THE MOST CHERISHED PRECEPTORS OF MY YOUTH,
THIS VOLUME IS AFFECTIONATELY INSCRIBED,

IN TESTIMONY OF

UNFEIGNED RESPECT FOR HIS TALENTS
AND PHILANTHROPY.

THE AUTHOR.

CONTENTS.

LETTER I.

The Voyage — Incidents at Sea — The Steamer — Our Passengers — A Romance at Sea — A Bear on Board — Amusements on Board — Life on the Ocean Wave — The Jolly Smoking-Room — Music on Board — Sabbath — Arrival at Havre — First Impressions — The Wines — Railroads — Arrival at Paris. 33

LETTER II.

Flitting about Paris; Its Streets; Houses — Shops of Paris — Sculpture — Garden of Plants — Its Museums — Cathedral of Notre Dame — Place Vendôme — Bird's-Eye View of Paris — Sunday in Paris — Hacks and Carriages — The Servants — Operas, Theatres.. 50

LETTER III.

The Grand Exposition — It is no Failure — Its Machinery Department — Mechanical Department — Its Saloons — Chinese Theatres — Negro Minstrels — American Contributions — Department of Fine Arts — Statue of the Dying Napoleon — Department of Jewelry — Dry Goods — Agricultural Department — Building of U. S. Sanitary Commission — Reserved

(xxi)

Garden — Aquarium in the Cave — Notabilities who visit the Exposition — M. A. F.'s (My American Friend) Opinion of the Exposition — The Rush for the Exposition — Expenses of Living — Princes and Potentates in Paris............................ 62

LETTER IV.

Amusements of the Parisians — About the Theatres — Romeo and Juliet, L'Africaine — Cafés Chantants — The Love of Flowers — The Races at the Bois de Boulogne — Grand Turnout — Balloon Ascension — A French Thimble-rigger — Imperial Palaces — The Soldiers — Police System of Paris — Mystery but Safety — Paris at Night — The Wines and the Water.. 79

LETTER V.

Medical Institutions of Paris — Boulevard de Sebastopol — The Hotel Dieu — Rue de l'École de Medecine — Medical Book and Instrument Shops — Professional Reflections — The Faculté of Paris — Examinations for Medical Doctorate — Colored Students — The Latin Quarter — Drs. Velpeau and Trousseau — The Hospitals.. 91

LETTER VI.

Memory of the Great Napoleon — His Tomb — The Invalides — Louvre — Imperial Museum — Palace of the Tuileries — The Imperial Family — The Champs Elysées — Jardin Mabille — An Adventure — Farewell to Paris.. 102

LETTER VII.

The Champagne District — Strasburg, its Cathedral — The Astronomical Clock — Going up the Steeple — The Storks — On top of the Steeple—My American Friend—An Incident, Interchange of Jewels—Monuments of Strasburg—How the Women Work—Freiburg—The Black Forest—The Höllenthal—The Inventor of Gunpowder.................................... 113

LETTER VIII.

Switzerland—Zurich—The Uetliberg—The Hotel Baur au Lac—Lake Zurich—Scholastic Institutions of Zurich—Curiosities of Zurich—Amusing Incidents—Pleasant Travelling Companions—An American Anecdote, in which M. A. F. spreads himself—He spins a Yarn and speaks a Piece—Indifference to American Affairs—Telegraphs and Newspapers—Comparisons Drawn....................................... 124

LETTER IX.

Switzerland—Up Lake Zurich—Hay-making—Trout-Fishing—A Swiss Cottage—Sojourn with a Swiss Family—A Knotty Question Solved—A Band of Minstrels—Lake Zug—Sunrise from the Rigi—Lucerne—Altdorf—Wm. Tell—Bürgeln—St. Gotthard—Andermatt—Snow-balling on the Alps—Lucerne.. 187

LETTER X.

Switzerland—Berne—Its Origin—Predilection for Bruin—The Bears in the Pen—Bears all over Town—Grindelwald—The Glacier—The Ice-Grotto—A Storm on the Alps—A Night on the Alps.. 152

LETTER XI.

Switzerland—Lake Brienz—The Giesbach Waterfall—Staubbach Cascade—Interlaken—Geneva—The Turner-Fest—

xxiv   CONTENTS.

PAGE

Trip to Chamouny — Among the Alps — Over the Tête-Noir Pass to Martigny — The Castle of Chillon — Down the Lake of Geneva — Return to Zurich — En Route to Munich — An Interesting Incident at Zurich.. 163

LETTER XII.

Munich — Passion of the People for Music — Gossip about the King—Art Galleries — Distinguished Portraits — Visit to the Bronze Foundry — A Monumental Colonnade — Beer — Stuttgardt — Its Palaces and other Buildings — Carlsruhe — Baden-Baden — The Archduke's Castle — The Conversation Hall — Gaming.. 176

LETTER XIII.

Heidelberg; Its Castle — Fourth of July — The American Flag — We meet a Friend and celebrate the Day — Manheim and its Surroundings—Visit to Worms — Drive to Bensheim—Religious Meeting in the Woods — My American Friend grows Eloquent over the Recollection of a Pennsylvania Campmeeting.. 194

LETTER XIV.

Mayence; Its Fortifications — Frankfurt — Notable Houses — Imperial Hall — Wiesbaden — A Marvellous Spring — The Cursaal — Visit to the Castle of Johannisberg — Down the Rhine — Scenery, Castles, etc. — Cologne — Its Cathedral — Interesting Features of the City — Opinion of the Rhine — Cassel — University of Göttingen — Arrival at Northeim..................... 212

CONTENTS.

LETTER XV.

A German Town — Rural Life — The Dwellings — A Dignified Game of Nine-Pins—My American Friend rolls and produces a "Pumpe"—A Fine Sulphur Spring — A Dancing Hall—The Delirious Waltz—Life at the Brunnen and in the Town—Close of the Day at the Hotel Sonne.................................. 226

LETTER XVI.

Growth of Berlin — Military Spirit of Prussia — The King and Bismarck — Their Visit to Napoleon — Unter den Linden — National Library — Museums and University — The House of Alexander Von Humboldt — Blücher's Monument — The Orpheum — Zoölogical and Botanical Gardens—The River Spree — A beautiful Forest.................................. 237

LETTER XVII.

My American Friend takes a Ramble through the Streets of Berlin — Gazes in the Shop-windows and sees Something — Finds out an Address and goes in Pursuit of it — What Happens there — An Accident — Does a little Doctoring — Makes the Acquaintance of a Prussian Soldier — Some Military Talk — An Heroic Action — Description of the Battle of Langensalza.................................. 248

LETTER XVIII.

City of Leipzig — Hahnemann's Monument — Gœthe's Faust, and Auerbach's Cellar — The Book-Trade and University of Leipzig — Dresden — Treasures and Works of Art—The Green Vaults — Kaufmann's Acoustic Cabinet — The Schützenfest of the Vogelwiese — A Trip up the Elbe to Königstein — Visit to the Battlefield of Sadowa, or Königsgrätz.................................. 259

LETTER XIX.

The Austrians — Their Personal Points — The Imperial Vaults in the Church of the Capuchins — Palace of Schönbrun — University of Vienna — The General Hospital — Rokitansky, the Pathologist — Rev. Dr. Mann, of Philadelphia............ 270

LETTER XX.

Visit to a Wonderful Cave at Adelsberg — The City of Trieste — The Adriatic — The Cholera Mortality in Italy — Superstition and Ignorance of the People — Venice — Fumigation Process on entering the City — Curiosities of the Place — Milan; Its Magnificent Cathedral — The Lake of Como — From Milan to Genoa — From Genoa to Pisa, Leghorn, and Florence............ 281

LETTER XXI.

Journey through Italy — Luxuriant Vegetation — The Italians — Beggars — Art — A Visit to the Studio of Hiram Powers — My American Friend's Adventures — The Galleries, Art Models, etc. — From Florence to Rome — A Fair Snuffer — Poetical Effusion of M. A. F. — Thoughts on the Eternal City — The Cathedrals of St. Peter and St. Paul — His Holiness Pius IX. 302

LETTER XXII.

Rome — The Appian Way — The Caracall Baths — The Catacombs — Circus Maxentius — Cholera — The Diet of the Romans — Visit to the Pope's Residence — The Pantheon — In Memoriam — Raphael — Adieu to Rome — En Route to Paris — Bologna — Turin — Susa — The Mt. Cenis Pass over the Alps — Arrival at Paris.................................. 323

CONTENTS.   xxvii

LETTER XXIII.

Paris — Professor Watts' Funeral — Doctors Trousseau, Velpeau, and Nelaton — Death of the two Former — The Writer has a Spell of Sickness — The Fashions of Paris — The Opera Season — Incidents — A Musical Anecdote — My American Friend in Trouble.. 337

LETTER XXIV.

Paris — A Thrilling Incident of Parisian Life — A Query — Anecdote — Reminiscences of the First Napoleon — Cemetery of Père La Chaise — Manufactory of the Gobelin Tapestry — Hotel de Ville — Jardin D'Acclimatation — Birds, Beasts, and Fishes therein... 350

LETTER XXV.

The Railroad Depots of Europe — Departure from Paris — Crossing the Channel — Sea-Sickness — Calais and Dover — Arrival at London — Good Cheer — Comfortable once more — The Tower — St. Paul's — Under-Ground and Over-Head Railroads — Westminster Abbey — London and Paris Compared — Hospitals of London — From London to Liverpool — Meet with Friends — Voyage Home — An Incident — M. A. F.'s "Pome" on the Occasion.. 365

LETTER XXVI.

Review of my Trip — European Manners, Customs, Politics, etc. — Topography of Europe; Of England; Of Italy; Of France and Germany — Sociality of Europeans — Selfishness of Parisians — Kindness of the Austrians — The Good-Natured Munichians — Temperate Habits of Europeans — Good Behavior of the Youth — The Armies of Europe — Importance of Understanding the Languages of Europe......................... 376

LETTER XXVII.

Concluding Letter by my American Friend — A Sea-Voyage a Humbug — Discomforts of a Ship — Of Landing in a Foreign Country — Bound to be Skinned — Kid Gloves of Paris — The Liquors and Wines of Europe — Endless Sight-Seeing — Sculpture — Tumble-Down Ruins of Europe — Climbing up the Alps — The Churches — The Railroads — Nothing like America — God Bless our Country.................................. 386

APOLOGY.

IN submitting these letters to the public, I would fain make a few observations of personal import between you, gracious reader, and myself. I did not at first intend to write more than a few cursory letters, in order to obviate the necessity of numerous communications of similar contents to my personal friends. I soon, however, found the work growing upon my affections, and assuming the shape of a conversation, wherein I did all the talking, supposing that your part of it was to take place on my return home, when I should faithfully do all the listening; and thus it was that this weekly writing became less a task than a pleasant companionship between us. I sincerely hope that I have not unreasonably bored you; but if I have, it was your own fault; for you could easily have gone over to Petroleum V. Nasby, the County Conventions, the sparkling editorials, or the Marriages and Deaths, — as the journal is a *cuisinier* of unbounded capacities, and caters sumptuously for many tastes, provided, only, that they are normal.

I know that, take it all in all, I have presented an incongruous *melange* of the would-be sublime and the ridiculous; and the transitions from the one to the other have frequently been so sudden as to outrage all scholastic rules and propriety. But then my theme has been such a mutatory one, so varied and diversified in character, that it was quite impossible to preserve the even dignity of a treatise on mathematical problems, or Locke (I had almost said, Padlock) on the Human Understanding. Nor am I quite clear about the grammatical character of these writings; my recollection of Kirkham's Grammar being principally confined to the fact that it contained a chart of twenty-four, or forty-four, or a hundred and four (I have forgotten which) rules, all numbered with Roman figures, as glaring as those on the dial of a town-clock; and that this chart, when unfolded, had the appearance of the constitution, articles, and by-laws of an infallible oil company. If every boy learned as much from that grammar — including the chart — as I did, then Mr. Kirkham had better saved his brains in its construction, and written a story about the wild Indians instead — which would have been much more interesting to study. Sometimes, with rather questionable taste, the *Profession* has slipped a little profusely into these letters; and I feel a misgiving that there are those who will attribute ulterior motives to this circumstance, or at least charge me with egotism. But, indeed, they are mistaken; for the dear knows there is nothing about me to warrant or cultivate such a feeling. It was so natural and thoughtless to mix these items with the rest, that if it was an error, I sincerely hope to be forgiven. After all, there is nothing that the shoemaker understands so well as leather; and I would rather hear him talk leather all day, than a brief period of things that he knows nothing about. Sometimes an observation has gone forth that, on subsequent reflection, I would have scratched out; but when the relentless mail authorities once have these matters in hand, there remains no alternative but to telegraph; and at a hundred dollars a line, this manner of sober second thinking becomes rather an extravagant recreation. So, upon the whole, I have let things go as people get married — " for better or worse." Should I at any time have made allusions at which any person could take umbrage, I want it distinctly understood that it was always in a Pickwickian sense, and as free from malice as the genial heart of that distinguished individual. And now let me add, supposing this to be the end of my last letter from Europe, that no child ever looked forward to the advent of Christmas morning, and all its joyous associations, with more heartfelt happiness than that with which I anticipate greeting you at an early day. With this assurance, believe me, dear reader,

Yours, truly,

C. H. H.

POTTSVILLE, PA., *October*, 1868.

ACROSS THE ATLANTIC.

LETTER I.

REFLECTIONS ON A SEA-VOYAGE.

THE VOYAGE ACROSS THE ATLANTIC.—INCIDENTS OF THE PASSAGE.—HAVRE.—RAILWAY TRIP TO PARIS.—AGRICULTURAL APPEARANCES OF THE COUNTRY.—ARRIVAL IN PARIS.

PARIS, *April*, 1867.

THERE are, in the physical nature and topography of our own country, all the grandeur and sublimity of scenery; in its population, all the diversity of human caste, color and character, to afford ample material for study throughout a lifetime of travel. But there is such a strange fascination, and almost superstitious feeling associated with the circumstance of sailing across a great ocean of water, as if, when the solid earth recedes from view, the life connected with it also passed away, and we were drifting to another and a strange region; so that, while the people of the Old World are eager to learn the wonders of the western hemisphere, there is always a peculiar charm to our own minds in the recital of European travels.

I could never realize, until I crossed the Atlantic, what a brave heart, what a clear head, and what an absolute confidence in the correctness of his theory Columbus must have had when he pioneered his course through that trackless waste. In our time, a voyage across the ocean is such a common occurrence, that it is generally passed over in a hurried manner by those who write letters. But, although the dangers and duration of such a voyage are greatly diminished by the use of steam, and the strong, colossal, and magnificent proportions of our ocean steamers, yet is the distance across, and the vastness and awful sublimity of that body of water, just as great now as it was in the time of Columbus; it is just as lonely now to be on its shoreless and echoless bosom as it was then. I have stood for hours by the side of our vessel, and watched it cleaving through the deep blue waves — watched how the ceaseless paddles of the huge side-wheels piled up the wild foam of the lashed waters like great long banks of drifted snow — watched along the straight, wide track in the rear of the keel until it faded away in the far-off horizon; nothing but water to be seen — deep, dark, limitless water all around. Nothing of life, save that on board our vessel; save, also, an occasional sea-gull, that seems like a condemned spirit, or an erratic comet, doomed to soar forever through the trackless air; or a spluttering porpoise that appears to look upon our ship as a monstrous fish — rushing along in playful admiration by our side, blowing and snorting imposingly, even as a little creature courtier does before the great magnates and lordlings of the earth. Nay, but we sometimes meet a sail coming from the direction to which we are journeying, and therefore we are, after all, not quite so lonely as was that little craft, under the guidance of the discoverer of our country. Methinks I could see him, with his faithful crew — but himself the only one whose faith did not falter in the end — sailing hopefully onward in the direction of the setting sun.

Methinks I could see that ocean now, with its countless white hillocks of foam, like the froth of anger, dancing on its vast surface, where no creation of human hands had ever ventured before; where the voices of the waves and the wail of the winds commingled with the sharp flapping of those intrusive sails. Methinks I could see the astonished porpoises, and spirting black-fish, and flitting sea-gulls bewildered and amazed at the little jauntily-rigged monster that was crowding its way before the breeze, where the silvery light of the moon, and the merry twinkle of the stars, and the bright radiance of the sun had never before shone on any solid fragment. There was no smoke-stack on that vessel, leaving a long, black cloud in its wake, like the tail of a comet — if comets' tails were black and formed of soot. There was no screw under the dark hull of that ship, the rotary motion of whose spiral flanks could have propelled it forward, like those of modern days; no side-wheels, making their steady revolutions in the direction of the unknown shore. There were no Cunard, or Inman, or Transatlantic lines of ocean palaces then; and the little world of people who floated under the direction of Columbus and the winds could have no daily hope of saluting another stray world of similar character during the whole period of their voyage. Things have greatly changed since then. Your vessel now cleaves through the water like a thing of life,— puffing, groaning, rolling, and pitching, grumbling and grinding and trembling and vibrating in every fibre of its timbers; and the hand-maidens of human ingenuity — steam, and improved marine architecture — have given us the possibility to traverse the ocean in a miraculously short space of time, and under the auspices of comparative pleasure.

What a thing is an ocean steamer! It constitutes a small world in itself; and when I saw the sun set right behind our rudder, and rise again, in the morning, directly in front of the prow, I beheld, indeed, that this little world observed the system of the planets, and floated along its own true orbit. It was isolated from all other worlds by a universe of water — a small satellite of the earth; and though we were repelled from it at New York, yet in accordance with the beautiful harmony of all things, we were graciously attracted again at Havre; nor did we induce the faintest manner of an earthquake by the collision. Yet I should do our ship an injustice if I omitted to say, that it was also a huge *churn;* and the manner of, and the extent to which we were churned was at first negatively visible by the few who represented our small community at the table during meal-times. Having had great experience, the first few days, of the melancholy effect of this churning, I could grow philosophical, nay, eloquent on the subject; but I prefer not to; yet I solemnly avow, that it detracts very materially from the romance of a voyage across the

Atlantic. It is not likely that I am misunderstood — I allude most respectfully to the infinitely unpoetical subject of sea-sickness. Yet we had fair weather, with the exception of one day, when it rained, nautically speaking, cats and dogs, and sandwiched us between two sheets of the same element. Nevertheless, without any wind or apparent cause, the sea was intensely agitated for a period of three days, tossing us about in a playful manner like a mere chip; but like a chip, too, that would remain and dance about in derisive dalliance upon the surface. The captain's explanation was, that it came from the north — blamed Canada and Greenland for it — and said, he was "veree much sorree, because it decommode ze passengers von great deal."

The enginery of an ocean steamer! what a noble theme it is for reflection! What a grand sight to watch its regular and ceaseless labors — to count the fifteen revolutions which the wheels make every minute — never caught napping, never fatigued; but sometimes warming up so exceedingly by their work, that a stream of cold water must be kept playing upon their journals, to keep them from igniting the contiguous wood-work. What an intricate multiplicity of wheels, and levers, and cylinders, pistons, gauges, and valves; and yet how harmoniously they all work together! They constitute the life, the heart that advance a ship in its motion, and make it pulsate in every plank of its construction. But like animal life, this motion is kept up only by combustion; and as an interesting item to all who have the prosperity of the coal trade at heart, it may be mentioned, that an ocean steamer consumes some eighty tons of coal daily; and ours had stored, before we sailed, about eighteen hundred tons.

We have had on board a melange of all sorts of people, from almost all habitable parts; from California, South America, Canada, Cuba, the different countries of Europe, and some from the Eastern, Western, Northern and Southern States of our own country. There were among us a number of celebrities in the arts and sciences, several congressmen, and any number of gentlemen with high-sounding military titles, which some had acquired in the union and some in the rebel service. The gentle sex was well represented, at the head of which was the charming and accomplished young wife of a United States senator, and the daughter of one of our ablest statesmen. We had a little sprinkling of romance, too, that is quite worthy of being recorded. The second day of our voyage, the weather being perfectly delightful, of course everybody who was not sick was on deck; and there was the beginning of that social recognition of each other, and exchange of politeness, which grew into familiarity, and terminated, in many instances, in doubtless long and lasting friendship. Suddenly a tall and handsome gentleman was observed confronting a beautiful young German girl, whom he scrutinized closely for a few moments, and then exclaimed, "Good heavens! is this possible, Theresa?" Thus accosted, the young lady started, and riveting her attention upon him who had pronounced these words, she appeared to recognize him at once. Her cheeks became pallid with emotion, and with the ringing exclamation. "Heinrich, my brother!" she rushed into his arms in the most beautifully theatrical style imaginable. Really it was quite affecting. The explanation is briefly this: the young girl was one whom the lady of the senator before alluded to, and who had visited Europe last year, had chosen for a friend and companion during her travels in France, Switzerland and Germany, and had prevailed upon her to accompany her to America in the fall, on condition of returning with her to Europe this Spring. The gentleman, who was her brother, had left home for South America some five years ago, where he had been sent as a civil engineer, to superintend the construction of a railroad. Thence he had come to the United States, and was now on his way back to Europe. Neither knew aught of the other's whereabouts. They had been orphans for many years, but were apparently of good family, and had enjoyed the advantage of an excellent education; and both were possessed of an adventurous turn of mind. I learned these particulars from the parties themselves, with whom I subsequently became right intimately acquainted; they being from my own native country, namely, Hanover.

Carmé, the French billiard-player of great fame, who caroms on two balls around a hat placed between them on the table, or on two balls placed on two different tables, was among the number of our passengers, and was quite a lion. Speaking of lions reminds me that there was another celebrity on board in the individuality of a bear; not the Wall Street article, but a real, genuine, quadrupedal, North

American black bear. A superscription on his cage showed forth that he was in care of the American Express Company, and sent by a gentleman from Ogdensburg, New York, to Monsieur le Compte Lubersal, of Paris. What the Count intends to do with this unique pet is not specified; perhaps he wants to "render" him, scent him with bergamot, and use him for a toilet article. At any rate, among his fellow-passengers he was the observed of all observers; the ladies daily amused themselves in feeding him with dainties; and, "how does the bear do this morning?" was their general matutinal concern. The cook baked little cakes for him; what he called these I do not know, but am quite sure that they were not "lady-fingers." At first Bruin was sea-sick for a while, but recovered after a few days, like the rest of us, and greeted us occasionally with a familiar and friendly growl that was quite refreshing on such a wilderness of water.

All manner of amusements is resorted to on board ship "*pour passer le temps*," the chief one, among gentlemen, being a game called "*Tonneau;*" which is a species of quoit-pitching with pewter quoits, about the size of a twenty-dollar gold-piece, (should any of my readers still retain a dim recollection of that size,) the object being to pitch them into the gaping mouth of a cast-iron frog, perched upon a box containing holes that represent different numbers, into one of which the frog drops the quoit; the game affords considerable sport. Then there is all manner of card-playing, chess, dominos, draughts, backgammon, &c. There was a great deal of playing for money, too; but fortunately all the participants so "mutually excelled each other," that none had lost or won to any extent at the end of our voyage. A small musical coterie enjoyed themselves greatly every evening in the ladies' saloon, which contained a fine piano. One of the gentlemen on board was an excellent performer; and the German lady, who met her brother so strangely, has a rich soprano voice, and sang for us enchantingly. Thus we had gems from Trovatore, Ernani, Traviata, and many other sterling operas; and on one occasion we had nearly the whole of the Bohemian Girl performed—without, of course, the acting and stage accessories.

Events on board a steamer do not always transpire in an uninterrupted course of serene dignity; on the contrary, a "life on the ocean wave" has its ludicrous phases also, that offer a pleasing contrast to the tiresome monotony which would otherwise prevail even during so short a period as a ten days' voyage. Wrapt up in your comfortable coat and shawls, you seat yourself languidly on an extension camp-chair, by the side of the officer at the compass, or promenade over a zigzag path up and down the quarter deck. Ignorant land-lubbers might think that you were a little muddled in the head; but it is not that — the defect is in the legs, whose sea-faring steadiness has not yet been developed. Perhaps you descend into the saloon, that is gorgeously fitted up and has the appearance of a first-class gambling establishment: directly you become an active member of the scene by joining some of your companions in a rubber of whist, or a game of chess. Presently the tableau changes: dinner is served; you are seated at one of the long tables; stewards and sub-stewards flit backward and forward, loaded with britannia-ware and bright silvery dishes, preserving a wonderful degree of steadiness under the circumstances. Suddenly the ship gives a lurch; and the cups and saucers, the platters and soup-tureens become extremely lively, and dance a jig to the music of their own clatter. Away goes a cruet of milk — and *such* milk! — into the ham and eggs; the coffee-pot upsets, and floods the leg of mutton with its savory contents, making a delicious gravy that can only be appreciated by those who have tasted it. While you look aghast at the lump of butter that has cosily nestled itself into your lap, the molasses-jug makes a sudden dart, and falling off the table, descends into and sweetens the lining of your neighbor's silk hat, that is standing on the floor; the potatoes roll about the table in a mad career of recklessness, as though they were engaged at billiards, and carom on each other and on every article of diet in their way. But — you don't feel very well — there's something wrong inside — an intestine commotion; yet you want to brave the lion in his den, and you go into the smoking-room. There you peer, as well as you may, through the thick volume of tobacco fume, and behold the dim outlines of some twenty of your comrades, like jolly spectres, that smoke and examine the ceiling through the bottoms of tumblers. Perhaps it is a French smoking-room; a polite *garçon*, observing your *wry* face, approaches you with — "*Desirez-vous quelque chose, monsieur?*" "*Oui, donnez-moi un cigar.*" "*Ne voulez-*

vous pas manger, monsieur?" "*Du tout! du tout! au contraire, je voudrais bien boire. Donnez-moi du cognac — ah! parbleu! du cognac.*" But perhaps the spectres are taking their flight to Hamburg or Bremen, and there is great yearning among them for lager-beer, Schweitzer-käse, pretzeln, and other Teutonic elements, but which I find are not *too tonic* to enter into the American constitution. Ah! but they are on one of the good ships of the Inman line — these spectres of the jolly smoking-room. One by one they approach the jolly panel of the partition that separates them from the treasures of the bar-room; the panel opens, like the door in the cave of the Forty Thieves, and — "A glars of Hallsops hale, hand another of Arf and Arf, hand be blarsted quick about it!" says the jolly spectre.

Evening is growing apace, and the saloon being brilliantly lighted, let us enter there, and be seated with the rest of the ladies and gentlemen. The piano is at the aft end of the apartment; and the beautiful and accomplished Miss Smith, after much persuasion from the part of our sea-faring audience, consents to play, and sings — " Believe me, if all those endearing young charms," or rattles away, on mid-ocean, "The Caliph of Bagdad;" breaks out hysterically with "Listen to the Mocking-bird!" then falls back on "Coming through the Rye," with variations, "We won't go home till morning," and other touching and appropriate melodies. Then there is little Willie Jones, just twelve years old, who plays on the violin, and sings with that sweet voice of his: —

> "For she was beautiful as a butterfly,
> And as proud as a queen,
> Was pretty little Polly Perkins,
> Of Paddington Green,"—

with all the passengers joining in the chorus, and making the ship vocal with melody, like the woods at Camp-meetings. Then Collins (who on the last day of the voyage fell and broke three ribs, poor fellow!) like a troubadour of the marine corps, accompanies himself with the most exquisite touch on his guitar to the sublime words of

> "Come, sit thee down, my bonnie, bonnie lass,
> Come sit thee down by me,
> And I will tell thee many a tale
> Of the dangers of the sea."

Although, as was said, our passenger list was composed of people from nearly all parts of the world, yet the prevailing tone of society on board was exceedingly French. The captain and entire crew, and fully one half of the passengers were French; the rules and regulations, and manners, and cooking, were all French; and the language that was spoken was almost exclusively French, either natural or acquired. In reference to this language, I overheard a conversation in English that disgusted me very much with the morals of "*la belle France.*" It was between a Frenchman who spoke but indifferent English, and an American. The latter expressed his hope of being able to acquire the French language during his sojourn at Paris. "Zat depend upon whezzer you are married or zingal," said the Frenchman. "I am married," replied the American. "Ah! mon Dieu! zat is von great pittee!" returned the Frenchman, "because ze bachelors learn ze French much quicker in Paris zan ze married man;" then the wretch added,—"but *il faut avoir* von dam bad memory—you must forget zat you are married." For the credit of the American I will say, that he appeared to be greatly shocked by this advice, and the conversation was discontinued.

And now—it is Sabbath morning. We glide along at the rate of thirteen knots an hour; nothing in sight, save the clear blue sky above, and the vast expanse of water all around. The bell on the foredeck tolls for divine service; and suddenly the ship is converted into a floating church. By degrees most of the sailors, attired in clean blue blouses, loose neckties, and jaunty flowing trowsers, as well as many of the passengers, congregate in the cabin, where the Captain, in full uniform, reads the morning service right impressively, for a brave sea-captain that he is; whilst a choir that is improvised for the occasion from the passengers acquits itself very creditably indeed.

To me worship to the Divine Author, held thus upon mid-ocean, is full of sublimity and solemn impressiveness, and I have seen many of the members of such a congregation moved with great, and doubtless heartfelt, emotion.

Arrived at Havre, we had but little trouble in debarking, and proceeding to the railway station to be in time for the next train for Paris. The much-dreaded annoyance from custom officers was scarcely worth mentioning. Many trunks were not opened, but their owners simply asked, whether they had any tobacco or cigars; those articles being a source of government revenue, are very strictly prohibited; not more than half a pound of the former, and fifty pieces of the latter being permitted to pass into France free of duty.

Who may describe the impressions that are awakened at the first sight of, and upon first placing foot on a foreign land? I may as well allude to myself, and say it out, that it had been the dream of my boyhood, and the ambition of my riper years, to be able one day to visit that historic land; and here I was — body and soul — with the whole of Europe lying bare before me at last. Here was altogether another section of the world; and, strange to say, it appeared to have all the elements and attributes of our own country. Here was ground like our own; sand and gravel and dust like our own; pebbles and stones and rocks like our own; hills and valleys and plains like our own; rivers and trees and houses, for all the world, just as natural and life-like as though they had been in the blessed United States themselves. The people were neither giants nor dwarfs; but middling-sized, nice-looking creatures like ourselves, dressed in strict conformity with the manifold complications of fashion; — the lordlings and great folks of society being no more precise in the suitableness of their attires than the hod-carriers and chimney-sweeps in theirs.

Thus, then, in general features, there was nothing in my first glimpse at Europe to surprise me, except in its resemblance to the surface of things that I had been accustomed to heretofore in our own country.

Nevertheless, in the details of that first day's life beyond the sea, there were many little incidents, trivial, it is true, that yet stamped themselves indelibly upon my memory. Among these was my first meal; I recollect every item of it: it was in a restaurant near the railroad depot, in the city of Havre, just previous to my departure for Paris, and consisted of bread and butter, oysters, sardines, and half a bottle of Medoc. The bread and butter was good; the sardines were good; the oysters were good, too, that is to say, they were good for nothing; and the wine — but stay! It is the general presumption in our own country, that the wines of Continental Europe so immeasurably transcend everything that we are accustomed to drinking, that the first mouthful might be supposed to beatify the brain, and captivate all the senses with its unspeakable deliciousness. Now, although the difference, especially to the palate, is not quite so great as all this, yet it may be safely asserted, that, whatever the cause may be, the effect of wine-drinking in Europe is not nearly so disagreeable as in America,— and, I may add, that when the half bottle of Medoc alluded to was drank out, it was empty — quite empty; there was no logwood or red sanders in the bottom of it. But let it not be understood that I emptied the half bottle myself — oh, no! I had an American friend with me, who was such a good-natured, whole-souled, congenial, and easily-pleased fellow, that he liked everything I did; was hungry, thirsty, and sleepy whenever I was; and was forever seeing the same sights, and going to the same places, at the same time with myself.

Another of those little things that made a strong impression upon my mind, was the great politeness that I experienced from all the railroad officials during that first ride in the Old World. The railway system of Europe has been so frequently described, that I will not dwell on the subject, but simply add my unqualified testimony to the many others who have preceded me, of its great superiority over our own. The comfort of their coupés far exceeds that of our long cars, and a choleric person, like one I wot of, can get his ticket, procure his seat, ride all day, and ask as many questions as his ignorance suggests, without being snubbed to death by every miserable little official, from the president to the brakesman, as is so frequently the case in our own country. The fare, however, for travelling on the railroads is somewhat higher here than in the United States, though there is a material difference between the prices of the first and second class cars, yet so little in the comforts and conveniences of the two, that hardly any persons but those belonging to the nobility ever ride in the first class; the extra charge being due to the exclusiveness of aristocratic souls and long purses. By giving the conductor a trifle, however, wherewith he can procure some choice beverage to quench his thirst, one may frequently secure the half, if not the entire whole, of the interior of a coach to one's self; an arrangement that is especially agreeable at night, when one may extend himself at full length on the lap of Morpheus—or, rather, if you will be particular about it, on one of the seats that are as pleasant to lie upon as a softly upholstered sofa.

We left Havre at twenty minutes past two in the afternoon, and journeyed through a country whose picturesque beauty, natural magnificence, and high state of cultivation, certainly eclipsed anything that one can conceive who has not seen it; and the scrupulous economy that is observed in the culture of the soil is, to an extent, almost amusing to an American, not a square foot being permitted to go to waste; and I could not help wondering how horrified these people would be, if they saw some of our worm-fences, and the band of six or eight feet of soil which they barricade against the plough. Indeed, the tract through which we passed appeared more like a vast and continuous garden and pleasure-ground, similar to the Central Park of New York, than ordinary farming country.

At last, when it was ten o'clock in the evening, we entered Paris. The moon was just full, and from a clear limpid sky was shedding its mellow radiance over our blessed earth, as it had shone at Pottsville, as it had shone also on mid-ocean, and was shining now on the two million inhabitants of this vast metropolis.

Paris! what historical recollections the name recalls! The city whose populace periodically breaks out into furious effervescence, like a living Vesuvius—whose great record consists of barricades—the guillotine—the Bastile! Well, I am not prepossessed in your favor; but "*nous verrons.*"

LETTER II.

PARIS.

FLITTING ABOUT PARIS.— ITS GENERAL APPEARANCE.— THE JARDIN DES PLANTES.— ITS NATURAL CURIOSITIES, AND WORKS OF ART.— VISIT TO THE CATHEDRAL OF NOTRE DAME. — PLACE VENDOME. — ASCENT OF THE COLUMN NAPOLEON THE FIRST.— HOW THE SABBATH IS OBSERVED IN PARIS.— THE FRENCH SERVANTS, HACKMEN, &c.— THE OPERA.

PARIS, *April*, 1867.

SO much has been written about Paris that one feels a natural hesitation in approaching the subject at all. Yet it is one so inexhaustible and ever varying,— one that exercises an influence over the whole civilized world, — so brilliant in its good, and so repulsive in its bad features, that the impressions which it induces, and which are as diversified as the theme is Promethean in character, may be recorded now, and by many writers hereafter, without danger of drifting entirely into trite and worn-out thoughts. And if I endeavor to describe what I see after my own fashion, and in accordance with my own feelings, without any reference whatever to what has been written before, it is hoped that the little egotism may be overlooked, and the true object — the desire to please — alone kept in view.

The day after my arrival here, I engaged a hack and had myself conducted through many of the most important thoroughfares of the city, bestowing a cursory glance upon many objects of interest, and accustoming my eyes once more to other things than the great, unsteady immensity of water over which I had just passed.

The first thing that attracts the attention of almost every one is the great cleanness of the streets of Paris, in which respect it surpasses by far any city that I have ever known. In many of the boulevards and other principal thoroughfares, one half of them is paved with cobblestones, and the other half, running along lengthways, is macadamized by a cement whose hardness is almost indestructible. The latter side of these streets is for carriages and all manner of light vehicles, which run over it almost noiselessly, and as easily as over the most perfect plank-road; but it is not practicable for heavy teams, as the exceedingly smooth surface yields no hold to the horses' feet, which in pulling at great loads would constantly glide out. The paved portion on the other side affords a good grappling for all heavy-draught animals, and is therefore appropriated to purposes of heavy transportation. Every real-estate proprietor is obliged by law to have the street and sidewalk in front of his own premises swept clean every morning, after which the refuse is taken away by means of so great a number of carts, that but a short time is necessary to complete the process.

The houses have a somewhat old and dingy look, even on the boulevards, where all the buildings have in every other respect a magnificence of style and palatial proportions. This faded appearance can only be owing to the character of the material that is used in their construction; namely, a kind of grayish, drab-colored stone, and bricks of pretty much the same hue. One misses very decidedly the cheerful red bricks, white marble, or rich, brown sandstone of New York and Philadelphia. Notwithstanding all this there is but little doubt, that of all the great cities of the world, the most beautiful and perfect specimen is Paris. You have here a gathering of nearly two million human beings housed away in systematic order, wherein beauty, comfort, and grandeur are harmoniously blended; and where obedience to the laws of the powers that be is as tacitly observed as in a hive of bees. It is indeed a pleasure to wander along its principal avenues, whose sidewalks, from ten to twenty feet wide, are almost continuously sheltered from the sun or falling weather by awnings; under which, especially in front of the numerous cafés and restaurants, are placed chairs and marble-covered tables, where the great world of Paris congregate to eat, drink, and smoke, and read the daily journals; but most of all to chat, laugh, and indulge in impromptu and miscellaneous merriment; or, perhaps, to hatch out the details of those social and political intrigues — those little affairs of the heart or of the brain, which send their fascinations all the world over, and envelop this fair city with a strange and peculiar charm. How grand are the long lines of high palaces, built in picturesque irregularity, that skirt both sides of these hundreds of pleasant streets, and are decorated with show-windows that display the very superexcellencies of ornamental art! — flaunting their trinkets and jewelry; their beautiful, patent-leather, high-heeled gaiters; their divine, raven chignons and auburn curls; their india-rubber proxies for nonexistent portions of the human frame; their corsets, marked No. 17 — God help the poor things doomed to wear them! — their glass eyes, and pearly, gold-mounted teeth; their ribbons, and silks, and broadcloth; shawls, dresses, and coats; tippets, and capes, and muffs, of otter, mink, and Russian sables; their tulles and point laces, satins and moire-antiques; their cashmeres from India and cashmeres from Paris; and oh! their ravishing little bonnets and hats, with feathers from pigeons, orioles, birds of Paradise, Chinese pheasants, ostriches, parrots, and peacocks! Yes, these and a thousand other little nameless things fill the windows for miles as you pass along the streets, and exert a marvellous attractiveness upon the gay throng of pedestrians, that are eternally migrating up and down, to admire and be admired in turn.

Aye, to be sure, it is here where you may see young gentlemen and ladies in their full glory! The former with unexceptionable well-waxed moustachios and imperials, fashionable hats, Bismarck-colored trowsers, and noses saddled with oracular eye-glasses. Even thus they may be seen, these sweet-scented, perishable Parisian exquisites, leading a "Divine creatchaw," in gorgeous array, like Villikins and his Dinah, on the one side, and a King Charles lap-dog by a pink ribbon on the other; and my American friend soon discovered, with his customary shrewdness of observation, that, as a general thing, the two poodles — one at each end of the ribbon — were distinguishable from each other only by the difference in their size.

The striking architectural feature that distinguishes this from our American cities, is the beautiful *sculpture* which everywhere embellishes the public and private buildings, columns, monuments, and triumphal arches. Indeed, it is impossible to conceive how a rising generation could grow up in ignorance amidst all the associations of a city like this, that appears like a vast school, in which object-teaching is the adopted method. The history not only of France, but in a great measure of all Europe, is graphically delineated in statuary, paintings and architecture everywhere. And in the Jardin des Plantes, amidst all the surroundings of the zoölogical, geological, and botanical departments, there is an amphitheatre in which free courses of lectures by the most eminent savans of France, on natural history and the different sciences, are held. Thus an education is rendered possible to every individual that desires it.

Not to skip over the beautiful subject of the Jardin des Plantes too hurriedly, let me here make the unqualified assertion, that to one who has helped to enrich the treasury of Van Amburg's menagerie with frequent quarter dollars, it is peculiarly gratifying to visit the numerous animals, reptiles, and birds that are here displayed in all their strength, beauty, and glory, "free, gratis, for nothing." Here we have every variety of animated nature, from the elephant to the chameleon, from the ostrich to the charming little butterfly. The wild animals are in cages, built very massively of stone, with strong iron gratings on one side to permit of their inspection, and sufficiently roomy for the animals within to be comfortable and display their qualities. I saw an immense grizzly bear walk about on his hind-legs, erect, like a huge giant, and measuring in that position some eight feet or more. The museum of comparative anatomy that is situated in this garden is truly wonderful, and said to be the greatest collection of the kind in the world. Here an anxious student has infinite opportunities for storing his mind with useful knowledge, whilst he cannot but be filled with wonder and admiration at the niceties of created things, which he can here examine in detail. There is also a geological museum that is quite monstrous in proportions, and to which I have not failed to contribute my mite, by presenting its superintendent with a few specimens from Schuylkill County; among which a small but rich piece of black band was pre-eminently the most interesting. It is impossible to convey any idea of the beauty of some of the mosaic work contained in this museum; among which there is a Madonna, equal in naturalness, color, and expression to the most finished paintings. Gold and precious stones, even diamonds, are displayed here in most gorgeous profusion, with substances of baser caste. Attached to this building is the botanical museum, wherein are contained specimens of woods, barks, leaves, seeds, &c., of all known plants.

One of the most interesting places to visit in this city is the Cathedral of Notre Dame. Accordingly I went there last Sunday morning, and it being Easter

Sunday, the ceremonies and music were more than ordinarily grand and impressive. I ascended one of the towers, from which an excellent view may be had of the whole city. While I was up there, they tolled the ponderous bell, it being the hour for high mass, and as access to the dome where the bell is suspended was permitted, I availed myself of the unique opportunity, and stood directly under it while it was in full swing. It is easily to be imagined, that the reverberating noise in such a position, amid the extensive scaffolding and tressel-work of that iron-clad cupola, must have been perfectly deafening. It still continued swinging, like a huge pendulum in a monstrous clock, long after the men ceased their manipulation of the levers; and its tones grew fainter and slower by degrees, dying out at last in an agony of vibration.

Notre Dame has been so much written about, that I shall say nothing more on the subject, except that it inspired me with a feeling of awe and veneration as I stood within its hallowed precincts, listening to the deep-toned organ, which is 45 feet in height, 36 in breadth, and contains 3,484 pipes. Yes, as the solemn music resounded tremulously throughout the naves, and aisles, and passages of that spacious edifice — in view, too, of those old scriptural representations in bas-relief all over the walls and side chapels, some of which were mutilated by the mob in the terrible times of the French Revolution, and "Liberty, Fraternity, Equality" chiselled into the outside stones of the sacred pile — where those words, though partially effaced, are still visible — when the great national creed was: "Death is an eternal sleep!" With all these associations passing like a panorama before the mind's eye, it filled me with emotion of no common order.

After leaving Notre Dame, I proceeded to Place Vendome, and ascended the high column that was there erected by Napoleon I., to commemorate the success of his arms in the German campaign of 1805. This column is 135 feet high, and only 12 in diameter, and is built in imitation of the pillar of Trajan at Rome, but on a somewhat larger scale. The whole pedestal and shaft are covered with bronze bas-reliefs, cast out of the cannon taken from the enemy. These bas-reliefs represent the progress and principal actions of the French army from the departure from Boulogne to the Battle of Austerlitz. The entrance to the interior of the column was guarded by a sentinel, an old soldier who had served with Napoleon at Moscow, and constituted one of his few attendants at St. Helena,— a proud old man, who seems more content now in having served under the great Napoleon, than Napoleon himself was while commanding the destinies of nations. He gave my American friend and myself a lantern, and together we ascended the high shaft. The spiral staircase was very narrow and tortuous, and my friend graphically remarked that it was like walking up a big corkscrew. Once on the top, the little breath left us was almost taken away on looking down the thin, long pillar, as it seemed; and one felt an instinctive fear of getting too near the railing that protects the platform, lest the whole concern might lose its balance and topple over. The view of the city, however, is very fair from this point, commanding a bird's-eye glance over the finest portions of Paris; only the roofs of the houses present a comic and ludicrous appearance, looking so very old and smoky, and being sprinkled over with such innumerable little, round chimneys, as though the city might have been blessed some centuries ago with a right smart shower of earthenware crockery, leaving the unharmed pots perched about in indiscriminate disorder. Then the general surface of the roofs is so excessively uneven; for every here and there is a low and squat dwelling between two tall and slender ones of five or six stories in height; whereof the general effect upon the eye is exceedingly amusing.

It will be recollected that it was Sunday when I ascended the column of Vendome,—not that it was particularly wicked to do a thing of that kind on the Sabbath, but it might have been—and much worse things are done on that day, for, to tell the truth, there is so little difference here between Sunday and other days, that it is difficult to keep the run of them, without referring to the heading of the morning papers—especially when one has no notes payable at the bank to come due. In general appearance on the streets, if there is any difference at all between Sundays and week-days, it is that on the former it is a little more lively, business a shade brisker, the cafés and restaurants a trifle fuller, and that the theatres offer two performances instead of one. Besides this, there are more of the prominent public places and palaces open to the people on this day than on any other. To these, as a general thing, admission is free; but in a number of them a polite Frenchman is stationed at the entrance, who insists upon taking care of one's cane or umbrella for the consideration of a few sous; and as the weather here is so capricious that the carrying of an umbrella is almost a constant necessity — and every Frenchman always has one in his hand or under his arm — why, one manages to get rid of his loose change.

Decidedly a blessing to the stranger in Paris are the public hacks, in which one can ride by the hour or single trip for a very moderate price. The drivers are kept under strict discipline, and no such thing as gouging or overcharging a passenger is tolerated. Generally, too, they are well informed, and if one is at all conversant with the French language, they will suffice as guides. I have had one of them conduct me in a very comfortable carriage, over many parts of the city, explaining the points of interest to me, during a period of five hours, and the whole expense only amounted to about two dollars and a half. Another great feature here is the thorough manner in which one is attended by the servants. It is true, they expect a great many "*pour boires*," (small fees,) but they are so very willing and cheerful, and polite withal, that it is impossible not to be pleased, or to recollect the slight inconvenience of the *pour boire*. You have them standing behind you, subject to the slightest nod, dressed up in black pants, dress-coat, white Marseilles vest, cravat of the same color, and, in some instances, white gloves also. So that, take it all in all, they are much more regardlessly gotten up than the generality of guests; and one almost feels like rising, and with a profound bow addressing their servantships with, "Really, monsieur, if it is n't putting you to too much trouble, you might be kind enough to bring me a plate of *cheval roti a la mode.*"

To-day, as I was walking down the boulevard des Italiens, I saw a gentleman black another gentleman's boots. Let me not be misunderstood: if "God makes the man, and the tailor the gentleman," then he who did this boot-blacking *was* a gentleman; for he was dressed neatly; had a nice, clean, well-starched and ironed blue blouse upon him; a moustache that was unequalled except by the dear little tuft of hair on his chin, and he was *smoking a cigarette*, and chatting familiarly with him whose boots he was polishing.

Last night I witnessed the representation of the opera of Don Carlos — the music by Verdi. It abounds with many passages of that brilliant style of music for which Verdi's compositions are so deservedly popular; still it lacks the beautiful and touching melodies that give such a charm to Il Trovatore; and for my part, I much prefer hearing an opera sung in Italian or German, — and this was in French. The scenic production of the opera was remarkably fine, and in the third act there was a ballet-dance of about one hundred damsels representing naiads, that was certainly the grandest thing of the kind I have ever witnessed. At the Chatelet, the largest theatre in the city, they are nightly performing a grand spectacular dramatization of Cinderella, which is somewhat similar to the Black Crook as it is performed at New York. Indeed, I find that performances of such a character are very much the rage here, and what has shocked the sense of refinement of so many Americans in the representation of the Black Crook is here looked upon as quite a *natural affair*. At the theatre Palais Royale they have been playing La Vie Parisienne, which must be seen and understood to be appreciated. It abounds in local hits, and delineates the manner in which foreigners are taken in by the wily Parisians.

LETTER III.

THE GRAND EXPOSITION.

THE GRAND EXPOSITION,— IT IS A SUCCESS.— THE UNITED STATES COMPARATIVELY POORLY REPRESENTED.— WHAT IT HAS ON EXHIBITION IS MUCH ADMIRED.— THE MANUFACTURING DEPARTMENT.— SALOONS OF DIFFERENT NATIONS.— NEW AMERICAN INVENTIONS.— THE NOTABILITIES WHO VISIT THE EXPOSITION.— WORKS OF ART DISPLAYED.— AGRICULTURAL DEPARTMENT.—COST OF LIVING IN PARIS.

PARIS, May, 1867.

THE Grand Exposition, although formally opened to the public more than a month ago, is still unfinished; nor will it be entirely complete for two or three weeks to come. Nevertheless, it is gorgeous and immense, almost beyond description; and those who have predicted that it would be a failure, have been greatly in error. It cannot, therefore, be other than a source of regret to every American who visits it, to see his country so poorly represented, in comparison with other nations, as it is.

When the arena of space allotted to the United States in the exhibition was first made known, it caused a deal of bombastic scolding and dissatisfaction among our editors, for not giving us more room; and yet, as it is, I am sorry to say that the space is not entirely taken up. It is but just, however, to add, that what there is on exhibition from our country is worthy of the genius of the nation, and compels the respect and admiration of all people. In some respects we even excite the jealousy of the French. Thus, in the *Figaro*, one of the dailies of this city, the editor, in reference to our pianos, says, " Let us be a little more patriotic, and not occupy ourselves entirely with American pianos. They have qualities to which we have done homage, but which should not fill us with enthusiasm to the extent of forgetfulness of our own." Then he tries very hard to extol the French instruments, but which lose their identity entirely beside our magnificent Chickering's and Steinway's.

A particularly interesting feature of the exhibition is the immense amount of beautiful machinery from all countries, which encircles it, and which is nearly all in motion; and that, too, for some purpose; for along a large section of this circle there is carried on the manufacture of almost all imaginable things, both useful and ornamental. In one department, for example, you can see them engaged in making gentlemen's hats, passing from the raw material through all the various stages unto the complete fashionable *chapeau*. The same may be said of boots and shoes; and it is astonishing to see how soon a young lady — for much of this work is done by females — can make a pair of boots. At another place may be seen operatives engaged in carving all manner of fancy work in wood, ivory, meerschaum, and cameo; where one can give them a photograph for a copy, and have an exact likeness engraved from it on a cameo breastpin or a meerschaum pipe. In this way a great amount of such goods is sold to the visitors, who are very eager for mementos of this description.

Here also can be witnessed the manufacture of jewelry, even to the polishing and setting of diamonds. Also the weaving of silks, silk scarfs, beautifully flowered, and brochét shawls. Then there is printing, book-binding, the making of envelopes by machinery, of pins and steel pens; of playing-cards, and a variety of trinkets and toys; of combs and buttons from bone, gutta-percha, turtle-shell, mother-of-pearl, &c. But it is impossible to enumerate all the different operations that are carried on here; and crowds of people are constantly looking on and admiring the workmanship as it progresses. In fact, next to the picture galleries, this seems to be the most attractive part of the exhibition. Stay! I may be in error; for probably, the most attractive places are the eating-saloons and cafés that constitute a zone which girdles the entire building; and to judge from the flushed faces that issue from these various retreats, it may be set down as being no very *temperate zone* at that.

Each one of these saloons has its own nationality, and is conducted just as it would be at home, in the country which it represents. Thus there is the English chop-house, with the imperative round table, and plump, jolly-looking fellows with mutton-chop whiskers, sitting up to it, and looking unctuously happy in the enjoyment of their slices from the delectable joint of beef or mutton, imbibing deep draughts from the big-bellied mugs of "arf and arf;" and smoking fine-cut tobacco in little clay pipes with long stems, and red sealing-wax at their ends. Then there is the French café, with always a goodly number of Messieurs drawing small whiffs of tobacco-smoke through tiny cigarettes, which they manufacture as fast as they require them — and chatter with fierce grimaces about Luxembourg (which they persist in calling "Lick-some-boor"), filling up the pauses with dainty sips at their *caffe noir*. The idea of calling such a thing coffee! Lo, how it is made: a solution of gypsum for water, chickory for coffee, brandy for milk, and sometimes rum for sugar! It is worse than an old-fashioned dose of senna-manna-and-salts, and would make an excellent hair-dye; but as the prevailing rage just now is to have *red* hair, they cannot, unfortunately, appropriate their coffee to this purpose. But, to resume, there is also the American saloon, where men stand up to the bar, and drink their mint-juleps, claret-punches, brandy-smashes, cocktails, &c.; but they cannot sit on high chairs and eat oysters; no, it is impossible — because there is no "R" in the month, and very much because they — have n't the oysters. Then there is the German *Wirtschaft*, with its bountiful provision of Bavarian beer, rye bread, and Strasburg sausage; where a few heavy philosophers sit in pensive contemplation, and enveloped in clouds of smoke exhaled from the *æchten Knaster*. Turks, Chinese, Japanese, and all the other odd branches and outcroppings of the human family have their own "ranches," and make it a matter of curious and gratifying import to go the "grand rounds," and visit them all. A Chinese theatre, built after their own fashion, wherein real Chinese do the performing, is another feature that excites considerable curiosity. The same may be said of a band of American negro minstrels, who exhibit daily, and attract, I am told, crowded audiences.

Notwithstanding what I have said of the comparatively small number of contributions from the United States, and in spite of all the delay in the completion of its department, there are presented many attractions that are well worthy of notice. Near the American locomotives, which, of course, cannot be excelled, may be seen the life-saving raft, an invention of Mr. Perry, which is rapidly coming into favor. The navy department, I believe, has recommended its general adoption. The raft cannot be overturned, and the one here exhibited is capable of saving the lives of fifty persons. So much confidence is felt, that a party of navigators propose to leave New York for Paris upon one of these rafts, during the Exposition. I should, however, respectfully decline being one of the party.

A large concourse of interested persons may always be seen in the vicinity of the models of street-cars, as exhibited by Mr. Eastman, our Consul at Bristol. By a practical use of this system, which is an improvement on that now in use, it is believed that all present objections to city railways will be removed. Mr. George Francis Train should look to his laurels; for Mr. Eastman's plans are remarkable for their adaptability to *any* kind of road. The famous Ferris Gun, ordered to be built by President Lincoln, is here, and being securely chained, one might be apprehensive of its liability to spontaneous explosion. Can it be feared that any one will run away with it? This gun has been fired several hundred times, with the result, that, at an incline of 35 degrees, the ball was projected to the distance of nine miles.

Considerable attention is drawn to the articles displayed by the Tucker Manufacturing Company of Boston. These consist of chandeliers, lamps, brackets, clocks, cases, statuettes, &c., made of bronzed iron, which are quite as handsome as, and hardly to be distinguished from, pure bronze, yet much cheaper. The Daball Patent Rotary Fog Trumpet is the invention of C. L. Daball, of New London, Connecticut. It can be heard from ten to twenty miles off in a fog, and produces a sound unlike to any other. In consequence, as a means of caution to ships at sea, it is destined to be of inestimable value.

In the English department there are some splendid paintings contributed by the South Kensington Museum; and it is in view of these that the distinguished visitors — consisting of kings and princes, of whom there are several every day — may be seen more frequently than at any other place. Here also all Britishers do mostly congregate; and Brown, Jones, and Robinson are comfortably seated with their better halves, or, perhaps, still dearer friends (to speak maliciously), and chat learnedly, or the reverse, about *chiar'oscuro* and the middle distance. The French display of paintings is also very good; though many of them are, in the eyes of the Parisians, old acquaintances, all the galleries of art whence they are principally taken being so liberally accessible to the people. Private studios and public galleries have alike contributed their treasures, and the result is highly creditable to the French as an artistic nation.

From the galleries, however, of the Louvre and the Luxembourg palace none of the paintings have been removed. As in all collections of French paintings that I have thus far seen, so also here do battle-pieces and war scenes predominate. Thus the battle of Solferino, and the taking of the Malakoff are very graphically delineated; and among the paintings of this description, the historical circumstance of Napoleon I. passing through his encamped army on the eve of the battle of Austerlitz, and the soldiers discovering the Emperor, by a spontaneous impulse illumined the whole camp with thousands of torches, has given rise to one of the rarest productions. As a set-off to these, the charming landscapes and scenes of animated nature by Rosa Bonheur, and some exquisitely drawn classic pieces, are exhibited. The Prussian and Austrian schools of art are also well represented. America, the very name of which suggests the vast and the sublime in nature, has a characteristic display of art. Some of our paintings are enormous, as perhaps they should be, considering the subjects they represent. Among them is Bierstadt's great painting of the Rocky Mountains, and Church's Niagara; and one of the most beautiful delineations here is an American Sunset by George Innes. Much has been said of the excellent qualities of portraits by Elliott of New York, and Hunt of Boston; but, however celebrated these may be, they lose very much by comparison with some of the portraits here exhibited. The portrait, by Hunt, of President Lincoln, which is here exposed, is really an excessively homely-looking production. It is true, the great original of the picture was not exactly a beau; but I have seen many handsomer likenesses of him that resembled him quite as much.

In Italy (for thus it is that the different sections assume the names of the different countries from which they are furnished; and friends, having occasion to separate in the spacious edifice, make appointments to meet again at a given hour in China, or Constantinople, &c.) there is a marble statue of the Dying Napoleon, which is exciting a great deal of admiration. The subject is depicted as seated in an arm-chair, clothed in a loose wrapper, his shoulders supported by a pillow, and a robe thrown lightly over his person, covering him as high as the lower portion of his chest. The wasted figure and sunken cheek, but large, broad forehead, and penetrating eye are graphically illustrated. The work is by an Italian sculptor by the name of Vela, whose reputation will be established by this production.

In India there is a large saloon, elegantly furnished with fauteuils and sofas, and supplied with light in such a manner as to enhance the effect of a bewildering display of cashmere shawls, over which many a covetous beauty wrecks her heart, and drags what is left of it to Lyons, where it founders again over the profusion of silks of all the colors of the rainbow, and all the textures imaginable, from a transparent zephyr-like web, to that compact tissue which causes such a delicious noise — and what man has not felt it — when it sweeps by you in the shape of a garment. Oh, what electricity there is in a silk dress! a fact, in which there is at least as much truth as poetry. If anything of the aforesaid wrecked heart be still remaining, it will barely escape to the orfevrerie of Christophel, the great jeweller of Paris, whose section of the Exposition recalls to mind the treasures of Alladin; for the mass of gold and silver ware, the profusion of crystals and jewels and precious stones, is almost painful to gaze upon,— and so we will leave it.

At Tunis a constant crowd is attracted by a Tunisian barber, who shaves gentlemen for a small consideration, and appears to enjoy a great rush of eager customers who seem anxious to have their noses pulled and chin scraped by this Oriental individual, though what there is in it I cannot for the life of me discover.

Mexico has a temple here in which I have no doubt Maximilian would be glad to worship just now. Chinese, Japanese, Turks, Arabs, and Indians — in fact, specimens of all the five races, may be seen rambling about in characteristic costumes, and appear generally to enjoy their situations.

Allusion has been made to the silks from Lyons, and shawls from India; but it is impossible to convey any adequate idea of the infinite variety and sumptuous attractiveness, taste, and arrangement with which these goods are displayed, to bait the desires of the ambulating visitor; nor of the stacks of linens from Holland, Ireland, and Saxony; nor of the surgical and medical appliances from Paris; the magnificent libraries from Leipzig, and the musical instruments from Munich. And what shall I say of the glorious statuary from Rome, the *bijouterie* from Geneva, the coral necklaces and diadems from Naples, and oh! the meerschaum pipes from Vienna and Turin? The subject is too great, — I see a book looming up before me, in attempting these descriptions, and dare allude to them but briefly.

One of the most interesting divisions of the Exposition, although one not containing anything of beauty to the eye, is the agricultural department; and an examination of the large collection of instruments and implements which it contains is interesting, especially of the numerous kinds of fertilizers of the soil — some of which make themselves known very forcibly to other senses than that of sight. In this branch of agricultural doctoring its practitioners have of late gone far ahead of the college of physicians in its relations to humanity. The science of chemistry has been brought to bear upon the soil, thanks to the discoveries of Professor Liebig. Farmers need no longer fertilize their soil empirically, but may only make up a small bag of it, and forward this to the professor of agricultural chemistry of this or that university. He analyzes it for a small fee, and tells them exactly in what essential element it is wanting. Not the least important feature of the "*Egsposissiong*," as it is here called, is the field with all its Arcadian and architectural embellishments, and of which the great gasometrical fair-building constitutes only the central point. And as a whole, the event is beginning to assume such monstrous proportions, that one will soon see Paris almost entirely translated to the Champ de Mars. This quondam field for sham-battles and other military manœuvres has been converted as by an act of enchantment, into a wilderness of pavilions, temples, kiosks, and cottages, which nothing but the fairy purse of an imperial treasury could have wrought into such miraculous existence during so short a time.

Among these buildings I was pleased to see one especially appropriated to the Sanitary Commission of the United States, in which specimens of all the articles that were made available by that philanthropic organization constituted an exhibition that was quite imposing. Indeed, I was astonished myself when I beheld here, within a sweep of the eye, the aggregate means that were presented for humanitarian purposes. The Prussians and Italians exhibit their resources of relief to the soldiers in a similar manner; but are far behind in this respect, as compared with our own country.

A very large pavilion is occupied by the French war department, where one may see the whole enginery of war in such close and collective proximity, that the appearance which théy present is enough to fill the reflective mind with horror.

Close to this, with rather questionable taste, is the Cathedral of the park, admission to which imposes an extra charge of half a franc, and in which are exhibited many curiosities of religious import. Then, there is an immense tower, iron-plated, which must be over a hundred feet high, and I think contains a reservoir somewhere near the top, from which to supply the great quantity of water used in the park for the fountains that are profusely scattered all about. There is an hydraulic engine close by that pumps the water from the Seine to this reservoir. Near this are erected on a scaffold of trestle-work, the chimes that are destined for the new cathedral at Buffalo, New York. They were manufactured here, and are displayed as a masterpiece of their kind. They toll the time every hour, and play an air, the whole being worked by machinery, like a clock. But the most pleasing part of the whole Exposition is the reserved garden, admission to which costs another ten sous extra. Within this enclosure are hot-houses, where the most beautiful tropical plants may be seen, comprising every variety of flowers, vegetables, and fruits, from the succulent cherry to the delicious pineapple. Outside of the hot-houses the place is laid out as a most beautiful garden, on an undulating surface, through which several small rivulets meander in serpentine directions, forming, at irregular intervals, delightful little lakes, with green, grassy borders, whose smooth surface reflect the pendent branches drooping over them from arbors and bowers that covet the votaries of Cupid, and which, under the mellow moonbeams of a summer evening, should awaken the melodies of the syrens.

Entering a cave, artificially created, one beholds the jutting protuberances of the rocks, and stalactites of irregular dimensions that stud the ceiling all around, and look threatening like the sword of Damocles, with a weird doom suspended especially over all silk hats. The sudden turns made by the walls of the excavation, which are lined with large aquariums, so artistically adjusted into the sides, as perfectly to bewilder the mind to know how it is possible for them to be there at all, present all in all a presumptuousness in art, that looks very much like flying in the face of nature. These aquariums afford the strange appearance of an interrupted wall of water and rock, and through the glass sides of the watery part of the wall may be seen any number of minnows, gold- and sunfish, in sportive dalliance with bigger fellows, such as mackerels, eels, shad, and a great variety of the finny tribe. Leaving the interior of the cave, one may ascend it from the outside by a winding path, and by the side of a cascade that splutters and foams and tumbles down the rocks as though it would like to be a little Niagara, but reminds me more of Southey's description of the Falls of Lodore than any other "waterfall" I ever beheld. This cataract is fed by a lake on the top of the cave, which in its turn is supplied from the reservoir heretofore mentioned. Indeed, the *tout ensemble* of this reserved park constitutes it a perfect fairy land, and almost realizes the descriptions given in the Arabian Nights' stories.

Yesterday the Fair was visited by the Emperor and Empress, who spent several hours among its wonders and novelties. Indeed, their Majesties may be seen there almost daily; so may many other nobilities and notabilities. The King of Greece, during his sojourn here, was a constant visitor, and the monarchs of Russia, Prussia, and Austria are positively expected to bedazzle Paris with their presence in the coming summer. During the past week I have visited the Exposition daily; and it certainly has been well patronized, notwithstanding the inclemency of the weather that we have had. There are many evidences of an unfinished condition still apparent; but every day adds something to the charms and to the wonders of the place. The vegetation in the various plots and gardens has very sensibly improved under the tutelage of bounteous Dame Nature, and all these places look fresh, verdant, and altogether lovely. The band of the *Garde de Paris* gives an additional charm to the grounds, and the crowds who listen to the lively strains look happy as the day is long. It would be exhilarating to hear the dear old melodies of Hail Columbia and the Star-Spangled Banner occasionally; but that is a pleasure to be deferred.

Somebody asked my American friend, what he thought of the Exposition, and he replied that, in his opinion, "It is the world done up in a small parcel, as if it was meant to swap it off in a retail speculation for a similar assortment from some other world; but in the face of too many difficulties of transportation, it will be found best to tear up the curious bundle again, and store away its component parts in their customary shelves." It is, indeed, a moving miniature of as much human exploit and handicraft, in operation and in result, as could well be crowded upon the limited portion of nature that was allotted for the purpose. It is a grand conception, carried out with wonderful success; and I shall ever feel an inward satisfaction at having been privileged to witness the extensive and beautiful experiment; for I do not believe that anything of a similar nature, in capacity and in detail, will be again produced for a long time to come. To see all of the enlightened, and many of the doubtfully civilized nations of the earth, with their different colors and complexions; languages and habits of life; mental and physical distinctive traits; natural products and creative genius, of primitive labor and inventive craft — to see all these commingled and displayed in such a narrow compass that the studious mind and observant eye may scan the whole of it, and draw instructive lessons therefrom, is an epoch in any man's life that may not reasonably be despised.

The detached, fragmentary manner in which this letter has been written will be understood, I trust, as the natural result of the scattered character of my observations. I have been enabled only to write hurriedly of what I have hurriedly seen; for to obtain a correct idea of the entirety of that great temple of art and industry, situate at present in the Champ de Mars, would demand the labor of a month of study. In fact, the croakers and grumblers who have indulged their ill tempers in speaking of the Exhibition, must now begin to feel that they have been in the wrong. If crowds of delighted visitors mean anything — and there is an average number of fifty thousand a day — then it has not been a failure, but is already a great success; and if it be so now, what will it be when Paris receives the scores of thousands who will undoubtedly come hither yet? The high prices charged at some of the leading hotels, however, added to a perhaps exaggerated fear of the expense of living here, has tended to keep many away who would otherwise have come. I will be practical, and state as nearly as I can what it costs me. I have a room on the third story of the Hotel du Monde, situated on Rue Lafayette, one of the pleasantest streets in the city, except the Boulevards. This room is quite comfortably furnished; containing an excellent bed, with spring and hair mattresses, a marble-covered toilet-stand, a table, four comfortable chairs, a lounge, a clock on the mantelpiece, and a large wardrobe, the door of which is a mirror. For all of this, including the service of the *concierge*, I pay four francs a day. Each breakfast costs me about two and a half francs, and dinner generally four francs. I have given these details to show how false the impression is that prevails abroad. Of course, one *can* spend a great deal more, but I doubt whether health and comfort would be enhanced thereby. Altogether it is possible to live very comfortably for about three dollars a day. If cabs are frequently hired, and the assistance of a guide (whose charges are generally five francs a day) is needed, which is almost a necessity to those unacquainted with the French language, then the expenses run up accordingly. I have met a number of Americans who complained greatly about the tariffs to which they were subjected; but I am satisfied, in almost every instance, that they were themselves to blame. They are reckless in the details of their expenditures; and are only laughed at by the shrewd Parisians in return.

The other day the King and Queen of Belgium arrived here, and were received by the Emperor in person at the depot. In fact there are just now a great many royal princes and princesses "and such" in this city; among whom are the king and queen just mentioned, the Queen of Portugal, the King of Greece, the Prince of Wales, Prince Alfred, Prince Oscar of Sweden, the Princess Clotilda, the Grand Duchess Maria of Russia, the Prince de Hohenlohe, the Duke of Lichtenberg, Lord and Lady Cowley, &c. Besides this, it is announced that the Shah of Persia and the Sultan of Turkey will come to France in July, to visit the Exposition; and it is also definitely asserted, that the Czar of Russia and King William of Prussia — the trouble between the latter magnate and Napoleon having been smoothed over — will arrive early in June, probably the first or second; and that King Victor Emanuel and the Emperor of Austria will be here shortly after. And thus we are in the sublime anticipation of great events. Many people and much money will hither wend their way, and *Paris mettra tout cela dans la poche.*

LETTER IV.

THE PARISIAN'S LOVE OF AMUSEMENTS.

AMUSEMENTS OF THE PARISIANS.— THE THEATRES.— THE NEW OPERA OF ROMEO AND JULIET.— THE CAFÉS CHANTANTS.—AN UNIQUE PERFORMANCE.— THE LOVE OF FLOWERS.—RACES IN THE BOIS DE BOULOGNE.—PALACES AT ST. CLOUD, FONTAINEBLEAU, AND VERSAILLES.—THE SOLDIERS.— POLICE SYSTEM.—PARIS AT NIGHT.—THE WINE AND THE WATER.

PARIS, *May*, 1867.

THE sources and opportunities for amusement to the people of this city are almost inexhaustible. Indeed, pleasure-seeking seems to be the prevailing business that preoccupies every individual. Of course, you see a sprinkling of work going on; such as houses being erected, old ones pulled down; streets being cleaned; carts loaded with vegetables and all other imaginable things, drawn about in every direction by little donkeys with bells, and, I am sorry to say, by women; — yet even these appear more like a species of recreation and enjoyment than real labor.

You see a fellow languidly mixing mortar with his hoe, and smoking his pipe at the same time; another carries it — the mortar, not the pipe — in a hod, to the fourth story of some building in process of erection, whistling all the while an air from Fra Diavolo, or holding an interesting and lively chat with some one on the sidewalk. He reminds you of the story of the Irishman in America, who wrote home to his cousin: "Och, Pat me boy, come to this counthry if you want to live at aise. You have only to carry bricks in a hod up four shtories of ladder, and there, be jabers! you will find a spalpeen that will do all the work for you."

My American friend who delivers himself at times of such gross absurdities that I would back him against any story-teller in Christendom, says: "I never see these Frenchmen perspire at labor; but often in the midst of an exciting conversation, when they get so fearfully argumentative, that I live in almost constant dread of witnessing the spilling of their calorific blood; but just when I think they are going to blow out each other's brains, they wind up with a hearty laugh and mutual understanding all round."

Theatre-going is probably more of an institution here than anywhere else in the world; for, although the prices of admission are quite as high as in America, and the remuneration for labor much less, yet the theatres—and there are some thirty at least—are crowded nightly, and that, too, with a full proportion of the laboring classes. It appears to me that they go to the theatres to save the trouble of reading books; and, consequently, the author and not the actors of a play stands uppermost in people's minds. Thus, they tell you, that they will go to this or that theatre, in order to witness this or that new piece by Dumas-fils, Meurice, or any other author; and its success will depend upon whether it is well and wittily written,—its representation on the stage, it is taken for granted, will be correct. While on this subject, it were as well to give some little account of the new opera of Romeo and Juliet (the music by Gounod, the composer of Faust) that was produced quite recently at the Theatre Lyrique. The whole opera bears the stamp of Shakspearean inspiration, and adheres with strict fidelity to the original text.

It is worthy of the composer of Faust, and may even displace that production in the race for popularity; indeed, it is always said by competent critics, that there are passages in Romeo which surpass, in richness and melody, the finest *morceaux* in Faust. The overture in itself is brilliant; at the end of which the curtain rises, and the Capulets, Montagues, Romeo, Juliet, Mercutio, the Friar and Nurse sing a chorus without accompaniment. The love-strains of the balcony-scenes convey a pathos that touches the heart. The marriage ceremony in the friar's cell is beautiful in its sweet simplicity. The marriage afterwards of Juliet with the County Paris is grand and imposing to a degree only equalled and not surpassed by the procession and march in Faust, or the Prophete. The death-scene by the tomb is made up of fragments of the love-passages in the preceding duets, so skilfully woven together that no objection can be made to their being served up again. Indeed, I have rarely listened to music that has had such an intoxicating effect over my senses as this opera of Romeo and Juliet.

At the Italian Opera, L'Africaine is performed alternately with Don Carlos. I once witnessed a representation of the former at Philadelphia, and was not particularly pleased with it. Whether it be that its production here on a scale almost approaching the miraculous, or its greater excellence in music, or my better appreciation of it on a second attendance, certain it is, that something has greatly revolutionized my opinion. But L'Africaine has been so frequently described, and any attempt on my part to depict its performance here would fall so far short of what it should be, that I will desist.

Popular places of resort to the Parisians are the *Cafés Chantants*—places where the pleasures of the palate are associated with those of the ear. To these, you are informed by placards on the outside, admission is free; but when you get within, you are obliged to take a cup of coffee or a glass of beer, for either of which it will be necessary to pay two francs. In one of these retreats, euphoniously distinguished as the Alcazar, I witnessed—besides a great deal of second-rate singing and first-rate dancing—a unique performance, in the way of a young Improvisatore, who came before the audience with a piece of white paper and a pencil; whereupon he bade the audience to call out any words they wished, which was complied with by a great many from different parts of the house, and in the most incongruous manner. But, as well as he could catch the words, he wrote them down in the order they were given, at the end of every line of his paper; and, when he had a page of such words, he filled up the lines so as to make the whole production a jingle of rhymes—and it was said to be excellent poetry. Apostrophizing the sublime genius, I whispered into the ear of my American friend the well-known quotation—

> "Shade of the mighty! can it be
> That this is all remains of thee?"

when he immediately responded: "That chap on the platform would say —

> 'Great muse of poetry! is it true,
> That this is all that's left of you?'"

In these cafés, amid volumes of smoke from the fragrant weed, the blouse and frock-coat are conspicuous, interspersed here and there with a muslin cap and merino gown, listening to the comic songs, or snatches from favorite operas, that are gushed out over them by the performers. On the Avenue des Champs Elysées there are concerts of this description, where the audience is accommodated in the open air, and the singers are under elegant kiosks, gayly painted and adorned with flowers.

The love of flowers among the people here amounts to a passion; their persons, their houses, and every object of love being decorated with a flowery vestment. Consequently there are some five or six large flower markets, of which that which is held on the Place de la Madeleine is one of the curiosities of the city. There, on Tuesdays and Fridays, the air is redolent with the intoxicating aroma that emanates from the vast quantity and variety of the genus flora that are displayed for purchase; and many are the little tokens of affection that are there culled and assorted to convey tender messages from one to another; and many the arch maiden and the sanguine youth who may be there seen tripping along between the beautiful bouquets, asking their prices here and there, with a burning, tell-tale cheek and swelling heart—a heart not yet charred and blistered by the torrid heats of exhausted passion, or frozen by the wintery winds of adversity; but full of joy, full of hope, full of the promise of a golden future.

Last Sunday was a great day in the Bois de Boulogne, it being a day appointed for the races to come off; and the weather being extremely warm and summer-like, thousands of people were attracted to that beautiful spot, which may truly be said to be the lungs of Paris. The races were very exciting, and betting was going on to a shocking extent. Indeed, to one not accustomed to such a desecration of the Sabbath, the scene was anything but agreeable.

The number of grand equipages that were present was perfectly astounding, and such a display of sumptuous livery and extravagant vassalage can only be appreciated by being seen—words can do no adequate justice to the subject. Among these was the Emperor himself, who was readily distinguished by the six horses attached to his carriage, (none other being allowed that number of horses,) and by the colors of his livery, green and gold. Hardly inferior to the equipage of Napoleon, were many others owned by the nobility, generals, ministers, plenipotentiary representatives of other nations, and by the wealthy citizens of Paris. On all occasions of parade and display, Prince Metternich, the Austrian minister, can be singled out most conspicuously by the gayety and magnificence of his turnouts.

On our return to the city from the Bois, these carriages constituted a crowded procession of miles in length; and while it was passing down the Avenue de l'Emperatrice, a man ascended with a 'monster balloon from the Hippodrome close by. I think, on the least calculation, there must have been sixty thousand people out at the races and other parts of the woods of Boulogne during the day.

One of the amusements on this occasion had been a little adventure which my American friend had with a French thimble-rigger, who was shuffling a number of cards, and turning three of them upon their faces so slowly and deliberately, that it appeared impossible not to see that they were three aces, of hearts, diamonds, and spades respectively; or to know exactly which of the three either of them was.

"I challenge any gentleman to tell me where the ace of hearts is," said he, in French, to the motley crowd who had gathered about him. My American friend, who had seen that sort of thing before in Jones' Wood and at Coney Island, looked curiously at the little, black-bearded professor of legerdemain, and then ventured to say, with a horrible English accent, that he thought he knew where the little joker was; and would back his opinion by a small wager of a Napoleon. This proposal was immediately accepted; the stakes were put up; and then being asked to produce the aforesaid ace of hearts, he seized the Frenchman's arm, and in an instant extracted from under the sleeve thereof the card in question.

The excitement that followed this dénoûement amid the observant crowd was a curious admixture of mirth and anger. The little thimble-rigger had been outwitted, and my American friend, who was looked upon as quite a hero, pocketed the two Napoleons, and went his way rejoicing.

The palaces at Versailles, St. Cloud, and Fontainebleau, also draw a great number from the city every day, and a greater number every Sunday, not only of strangers who visit Paris, but to a great extent of Parisians themselves; who never get done looking at those magnificent monuments of art and royalty; but return to them over and over again; and each one appears to take as much interest in any one of the palaces as if he owned it himself, and was its lordling "to the manor born." Whichever of its many residences the Imperial family occupies is not accessible to visitors at the time being; but the others are all thrown open to satisfy the eager curiosity of the public, and the foot of the stranger may tread through all their rooms, nor is the sanctity respected even of the chamber of the Empress.

Nevertheless, there is always an ample guard of magnificently uniformed soldiers, who parade about in great pomp and circumstance, and although one may go everywhere and *look* at everything, yet under no condition is a person allowed to *touch* anything whatever.

Speaking of the soldiers, what a great element they constitute in France, and especially in Paris! They may be seen at all hours of the day or night, singly or in groups; and the many uniforms of the different arms of the service, but all gay and beautiful, produce a pretty effect in the general sprinkling of them through the thickly populous streets. Indeed, the dress of the soldiers is unexceptionable, in regard to the elegance of the fit, and the neatness and cleanliness in which it is kept; and what with all its stripes and decorations and tinselled embellishments, a private soldier here looks far more gorgeous than General Grant in full uniform.

Then the Sergeants de Ville, or policemen, are another set of splendidly attired fellows; and there are so many of them, that by the time night comes, your eyes ache from the everlasting deep-blue coats and shining brass buttons they have encountered during the live-long day. But it must be admitted in connection with this subject, that the police system here is as near perfection as such a thing may possibly be. I have been here almost a month now, and have not read of a single theft, to say nothing of murder and any of the bolder catalogue of crimes having been committed. Although there is doubtless a great deal of vice; yet actual, open, and defiant crime is extremely rare. This is the more apparent from the extreme horror with which the ideas of New York and a disregard of the laws are associated in every Frenchman's mind. True, their system here is one of espionage; and although one feels a trifle less free than in New York, for instance, yet one certainly feels, at the same time, a great deal more safe. Voila! the extent of their system. You arrive at a hotel; by-and-by the landlord gives you, with much obsequious politeness, a blank statement to fill up, which requires your name, nativity, age, occupation, last residence, how long you expect to stay at Paris, and whether (if a foreigner) you have a passport. Thus they know all about you, and know exactly who, and how many strangers are in the city. Besides this, there is a certain mystery in almost everything that lays heavy on one's Yankee curiosity. Thus you come home from the theatre at night, and find the door or porter's gate locked. You ring the bell, and instantly the door flies open, as if some magic "sesame" had been pronounced. You are startled by this sudden response of invisible agents to your touch of the bell-knob, but you glide in notwithstanding, and push the door back, which closes with a sharp click, as if it had closed between you and liberty forever. You see no person whatever, but reflect and make up your mind that you have been let into the house by some horrible French machination. You sit down in your own room in thoughtful contemplation, wondering whether some "iron mask" will be clapped upon your face soon.

With the resignation of true philosophy, you retire and go to sleep, and in the morning when you awake again, with the heavenly light streaming into your chamber-window, you feel jubilant to find that you are not a prisoner after all; for the door is unlocked, your pocket-book with all its important contents still occupies the pocket of your nether garment, as you flung them on the chair the evening before; the watch — the bright yellow golden watch — is still hanging on the nail in the wall, and ticking away as if its mainspring was on a great bender, and having a jolly old time on tick. Temptingly it hangs there; but no ruthless hands have touched its pretty face, except those that describe their daily circuit from its centre, and indicate the progress of fleet-footed time. Another mystery that is difficult to unravel, is, to know when people — or whether they ever do — go to bed. I have returned to "mine inn" from the various attractions which the night affords as late as one o'clock, and found the Boulevards just as crowded, and the cafés as noisy and brilliant and full as during any time of the twenty-four hours. I entered one of them, took a little *eau de Seltz*, and smoked a cigar, thinking I would wait and find out the Parisian bedtime; but at two o'clock I gave up the contest, and retired myself, no wiser than I was before.

Mystery number three is, where all the wine comes from that these people drink. It seems to me, that if the entire surface of the earth was planted with grapevines, and there never was a failure in the crop, they could not produce grapes enough from which to squeeze out all the wine that is consumed here. You walk into a restaurant for your dinner, the first thing the "garçon" asks is, *what kind* of wine you will have, and not whether you will have any at all; and when told that you desire *no* wine, he seems paralyzed with astonishment, and looks at you with such an air of pity and commiseration, that you drink a bottle of Bordeaux, just to save the poor boy's life. To tell the truth, however, the water that one gets here is not fit to drink; it is obtained from the Seine, and although filtered and taken from above the city, the association is anything but pleasant. In course of time it is hoped that they will have artesian wells to supply the water in sufficient quantity for the city. Already at the Bois de Boulogne they have a well of this kind, that produces a very large stream of water. It is, I believe, the deepest in the world, with the exception of that in Columbus, Ohio; so deep, in fact, that the water is quite warm — warm enough to create a suspicion that —— well, the reader may draw the inference, while the Parisians draw the water.

My American friend, who has just read this letter, calls it a light and trivial affair; but *parbleu!* what else can one write on such an effervescent subject as the amusements of the French?

LETTER V.

BOULEVARD DE SEBASTOPOL.

MEDICAL INSTITUTIONS OF PARIS.

PARIS, *May*, 1867.

IT is my purpose to devote this letter principally to a subject in which it is but natural that I should feel interested, namely, the medical institutions of this good city.

In order to approach these, let us enter one of the most beautiful, though not, perhaps, most fashionable thoroughfares of Paris — the comparatively new Boulevard de Sebastopol. Although in the morning it represents the scene of a long and extensive market, being literally crowded with wagons and carts, so as to make it almost impossible to pass through it with a carriage, yet the sidewalks are so wide and free from obstructions, that no difficulty is experienced in one's pedestrian progress of reviewing this extraordinary living panorama.

Having passed southward, we traverse the Place du Chatelet, with the Imperial Theatre du Chatelet on our right, and the Lyrique on the left, with the beautiful fountain that adorns that square, in the centre. The fountain was the first monument erected in commemoration of the victories of the Republic and the Empire. It consists of a circular basin, some twenty-five feet in diameter, with a high stone column in the form of a palm-tree in the centre. On the pedestal are four statues, representing Justice, Strength, Prudence and Vigilance, which join hands and encircle the column. The shaft is intersected with bands of gilt bronze, inscribed with the names of the principal victories of Napoleon.

The water issues from four cornucopiæ, terminating in fishes' heads, and from the mouths of four sphynxes; on two sides are eagles encircled by wreaths of laurels; and on the summit of the shaft is a gilt statue of Victory.

Passing on, we arrive at the river's side, and cross it by the bridge (Pont au Change), and will be in the *Cité* — an island where, it is said, the first Roman squatter sovereigns located themselves some sixty years before the birth of Christ, and formed the nucleus of Paris, and where, besides other buildings, the important edifices of Notre Dame, the Hotel Dieu, and the Palais de Justice were afterwards erected.

The Hotel Dieu consists of two long, old and shabby-looking stone buildings, extending along the two banks of the southern portion of the river, of the two arms that form the island; and you pass from one building to the other by means of a covered bridge or passage-way.

This, then, is the world-renowned and most ancient hospital of Paris. I confess that, when I first saw it, I was somewhat disappointed; but falling back on its time-honored history, and the great men who have taught and practised in its wards the alleviation of suffering humanity, I could not but look at it with a feeling of reverence and admiration. We will pass it by, however, for the present, and proceed across the second bridge (Pont St. Michel), along the beautiful fountain where the Archangel is represented as destroying Satan, and from the rock forming the basement of which, and the mouths of two dragons, streams of water gush into the basins below. We continue a short distance down the Boulevard St. Michel, pass the Boulevard St. Germain, and in doing so, glance at the Hotel de Cluny, a museum of antiquities, and the Palais des Thermes, which is a still remaining ruin of a castle built by Julius Cæsar, —and turn at last to the right, into the *Rue de l'École de Médecine*. This is a narrow street, with very narrow sidewalks; but as thoroughly devoted to the goddess of Medicine as Wall Street in New York is to Mammon. Here the windows of the shops exhibit a profusion of skeletons, in picturesque and artistic attitudes, most tempting to the covetous student; a fine display of anatomical plates and preparations; casts in wax of the muscular system, and manikins of every description. Next door is a gorgeous assortment of surgical instruments, of quaint and curious fabric, bright and glittering, like diamonds in the sunshine, that make a cut here and a stab there, and the sawing off of an occasional bone, look like fascinating little affairs rather to be desired than otherwise.

Next door again you have a medical library displayed in the windows. Pamphlets, and monographs, and treatises, and elaborate French and ponderous German works, that would take ages to read, and the very sight of which makes one wonder how it is possible — in the face of all this learning — that human beings are ever permitted to die. I have seen some of the learned authors of these books rub their hands in glee at the discovery on a post-mortem examination, of a pathological condition, "Just as they had predicted." But the poor body was dead. Ah! how well we understand the infirmities that flesh and blood are heir to! If men were crystallized we could not see any better than we do now the fatal tubercles gnawing at their lungs, or the refractory valves that will not serve their functions in the heart. But where is the remedial agent? Shades of Hippocrates and Galen! we know the bane; but where, oh where is the antidote? We diagnose diseases so nicely now as to discriminate, in a case of *mania a potu*, the species of stimulant by which it was produced; if by whiskey, the face will be pale; by wine, it will be red; and if caused by a malt beverage, the nose alone will stand out as "a burning and a shining light." Now this is very well; but how about the treatment? A young fellow, who professes to be very scientific, says: "In the first instance give wine; in the second, whiskey; and in the third, wine and whiskey alternately, frequently, and in large doses." *Medica aliquid dandum est.*" The American friend, who is my oracle and a doctor, again prompts me, and says, that "the science of disease, by the aid of chemistry and the microscope, has become a beautiful perfection; but all the various systems of therapeutics, or modes of treatment, are a hum— a very imperfect thing indeed."

But I am getting into my old habits — it is time to stop this abusing of my bread and butter.

Next to the bookstore you will see another window studded with optical instruments, among which microscopes are most conspicuous; and some of them are so powerful — you will be told — that if you place a small particle of *brain* under their lenses, you can almost *see it think*.

Thus a succession of professional appliances will be met in the shops all along the street, until you arrive at the College, where the Faculté of France give their medical instruction. This faculty consists of twenty-nine professors, and the same number of sub-professors. They deliver lectures on fourteen different branches of science applicable to the practice of medicine and surgery. The lectures are free to all; but in order to obtain the diploma of the Faculty, which entitles the possessor to practise his profession in France, a course of study during four years, and a tri-monthly subjection to examination, are necessary.

As these examinations are conducted in public, I have attended some of them; and must confess, that I have been very favorably impressed with the careful manner in which doctors are created in this country. The place where the examinations are held is a large and magnificently furnished apartment, carpeted with heavy Brussels tapestry, to prevent the noise of footsteps. The walls are hung with allegorical paintings and portraits of the eminent fathers of medicine and surgery, copiously interspersed with marble busts representing the same, and a very excellent one, occupying the place of honor on a special pedestal, and bearing the well-known features of the present Emperor. Along the sides of the room are sofas and chairs, covered with crimson plush, for the accommodation of the visitors who desire to witness the examinations. In the rear end of the room is a long table covered with green baize, before which are seated three candidates (during these ceremonies), and behind it, fronting the auditory, are the three professors who examine in turn. They are attired in deep scarlet robes of satin, and crowned with black caps, glittering with broad and heavy gold bands. Amidst the breathless silence is only heard the distinct question, followed, after a pause, by the subdued and modest answer.

At one examination that I witnessed, on the subject of Materia Medica, the table was covered with bottles and jars, filled with different medicaments, but without any labels to denote their contents. These articles the candidates were required to denominate and describe, giving their history, chemical reagencies, physical and medical properties, &c. At another examination on Anatomy which I saw conducted, the candidate was placed before an anatomical subject, into which a long knife or catline was plunged at hap-hazard up to the hilt, and he was then directed to enumerate and describe all the blood-vessels, nerves, muscles, and organs of the body that had been transpierced by the knife; after which he was asked to expose a given nerve, or artery, or muscle; and finally, to perform, on the subject before him, this or that man's mode of operation for this or that pathological condition.

After the examination is over, which generally continues about three hours, the audience is required to withdraw; a private conference is had between the three judges, the result of which is afterwards made known by a clerk to the assembled students in an adjoining room, by whom, if favorable, it is generally received with demonstrations of joy and satisfaction; if unfavorable, with long and thoughtful faces, and expressive silence.

Among the audiences in attendance upon the lectures, I constantly see men of all ages, from the youthful student to the venerable old man, who has evidently seen a great deal of service in the profession; but comes here to refresh his mind on special subjects, or listen to the promulgation of some new theory or mode of treatment. Men from all countries, too, are heré; a large number from the United States, several from Mexico, and many from England, Germany, and other European sections. But, strangest of all, there are six or seven black men in daily attendance on the lectures. They are young men, dressed genteelly, and associate with the other students as if they were not at all proud; walking along the streets, engaged all the while in animated conversation with white men, or entering a restaurant, and partaking of an "absinthe" or "caffe noir" with some Caucasian friend, who never thinks of drawing any lines of social distinction between his sable companion and himself. These people are here called Egyptians, as we would speak of Germans, Englishmen, Italians, &c., distinguishing them from other people by the country they come from, rather than by the color of their skin. At home we would call these medical students "niggers;" at least, such is the opinion of my American friend, and I am sure *he* knows.

The section of Paris where the medical colleges are located was formerly distinguished as the Latin Quarter, and all students resided in its precincts, leading a rather loose and Bohemian life. Of late years, however, that portion of the city has been much improved by stately mansions, taking the place of inelegant houses, and splendid boulevards in lieu of the labyrinthine thoroughfares that constituted the haunts and purlieus of debauchery in former days. An old relic of the olden time, however, is still retained in what is known as the *Closerie des Lilas*, which is a special resort for students, and, like the *Jardin Mabille*, constitutes an arena for the midnight saturnalia, where the gay and licentious of both sexes congregate, passing the hours, that should be devoted to better purposes, in very questionable propriety, where the *can-can* dance runs through the whole order of exercises, and voluptuous abandonment characterizes the entire proceeding.

One of the most popular hospitals of Paris, if not *the* most popular, is La Charité, where Drs. Malgaigne, Bouillaud, and the venerable and world-renowned Velpeau* prescribe for the sick, and give their clinical instructions. The latter-named gentleman is some eighty years of age, yet performs operations for cataract on the eye with a steady hand, and without spectacles. Indeed, it is touching

* Since dead.

to see the poor patients brighten in the face when he approaches their bedside; for he is greatly venerated by the citizens of Paris, who look upon him as a kind of medical demigod. And for myself I must say that I feel it as a great privilege, being enabled at this late period of his life to follow the teachings of this experienced man; one of whose principal works I read many years ago, as it was then translated by our own eminent but now deceased Dr. Mott of New York.

I regret exceedingly that another venerable patriarch in the profession, Dr. Trousseau, whom I had hoped to be enabled to see, is so ill that his recovery is despaired of.*

The Hotel-Dieu, the most ancient asylum for the sick in Paris, still retains a reputation worthy of its past record. Here, where Bichat, Dupuytren, Desault, and more recently, Trousseau and Jobert de Lamballe, have ministered to their suffering fellow-beings, and covered the place with a classic halo, it is still evident that the work of humanity is in the hands of skilful servants, who have dedicated their lives to its faithful performance. Of these, I doubt not, that M. Fournier, whose teachings are of the rarest merit, and who has his whole heart in his occupation, will one day, if he lives, shed as fair a lustre upon science and the healing art as any one in the bright galaxy of names whose illustrious labors have preceded, but not eclipsed his own.

The hospital Salpetrière is remarkable for its construction, as well as for its extent and capacity. It consists of no less than forty-five different buildings,

* Since also dead.

which in all reach to the length of 1,680 feet, and has 5,204 beds. From these few facts some idea can be formed of the dimensions of this institution. Its purpose is to receive, first, Reposantes, or women who have been in its service thirty years, and are upwards of sixty years of age; second, women upwards of seventy, who are afflicted with incurable diseases; third, insane and epileptic females. Not fewer than 484 persons are employed in its service. The hospital St. Louis is chiefly designed for the treatment of skin-diseases and scrofula, although it also receives other cases, and had a great many patients during the prevalence of the cholera. It would be an excellent place for some of the sufferers of that very fashionable and "popular eruption" that has prevailed so extensively in the United States during and since the late war; for they have a method here of curing the itch in two hours. It has a very large bathing establishment, justly celebrated for its medicated and mineral baths, particularly those of a sulphurous nature. There is also a large vapor-bath, admitting by distinct entries eight patients at the same time.

As a general thing, I find that throughout all the hospitals very little medicine is given; indeed, it is surprising to what a degree this entire dependence upon the restorative powers of nature is carried, and that too, I am bound to say, with a very favorable result. A strict discipline of dietetics, and close attention to all hygienic laws, are enforced, and that with the administration of Bordeaux wine, which they give under almost all circumstances, constitutes nearly their sole treatment. Yet in cases of hopeless diseases they make exceptions to this treatment, and experiment with medicines to a fearful extent. Of these medicines, strychnine and arsenic are, just now, those that are most highly favored, and, of course, these are things not to be trifled with.

There are a great many more hospitals and charitable institutions that might be enumerated; but I fear the reader is wearied of the subject, as it is not exactly that which is calculated to interest the general mind, yet not altogether without curious import to many.

LETTER VI.

THE GREAT NAPOLEON.

THE MEMORY OF THE GREAT NAPOLEON.—HIS TOMB.— HOTEL DES INVALIDES.—ITS VETERAN INMATES.—IMPERIAL MUSEUM IN THE GALLERIES OF THE LOUVRE.— THE GALLERY CONTAINING RELICS OF NAPOLEON I.— THE TUILERIES.—THE IMPERIAL FAMILY.—THE JARDIN MABILLE.—ADVENTURE WITH A FAIR MAIDEN AND A STERN LANDLORD.

Paris, *May*. 1867.

IT is a truth admitting of no dispute, that the memory of the great Napoleon has a strong hold upon the affections of the French people. A clear evidence of this may be seen on those days when the public is allowed ingress to that magnificent dome where the mortal remains of that wonderful man repose. Although a large proportion of the visitors are strangers, yet the majority are Frenchmen; and of these the greatest number wear blouses, showing that they are of the great masses. It is affecting to see with what veneration they uncover their heads as they enter the portals of that, to them, hallowed precinct. Over the door to the entrance of the marble crypt are inscribed, in letters of gold, these words from the last will and testament of the Prisoner at St. Helena:

"*Je désire que mes cendres reposent sur les bords de la Seine, au milieu de ce peuple Français que j'ai tant aimé.*" I saw a Frenchman reading these words audibly to his wife and child, whom he had with him, and while he did so the tears moistened his eyelids.

It is but natural to any ardent admirer of the proud warrior, to feel himself there as in the presence of a great spirit that slumbers. It gratifies one's sense of justice, too, to see, at the right and left of him, grandly reposing the ashes of the two faithful friends who remained true to him in the dark hour of his adversity, Generals Duroc and Bertrand, the latter of whom shared with him the dying glory of his island solitude.

Quitting the presence of the august dead, I proceeded to the Hotel des Invalides, where a number of the brave comrades of the conquering hero still survive, some of them from seventy-five to eighty years of age; in fact, none of the veteran invalids who enjoy the hospitality of this refuge appear to be less than sixty.

When I entered their *salle à manger*, they were seated at breakfast around two long rows of circular tables, about ten men to each table. With their neat attire, venerable aspect, and precise, orderly, and dignified deportment, these old men presented the appearance more of a council of reverend senators at a state banquet, than of soldiers in the ordinary participation of their frugal meal. Many of them have lost an arm or a leg, and all are more or less disabled by wounds or infirmities, making a crutch or staff necessary to them in walking. They all have clean-shaved faces, except in some instances, where small, gray side-whiskers on the upper part of the cheeks, or, here and there, a thick gray moustache may be seen among them. All these things lend a charm to their assemblage that is difficult to describe. An interesting part of this building to the visitor, is the gallery containing the models in cast of all the principal cities and fortifications in France, some of them being perfectly level, like Paris, and others, like Grenoble, on the side of a towering mountain or the crest of some fearful gorge. There is also a miniature model of the Battle of the Bridge of Lodi, where Napoleon so eminently distinguished himself in the early part of his career; and another of the storming of Sebastopol.

One of the most noteworthy places to visit in Paris, is the Imperial Museum in the galleries of the Louvre, where hundreds of the most magnificent oil-paintings, by the old masters, may be inspected and studied daily by all who desire to do so. Here one may feast his eyes on such choice productions as the frescos by Guichard and Lebrun, the Triumph of the Earth, and the Triumph of the Water; the Four Seasons, respectively by Callet, Durameau, Taravall, and Lagrance; the Feast of Cana, and Mary anointing the feet of Jesus, by Paolo Veronese; Charles the First, of England, by Vandyck; the Conception, by Murillo; and the Apotheosis of Homer, by Ingress. Here, too, is the celebrated Galerie de Rubens, containing many of the most admired works of that great artist. None but the works of deceased masters are admitted into this gallery, which was chiefly formed by Napoleon, and enriched with the masterpieces of Europe. In the Musée Napoleon

III. is a collection of antiquities from Syria, Macedonia, Thessaly, and Asia Minor; and in the Musée des Souverains are relics, consisting of armors, spears, battle-axes, swords, crowns, &c., that belonged to the different monarchs of France, as far back as the earliest periods. The *Salle de l'Empereur* is devoted exclusively to articles relating to Napoleon I., including the full-dress uniform worn by him on state occasions; his saddle, sword, gloves, &c.; his uniform which he wore at Marengo; his sword of First Consul; his horse's bridle-bit; the hat he wore in the campaign of 1814, and the small round one which he wore at St. Helena; besides numerous other things too trivial to mention. In the picture-galleries, scores of artists, ladies as well as gentlemen, may be daily seen engaged in copying the eminent productions, and it is interesting to compare the copies with the originals. In several instances I have found the similitude so exact as hardly to be able to distinguish the old from the new picture, and in such cases my American friend invariably wondered why the imitation should not be worth just as much as the original.

Contiguous to the Louvre is the Palace of the Tuileries, the principal town-residence of the Imperial family. As it has thus far, during my stay in Paris, been occupied by the illustrious trio who constitute that family, with their numerous attendants, I have not been privileged to perambulate through its interior, with a curious eye on the regality thereof, of which report says many precious things. It looks imposing enough from the outside, to be sure; and I suspect that it is possible to dwell within it with much ease and comfort. Yet there is trouble inside of it, too, just now — even as it gets into the abode of more plebeian mortals; for the Prince Imperial is sick, and Dr. Nelaton is in almost constant attendance. The little invalid has certainly very great expectations; and if the principal one of them, that of recovery from what is threatening to be hip-disease, will only be realized, it will be a blessed thing for himself, and a great feather in the doctor's cap. Upon the whole, though, just at this juncture, I doubt whether that professional gentleman's position is greatly to be envied; for his imperial patient might die, and then — like to a general after a lost battle — things might look rather squally with his future prospects. It is a pity that the boy has not a half dozen brothers and sisters to share his responsible situation, as they could possibly come in very handy some day, as a kind of collateral security for the Napoleonic dynasty. His mother, Eugénie, is a splendid woman to look at, and might displace many a younger one in the race for admiration; but, unfortunately, she has thus far been somewhat defective in the greatest quality of her sex, one in which the reigning queens of England and Spain have so eminently excelled her! The boy's father, old Mr. Napoleon, must be closely running on to sixty, and is beginning to look a little the worse for wear. Still, come to look at his physiognomy, there's a good bit of authority enthroned there; and his large Roman nose appears as vigorously on the lookout for breakers ahead, or to smell out diplomatic schemes, as ever. What the papers say about his precarious health is all fudge; for to see the elasticity with which he mounts his horse, and the ease and gracefulness with which he rides him at reviews in the Place du Carrousel, or the firm, yet muscular springiness of his gait in walking, must convince any reasonable person that the Emperor has still all the outward appearances of a pretty long lease on his sublunary life.

Strolling along the Champs Elysées, in the vicinity of the Jardin Mabille, one evening, I was tempted, by the wonderful renown thereof, to enter that enchanted enclosure, and behold with mine own eyes the hidden glories it affords. Presently I was wandering over the labyrinthine paths of a beautiful grove of the choicest shrubberies and aromatic trees, that filled the air with delicious perfume and a freshness that was truly charming; amid all manner of curiously contrived fountains, that bathed voluptuous figures, in marble, of dolphins, naiads and Venuses, covering them with aqueous veils, in which the many-colored lights from hundreds of Chinese lanterns, that were tastefully arranged all around, trembled and glittered in phosphorescent effulgence, like a shower of diamonds and rubies and emeralds in the full blaze of the noon-day sun. From the more central focuses of this bewildering splendor many little by-paths terminated in cosy half-concealed retreats, bowers, and grottos, where rustic seats were constructed to afford comfortable resting-places, or sentimental *tête-a-têtes* for the votaries of Cupid.

Within an inner circle, in a pagóda of Oriental magnificence, were a string-band of musicians, discoursing such dulcet strains into the mellow night, that a concert of æolian harps could not have more entranced the soul with the dreamy and blissful imagery of sound. Within this magic circle, too, were figures in rustling silks, tripping along on the light fantastic toe, in the wildest coquetry of graceful flexibility, that should gratify the terpsichorean Muse in her most fanciful exactions.

I seated myself by a table, in an arbor of trellis-work, thickly covered by the foliage of a creeping vine, and studied the scene before me with all the enthusiasm of a visionary soul.

Presently there appeared, dispelling the solitude of my retreat, one of those sylph-like beings whom I had seen in the airy dance tilting with tiny feet the hats from their partners' heads. Panting with apparent physical exhaustion, she sank upon a seat at the opposite side of the table, and exclaimed, in the most captivating vernacular: "*Mon Dieu! J'ai une grande soif!*" Moved by her distressed appearance, I made bold enough to ask whether I could serve her with a glass of water; whereupon she gazed at me with a world of gratitude, and replied with a gushing vehemence of French eloquence: "*Merci, merci bien, monsieur, mais je crois qu'un verre de vin me sauviez la vie.*" "*Vous l'aurez immédiatement, madame,*" responded I with heedless precipitation, and ordered a waiter to produce the life-saving beverage required by the unnerved danseuse.

She was beautiful as a houri, and the look of deep tenderness with which she accompanied her profuse expressions of thanks somewhat disconcerted my equanimity. Directly the wine arrived, and she drank down a goodly portion of a gobletful, with much apparent benefit to her sinking spirits. But, soon after, while she was yet sipping at a second libation of the purple-tinted nectarine juice — as sip the muses from the fountains of Helicon — and lost as it were in a revery of a serious drift, a burly-looking Frenchman entered the arbor abruptly, and accosted her rudely, at the same time thrusting a piece of paper into her face, saying: " There, madam, is that bill of a hundred francs which you owe me for rent, and if you do not pay me immediately, you shall not enter your apartments again; and I will seize upon your effects the first thing in the morning."

Frightened and chagrined at this coarse informality, in the presence of a stranger too, and from a countryman, in the land whose politeness is set forth as an example to all other nations, she first upbraided her intrusive landlord; but finding, from a responsive frown, that this would only tend to make matters worse, she implored him to grant her time until the following afternoon; that she was quite certain of receiving a remittance in the morning, and would then be enabled to meet his demand.

The creditor was inexorable, and said that he had purposely followed her to this resort of pleasure and dissipation to convince himself of her luxurious habits, and insisted on being paid. At this she began to weep bitterly, and wrung her pretty hands with anguish, presenting a scene that was altogether painful to behold. I could now endure the situation no longer; all the impulses of a naturally philanthropic disposition were awakened within me, and I ventured to expostulate with this heartless creditor about the matter in question, with the hope of mollifying his stern and unfeeling purposes. He was an obdurate, hard-fisted old wretch, whose veins did not pulsate with the generous flow of the milk of human kindness; and he continued as steadfast in his importunities for the amount of his bill as any Shylock that ever harped upon a forfeited pound of flesh. "*Ah, mon Dieu!*" said the poor girl in distress, "if I only knew some kind, generous person to lend me this sum until to-morrow, when I should be amply able to refund it;" then, as if endeavoring to overcome with a desperate plunge the reserve that had governed her thus far, she turned with an appealing look to me, and exclaimed: "Oh, sir, you see how this man has outraged my feelings. I have no friends here, and would not know where to go for the night; but you, you are kind, sir, I see it in your face; you are sure, sir, that you can safely trust to my integrity; you will lend me this paltry sum, will you not, *dear* sir? with your address, too, so that I may send the amount back to you — with my unbounded gratitude — to-morrow afternoon, d-e-a-r sir."

She looked honest; her eyes were suffused in tears; her cheeks crimsoned with conscious shame at her temerity; her whole attitude was so gracefully imploring — and she certainly was *very* pretty. Undoubtedly, thought I, it is my duty to relieve this poor, sweet lady from her embarrassment. "I will do it — yes, I will do it — come what may; by jingo! I will do it! It is a precious comfortable thing to perform a kind action — makes a body sleep so soundly, gives one a good appetite, and does lots of agreeable things for you." Thus reflecting over the matter, I was about to take out my pocket-book and look for a hundred francs, when suddenly a hand came down with a heavy force upon my shoulder. I looked around — it was my American friend. "Are you going to make a darned fool of yourself?" said he, "don't you see that this is a regular game here — a common ruse — and that the fellow yonder is only a flunky, who operates in concert with the girl for half the proceeds? Is this at all a likely place or season to be dunned by a landlord for rent? Ha! ha! ha! why, what a regular old greeny you are, to be caught with a lot of French chaff like that!" I was thunderstruck; could it be possible? could such things be? They evidently could; for my American friend continued to laugh immoderately; and while I could only see myself in the light of a benevolent benefactor, he, it was clear, could only look at me as a great simpleton. Aye! and my friend's sagacity was not long in being proved; for directly upon his interference with the affairs of the pretty tenant in default, the landlord turned ferociously upon him with, "*Sacre bleu! que voulez-vous dire, monsieur?*" "*You* mind your own business, mounseer," said my friend, confronting him with a defiant look, and not deigning to use the Frenchman's mother-tongue, "or I'll give you such a dab in the eye that the *blue* around it will be anything but *sacred* to you."

The fellow now spluttered out a lot of very heroic phrases, accompanied by suitable flashes of an ugly pair of eyes, shrugging of shoulders, and clenching of fists. "Look there," said my American friend, "do you see that *sergeant de ville?* Now mizzle instantly, or I will place you under his tender protection." No sooner did he see the public functionary pointed out to him, than he gathered himself up and prepared to leave. The fair damsel too, seeing herself check-mated, dropped her troubled and injured look, and taking the arm of her terrible creditor, deigned to laugh, probably at my tender simplicity, and to scowl at my American friend; then the two passed out of sight, and only figure in my mind now as it were a ridiculous dream.

Farewell, for a while, to Paris. As a general thing, you have pleased me, but I must further go. I hesitated some time, whether I had not better devote all my time in Europe to this city; but my American friend, to whom I confided the matter, and who sometimes addresses me in German, especially when he is in earnest, now opened on me with: "*Was, der Henker! Soll man von dir sagen, du bist in Rome gewesen und hast den Papst nicht gesehen?* That's what Smith and Jones and Brown and Mrs. Grundy will say to you, if you don't proceed farther. No, no, my lad, it will never do to get sea-sick for the sake of Paris alone." Enough, my friend, *that* argument is unanswerable. I leave to-morrow, and you shall go with me.

LETTER VII.

THE CHAMPAGNE DISTRICT.

*EN ROUTE TO ZURICH.—THE CHAMPAGNE DISTRICT.—
STRASBURG.—ITS CATHEDRAL.—THE WONDERFUL CLOCK.
ASCENT OF THE STEEPLE, THE HIGHEST IN THE WORLD.
INTERCHANGE OF COURTESIES WITH A BOSTONIAN.—
MY AMERICAN FRIEND'S GHOST-POEM.—THE MONUMENTS
OF STRASBURG.—INDUSTRIAL HABITS OF THE PEOPLE.—
OPPRESSION OF WOMEN.—THE BLACK FOREST OF THE
DUCHY OF BADEN.—THE SCENERY.—CURIOSITIES OF
FREIBURG.*

ZURICH, SWITZERLAND, *June*, 1867.

LEAVING Paris, I passed through the District of Champagne, which is remarkable in nothing so much as in its contrast with the rich soil of Normandy that I had traversed on my way from Havre. This I fancifully accounted for on the strength of the supposition, that if all the beverage which is drank for Champagne wine is grown in this country, then the poor soil is quite excusable in looking as parched, impoverished, and starved-out as it does. I had no previous idea that the delicious nectarine juice — so unctuous to the popular palate of the evening, and so melancholy on the popular brain of the following morning — grew upon vines as dwarfish as those I have seen; but rather upon such as that which shaded Jonah, to say nothing of the grape that should rival the magnitude of the pumpkin. The moment we reached the district of Alsace, it was observable in the greener and more advanced condition of the fields, and the prettier villages of whitewashed houses, that had at least been furnished with windows, which many of those in the reputed wine district we had passed were in want of.

Arrived at Strasburg, the great and first object of interest was, of course, the Münster, or cathedral, with its high dome and wonderful astronomical clock. The size of this cathedral is very great, being some hundred and eighty yards in length, and seventy in breadth. The style of its architecture is of the Gothic order, though not entirely so; and it is doubtless surpassed in beauty by many other buildings of less pretension. It has some of the richest painted glass windows of the fourteenth century that may anywhere be seen — one of which, in particular, sparkles as though studded with the most precious gems, and has colors that cannot be imitated at the present day. In the interior of the church, to the left of the altar, is the celebrated clock, whose ingenious workmanship is almost beyond the bounds of credibility. On the left side is a construction that shows the ecclesiastical calculation of time, and on the right the conjoint movements of the sun and moon; below which is a globe exhibiting the course of the stars, before an almanac that is said to have a correct reckoning for a thousand years. Then follows a dial showing the diurnal time, above which the moon — the one half gilded, and the other half black — moves in perfect accord with that orb in the heavens; so that at full moon it shows all the gilded surface, and at new moon but the faintest cycle of it. Once in twenty-four hours, when it is about to indicate twelve at noon, an angel strikes a bell, when another angel, to the left, immediately turns a sand-glass which he holds in his hand. Above these is Time, in the shape of a skeleton, which strikes a bell twelve times; and this is surrounded by smaller figures, representing Infancy, Youth, Manhood, and Old Age, which respectively strike the quarter hours in rotation. From a niche, the symbolic figure of each day, as Apollo for Sunday, Diana for Monday, &c., steps out; and from a niche near the top of the whole construction, figures of the twelve Apostles move successively forward, and pass in front of a representation of Christ, bowing as they do so. Meanwhile, during the time that the clock slowly strikes twelve, at every fourth stroke a cock, perched upon a tower to the right, flaps his wings, stretches his neck, and crows so loud and natural that the sound cannot be distinguished from that of the genuine barn-yard prototype, and reverberates through every nook and corner of the spacious edifice. This performance of the clock occurs only once every twenty-four hours, at mid-day, when a concourse of strangers is generally present to witness it. An old used-up bird of this description, that announced the sun at high meridian during more than three hundred and fifty years, is still on exhibition, together with many other curiosities, in the house once occupied by Erwin, the sculptor and architect of the church, and his daughter Sabina, who succeeded him in the work. By manipulating the intestine machinery of his roostership, he will yet flap his wings and stretch his neck; but his larynx is broken, and he is voiceless forever.

To "get up in the world" is one of the instinctive tendencies of the human family; in accordance with which natural proclivity I now began my pilgrimage heavenwards in that ecclesiastical dome; and I can say in very truth that the "way" was both "crooked and narrow." I was accompanied by a young gentleman from Boston, and together we arrived at an elevation of three hundred feet, upon a large platform partly roofed over, where we could inspect the machinery of the great clock, and where the keeper dwells, or rather roosts, in order to watch the place, and guide pilgrims further up, if they desire it. Here is also, at the visitor's disposal, a fine telescope, through which one can view the distant Schwarzwald, the serpentine course of the Rhine, and the beautiful landscape all around for many miles in extent.

On the chimneys of the city below, a great curiosity are the storks' nests, of which there are some fifty, one having been in existence and inhabited by the same family of storks these twenty years. By the aid of the telescope the storks appear the size of large geese, generally four or five of them to a nest, standing calm, dignified, and motionless upon one leg. After having recovered our exhausted breath at this stage of the ascent, we renewed the journey, and soon arrived at another abutment, a hundred feet higher, where our upward tendency was abruptly blockaded by a bolted door — permission from the Mayor being necessary to proceed farther. As we had neglected to obtain this permission, and as the running down after one was rather an uninviting task, why, therefore this closed door presented quite an ugly obstruction to our rising ambition. But, fortunately, our guide the keeper was human, with a conscience not over-scrupulous, nor wedded to the Bürgomaster's cause: so, through kindness of heart and the persuasive eloquence of a franc-piece, he unlocked the intrusive portal, and bade us rise, follow him, and fear no danger. Thus encouraged, we ascended again, another ninety feet, through a turret of open work, so narrow and tortuous that it was impossible to bend our knees to any extent, but we had to draw ourselves up mainly by the hands; and at one place, near the top, it was necessary to hang on absolutely outside of the steeple. The young Bostonian and myself crowded our bodies with much difficulty into the narrow cage at the top, directly under the cross that forms its highest pinnacle,— and then we were four hundred and ninety feet above the foundation of the church — higher than any other point raised by human hands in the known world, since the top of the pyramid of Cheops was shattered by lightning some years ago. Thus situated, I asked my companion how he felt. He replied, that he felt a little dubious about his identity, and, upon a look of inquiry, continued, that he would like to know whether he was still an individual of the *genus homo*, or a weather-cock; then abruptly changing the subject, he propounded the following question: "Have you ever been at Jerusalem?" I replied him, "Nay;" whereupon he responded, "I have just arrived from there, and have in my pocket a number of so-called Jerusalem agates; accept one, sir, in commemoration of this interesting occasion." Taking from him the proffered precious stone, I asked him, "Have you ever been in a Pennsylvania coal-mine?" He answered me, "Never." Whereupon I drew from my vest-pocket a perfect little jewel of Peacock coal, and said, "Behold this carbonic beauty — of no intrinsic value, but glorious to gaze upon as a rainbow in the heavens. It was once as deeply imbedded in the earth as it is now elevated above it. Accept it, sir, in return for the little treasure you have given me." "Ah!" said he, "a black diamond is at all times worth more than a Jerusalem agate."

As a matter of curiosity be it recorded, that on this occasion of eventful import my American friend had nothing to say. But when we had descended again into the body of the church, we found him after quite a search, leaning against a saintly-looking statue, writing with his pencil into his pocket-diary the following lines, which he said were a reminiscence of his childhood, recalled to memory by the sombre and ghostly atmosphere that pervaded the interior of this church:

> "That dreadful night I never will,—
>   I never can, forget,
> When I did battle with a ghost,
>   Whose shadow haunts me yet.
>
> I was a little shaver then—
>   Some thirteen years or so—
> And that I was a valiant one
>   This presently will show.

My bed was in the haunted room —
  At least so people said —
But what cared I for haunted rooms,
  So I laid down in bed.

My arms were coiled around my head,
  As I lay sleeping there;
When suddenly I screamed, sprang up,
  And met a ghastly stare!

Oh! horror indescribable!
  All scantily begirt,
There stood a ghost — with nothing on —
  With nothing — but his shirt!

I started back — he did the same,
  And this subdued my fear;
So I demanded tremblingly,
  'What is your business here?'

I saw his lips move mockingly,
  But could not hear a tone;
'Ill-mannered ghost!' I fiercely cried,
  'I'll thrash you all alone!'

I struck a hostile attitude,
  The ghost, he did so too;
We sparred — a dreadful pause, and then
  We pitched — *the mirror through!*

The glass went smash — and there I stood,
  Victorious, I suppose!
But, oh! with what a ruined fist,
  And what a bloody nose!"

Among the monuments of the city of Strasburg, that are worthy of mention, are those of General Kleber, who was born here, and suffered death at the assassin's hand, in the midst of his successes in Egypt; and of Guttenberg, the inventor of the art of printing, who, although born at Mayence, carried on the principal part of his labors in this city. These monuments both adorn squares bearing their respective names.

Much might be written of Strasburg — of the church of St. Thomas, with its beautiful and very costly monument to Marshal Moritz of Saxe, by order of Louis XV.; of the very complete museum of natural history; of the enormous tobacco establishment, where the French government, with French generosity almost equal to that of our *ci devant* Southern chivalry, gives the preference of making cigars, snuff, chewing and smoking tobacco, to females, of whom some five hundred work here for thirty cents a day, in an atmosphere charged with the seeds of pulmonary disease to such an extent, that I, who have used tobacco the latter moiety of my life, could not walk through these rooms without coughing and sneezing almost constantly. I never saw anything in my life that excited my indignation so much as this; never anything like this, that I could only look upon as a murderous and criminal proceeding on an enormous scale; and this in the land where civilization and education, polish and refinement — heaven save the mark! — are reputed to have attained a greater perfection than in any other country.

Oh! a glorious country indeed! where the men loaf about in idleness, decorated in motley soldier clothes, talking big, like ancient Pistol, of national grievances, wars, and bloodshed, while the women, in the proportion of three to every one man, work in the fields and on the dunghill, bareheaded, and under the scorching rays of a summer sun. I have seen it over and over again, and felt the blood rushing to my brain at this gross indignity, this violence upon the laws of nature. There! I did not mean to write all this; but it's honest, and I won't scratch it out. Much there is in this country that is truly charming and delightful; but I cannot help raising my voice against that which is obnoxious to the finer feelings of, thanks be to God! an American heart.

About three miles south of Strasburg, on the opposite side of the river Rhine, (which is here spanned by a handsome railroad bridge, and another of pontoons,) is the town of Kehl, where I took the cars and proceeded to Freiburg, in the Grand Duchy of Baden. Here is the beginning of that chain of mountains which constitute the Black Forest, many of which, in towering and majestic proportions, are second only to the Alps. One of these, the Schlossberg, bears about the same relation to Freiburg that the Sharp Mountain does to Pottsville — only that the former is about twice as high as the latter. On its loftiest point is a small pavilion, called by the people here the "pepper-box," from which there is a very extended view in every direction; so that with a good glass, the steeple of the Strasburg Cathedral, though more than twenty miles distant, may be seen; as also many mountains of the Black Forest, whose tops are still covered with snow, such as the Belchen and the Feldberg.

On the top of this Schlossberg there is also a circular level field, called the Moon, where the students of the Freiburg University generally resort to fight their duels, for I understand that this barbarous practice is still in vogue here; though the first "scratch" generally terminates these rencontres. Beautiful roads wind in zigzag directions along the sides of this mountain, that are verdant with the rich drapery of the vine, and whence rises a spring whose water is as cold as ice, and has the reputation of great healing virtues hereabouts. The valley below is irrigated by a beautiful and swift stream, called the Dreisam, in which I caught, by permission, thirteen splendid trout, from eight to ten inches in length, in about an hour and a half. The limpid water of this river is led in small streams through nearly all the streets of Freiburg, making of this city, in the summer season, an exceedingly fresh and agreeable place to reside in; and I understand that many English families with shattered or limited fortunes take advantage of the inducements of cheap living and delightful scenery that are here offered, to settle down as permanent citizens of the town.

From hence I made a journey afoot through the Höllenthal, over the road that the unfortunate Marie Antoinette traversed on her way to Paris, previous to her marriage with the Dauphin, afterward Louis XVI. It is also the same pass that General Moreau took in his famous retreat, when pursued by the Archduke Charles, in 1796.

This ravine is perfectly fearful, with its towering and overhanging rocks, some of which are hundreds of feet in height, and on the top of one of which are the ruins of the castle of the robber, Count Falkenstein, who was at one time the terror of the whole district.

Freiburg contains a handsome monument to the

memory of Berthold Schwarz, the inventor of gunpowder. On one side of the pedestal is a bas-relief representing him in his laboratory, triturating the ingredients of gunpowder in a mortar, while on the opposite side another bas-relief depicts him in an attitude of great fright, gazing with well-expressed consternation on a volume of smoke emanating from the mortar, the pestle lying on the floor, the whole indicating an explosion. This base is surmounted by a life-size statue of Schwarz. My American friend thinks it very questionable whether the inventor of gunpowder deserves a monument at all.

LETTER VIII.

ZURICH—SWITZERLAND.

DESCRIPTION OF ZURICH.—THE UETLIBERG.—THE BAUR AU LAC HOTEL.—THE CHURCH-BELLS ON A SABBATH MORNING.—THE SCHOLASTIC INSTITUTIONS, &c.—MEETING WITH ENGLISH TOURISTS.—AMUSING INCIDENTS.—IGNORANCE OF EUROPEANS ON AMERICAN AFFAIRS.—A LITTLE MORALIZING.

ZURICH, SWITZERLAND, *June*, 1867.

ZURICH, the Turicum of the Romans, a city of some twenty-five thousand inhabitants, without including those of the surrounding hamlets of the canton, endowed by nature with all the associations that can charm the eye and please the senses, lies on the northern shore of a beautiful lake that bears its name, and from which the emerald current of the river Limmat takes its source, passing directly after through the centre of the city.

All along the shores of the lake, as far as the eye can reach, pretty Swiss cottages and magnificent villas seem to have rained down, once upon a time, so thickly they are sprinkled over the green swards and hill-sides hereabouts. On the east is a richly vine-clad slope, along which, about midway up, runs the "High Promenade," which formerly constituted the ramparts of the city.

On the west is the majestic Uetliberg, from whose high altitude one may see far along the valley of the

Rhine, with its cataract at Schaffhausen. To the northward is the dark chain of the Black Forest; and in the direction of the south, the long line of the snow-capped mountains of the Alps.

From the Uetliberg I have gazed westward to see the sun set; and while he emblazoned the horizon in gilded glory, I have thought, what an optical illusion! what a strange paradox in physics! that I should behold this sublime spectacle, yet not be able to see, through the thin air, that which is much nearer, and should be illumined radiantly by the bright light of Phœbus, namely, the associations of my own home — the dear old hills of Schuylkill, that are now doubtlessly attired in their bridal vestment of laurels, *spruced* up in gorgeous splendor, and *pineing* under the excess of their perennial greenness.

In a dreamy revery I remain gazing through that long vista of vacancy, until "darkness" comes again "over the face of the earth," when, turning, I behold, at the foot of the mountain, Zurich, like a thing of enchantment, brilliantly lighted by thousands of gas-jets; so that between the star-lit vault of heaven above, and the gas-lit city below, that appears in the surrounding darkness like another sidereal region — when

>"Naught but the torrent is heard on the hill,
>And naught but the nightingale's song in the grove,"

I feel myself in a church, the like of which is not built by mortal hands, listening to a sermon, the like of which issues not from mortal tongue. Thus serenely occupying the hour of Vespers, I linger on until the evening wanes apace; and as there is an auberge here, that extends its hospitality for lucre, I conclude to remain all night, breathe the rare atmosphere so much nearer to the stars, and dream of a glorious sunrise in the morning. The morning comes; but it is misty, and the sky is cloudy, and the sunrise is a failure.

Somewhat disappointed and abashed, I descend again to the common level of ordinary life and habitations, arriving at my hotel with a right unpoetical appetite for breakfast. And this hotel is not the least of the attractions of Zurich. It exceeds, in romantic situation, princely elegance, and home-like comfort, any other that I have seen in Europe, not excepting the Grande Hotel at Paris. The building itself is a magnificent structure of granite-colored sand-stone, three stories high, and so large in extent that it has two hundred comfortable rooms for guests. Attached to it is a reading-room, with a fine library, and both European and American newspapers and periodicals, in numbers and selection second to none on the continent. There is also a fine billiard and smoking-room, and a large, extraordinarily splendid dining-room.

At one end of the latter is a handsome fountain, whose many jets of water, issuing from curiously sculptured figures, shower a refreshing spray over a large variety of flowers and plants in great china vases artistically arranged, cooling the air, and making it redolent with delightful perfume; while at the other end, on a raised balcony, an excellent band of musicians discourses harmoniously every day to a delighted audience of guests when seated to dinner at three long rows of tables that occupy the room. In front of the building is a garden, laid out with numerous gravelly walks, most excellently designed for promenades, through a profusion of flowers, shrubbery, and trees, to the very edge of the water; whence, from arbors and summer-houses, a fine view is presented of the lake, whose water is of a light green color, and as clear as crystal, yet has a depth at some places, I am told, of thirteen hundred feet.

Nothing is more enchanting than, on a Sabbath morning, to hear the music of the church-bells of Zurich and the many villages that surround this lake reverberating back from the mountain sides in regular waves of delicious melody; or, in the evening, to see this placid water studded with innumerable small boats of light and jaunty proportions, under clean, white sails, skipping along coquettishly before the slightest breeze, and from which you may hear issuing, perchance, the dulcet strains of many flutes, or witness the silent rapture of —— ah! I think that will do;—going up that mountain has been a Jacob's ladder to me, and my visions and things are becoming quite angelic.

Zurich stands pre-eminent as the most prosperous manufacturing city, as well as the literary centre, of Switzerland. Its scholastic institutions are numerous and of an excellent character. The Polytechnic School is a model of its kind; and in the Medical University one branch, that of Microscopy, is taught by Professor Heinrich Frey, whose great work on this science is the text-book of Professor Rokitansky's class, at Vienna, and who is probably the ablest teacher now living, save, perhaps, Mr. Beale, of England, on that interesting and important branch of a thorough medical education. There is also a hospital here, through the various departments of which Professor Frey has kindly conducted me. It is a handsome, new building, of granite, with airy and comfortable wards; and from the cooking department up to the treatment of the sick, the management seems to be of the best possible order; and the percentage of mortality is comparatively small, owing, doubtless, in a great measure, to climatic and other local advantages.

This city has been the birth-place and subsequent field of labor of many eminent men, among which may be cited the names of Levater, Hess, Pestalozzi, Heinrich Meyer, the friend of Gœthe, and many others.

A botanical garden of some eight hundred different Alpine plants alone is situated here, and is well worthy of a visit.

In a museum of old weapons are exhibited, among many interesting curiosities, the battle-axe of Zwingli; and a bow which is represented as that with which Tell shot the apple from his son's head; but I take the liberty to doubt the genuineness of this bow very seriously; for it does not look to me like a thing with which it would be at all possible to shoot very straight. If the truth were always known, probably, many of the wonders and curiosities that are stared at, all over Europe, by admiring antiquaries, for francs and groschens and gilders, would dwindle into extraordinary characters of proxyship, and should be gazed upon with a huge grain of allowance.

The United States are well represented here in the person of Mr. Page, a correspondent of the *New York Tribune*, who is exceedingly kind and attentive to his fellow-citizens sojourning at Zurich.

With its fine scenery, healthy locality, and many other attractions offered by this city, it naturally becomes an important landmark for travellers, many of whom may at all times be met here.

Indeed, quite a number of English families have made their permanent residence here; and an American family from New York occupy — and have done so during a number of years — the most beautiful villa on the lake-shore, far excelling, in style and costly splendor, that of the ex-Queen of Naples, which is quite contiguous to it.

Not the least interesting feature of a journey through Europe, is the constant and ever-changing opportunity that is offered for the study of characters of different nationalities and conditions in life, and to observe the different opinions entertained by them. I was greatly amused the other day at an old English lady, with a strong cockney accent, who desired to know whether the " 'ay fever was as fatal in Hamerica as it is in Hingland;" and after I had delivered my opinion on the subject, the husband — stern and consequential old pater familias — broke in with the rapturous declaration, that it was "very jolly to 'ear 'ow well a Hamerican can speak Hinglish;" but added, I thought a little reproachfully —

"they tell me that you carnt make a good bitter-beer, because, you know, you 'aven't the ops."

A couple of young Londoners, who are "doing" Switzerland, were scudding about the lake in a little sail-boat, when, approaching the "frail bark" that I was rowing for exercise, one of them asked me whether we "ever had any yacht races in America?" Astonished at such a question, which, nevertheless, I took for a joke, I laughingly inquired what he thought of the Henrietta, alluding, of course, to the yacht of that name; whereupon he rejoined that he hadn't the pleasure of her acquaintance; that she must be a German lady; for if she was English, she would be called "'Arriet."

On explaining the matter to him, I found that he either did not know, or did not wish to know, anything about James Gordon Bennett, Jr., or his yacht, or anything else appertaining to the race across the Atlantic.

Upon the whole, however, the English people make very pleasant *compagnons du voyage;* and there are quite a number of them, just now, sojourning at the hotel I am staying at — the elegant and princely Baur au Lac. Not the least interesting pastime that we have among ourselves, is that afforded by our gathering in a social group, these beautiful twilight evenings, in the garden at the edge of the lake; where, comfortably disposed in rustic simplicity along the grassy earth, or on rudely constructed seats, we indulge with unreserved and companionable pleasantry in lively conversation, merry jests, and spicy, humorous anecdotes, of the latter of which, especially, my American friend has always a goodly stock on hand. Our English confreres are good listeners to Yankee yarns; and he gets off, occasionally, some very eloquent efforts.

Thus, but an evening or two ago, in relating an incident connected with a country debating-society in the far-off home beyond the sea, he threw himself into a declamatory posture, and went on as follows: "Gentlemen, there once flourished a fraternity of sages, young and old, distinguished collectively as 'The Diagnothian Literary Society of Hellerstettle.' Hellerstettle is a village situated in one of the loveliest valleys of Pennsylvania; and its principal feature was dignified with the appellation of 'The Academy,' which flourished under the learned superintendence of Professor Wittyman. The school consisted of lads and lasses, varying in age from five to twenty-five years; and in studies, from the English alphabet to anything under the sun, not beyond the limits of the human understanding. From the male department of this school was formed the aforesaid Diagnothian Literary Society. The Professor was pompous and high-wrought in his notions, and the thing that of all others he strained most after, was *originality of thought*. Probably to this end he suggested the strange question to be debated, "*Is Man an Animal?*" and challenged the youngest doctor of the place to establish a reputation by proving the affirmative, if he could. The Doctor was an unassuming young man, but vain enough to believe that he would come off victorious on a question of this kind, and accordingly accepted the challenge. Aye, he was even anxious to do so, as he desired to become illustrious in the eyes of one with whom he had fallen desperately in love — one who was the fairest of the village — the pet and pride of the community in which she lived — and by far the best scholar of the 'Academy.' The evening appointed for the debate at length arrived, and the Doctor hired a small boy to convey his text-books of authority in a wheelbarrow down to the school-house. There were Dunglison, Carpenter, Kirk and Paget, Locke and Noah Webster, all jumbled up together, and had probably never enjoyed so democratic a ride before. The room became crowded with the fashion, the beauty, the learning of the village.

"All things being in order, the Doctor opened the debate in a calm, sensible, and logical way; explaining how it could not be possible for man — being constituted of flesh and blood, of bone and sinews, and all the elements of other animals — to be anything but an animal himself. How all creation was divided into three kingdoms — the animal, the vegetable, and the mineral; and that man, being neither of the latter two, must of necessity belong to the former — unless, indeed, his worthy and learned opponent would 'acknowledge the *corn*,' and own *his* relationship with *cabbage-heads* and *small potatoes*. Here a burst of laughter interrupted the speaker for fully a minute and a half. He then proceeded, submitting that it was a common custom, even with ladies, to consider *some* men as 'brutes' and 'bears,' and, sometimes, 'lions;' to say nothing of the complimentary terms with which men sometimes refer to each other, as a 'sheep,' a 'mule,' a 'goose,' &c. In short, he went over the whole ground very fully, in a good-natured, and, what he deemed, a rational way; and concluded by asking his friend to state what then man *is*, if not an animal? During the speaker's harangue, his little hits and witticisms were followed by an audible and good-natured titter through the appreciative audience; and his eye wandered to the loadstone of his affections, who, he perceived, was quite convinced that women, as well as men, are, after all, but mortal, yet glorious and most bewitching animals. In fact, all his hearers appeared to take his view of the matter, without exception. But the Professor had not yet opened his battery of argument upon them; and presently there was to come a wondrous change over the spirit of that audience. He arose with the imposing grandeur of Ulysses, and commenced as follows: 'Mr. Chairman!'—(the chairman was aged eleven years, and could actually read words of three syllables)—'Mr. Chairman, must man be an animal? an *animal?* Who *says* he must? My opponent? Has *he* the hardihood—the undaunted, bare-faced, *brazen* hardihood to stand up, erect and *unabashed*, before God and this intelligent and philosophical assemblage, and be so base, so altogether bereft of shame, as to proclaim man an animal —a *very* animal? though it be in express and direct contradiction of that Writ divine, which says, 'in phrases not equivocal,' that *man* is DUST? Does *dust* belong to the animal kingdom? Let the *air* take up the question—let *America*—let every corner of our *continent* resound—let the welkin burst with a tremendous 'No!' And, sir, am I *asked*—deliberately asked the question, what *is* man, if not an animal? Why, Mr. Chairman, man is the magnetic element of the dynamic condition of the concentrated quintessence of the electrical affinity of the theistical presence with the sublunary chemistry of eternal and everlasting mortality! Man, I say, is the auricular, perceptive, declamatory, odoriferous ideality of the innate spark of the highest and most exalted order of vital *progressiveness!* Man' (here he struck an attitude, as Forrest does in the Syracusan senate, grand and terrible to behold.—O gentlemen! have you ever heard Forrest? No? well, I pity you; but to proceed) 'Man,' said the Professor, 'is the climacteric handiwork of *Jehovah!*—the great phenomenon of *creation!*—the spirituality of flesh, and the carnal embodiment of *spirit! Man* an *animal?* Oh!' (the 'oh!' pronounced as Mr. Whitfield could, and for the power of which Garrick would have given a hundred guineas) "O-o-o-oh! how RECreant! how false to *God!*—how traitorous to his *country!*—how slanderous of all that's chaste and lovely and divine must *that* man be who deems himself an animal! No, Mr. Chairman,' (subdued and melancholy,) 'man is *not* an animal. Man, in short, *is* man—and nothing shorter.'

"The Professor sat down amid the applause of the delighted multitude who had listened to his eloquence, and were overwhelmed with the grand truths they had heard. And the poor Doctor departed, crestfallen and abashed, from the presence of such superior intellect, and not long after left the entire neighborhood; not, however, without a head somewhat muddled on the subject of 'man,' and a heart full of regrets on the subject of woman."

This story of my American friend, and the manner

in which he recited it, was almost as good as a circus —clown, acrobats, riders and all—and raised him wonderfully in the estimation of our British companions.

Generally speaking, little interest is taken by Europeans in matters of any national import concerning the United States. I have heard more palaver about Maximilian and the miserable Mexican affair, in a single day, both in France and Switzerland, than of our four years' war, during all the time that I have been here. A French gentleman at Paris, and really an intelligent man, to whom, in the course of conversation, I mentioned the battle of Gettysburg, actually did not even recollect the name of that great and decisive conflict; but apologetically remarked, that we had fought so many battles, he had forgotten their names. I asked him whether he would not suspect a man—no matter in what part of the world he lived—to be excessively stupid, who did not know, at least by name, the battles of Waterloo, Solferino, or Sadowa? "*Oh! certainement, monsieur; mais c'est une ôtre chose;*" and I really don't believe that he took my pointed inference at all. Whereas, our newspapers contain one or two columns of telegraphic news from Europe every day, here the whole subject is passed over with a simple announcement of the price of gold, five-twenties, and cotton; and this is the case with all the journals, without a single exception, no more being found in the London Times and Paris Moniteur than in the humblest sheet that is published. In scientific attainments we have men that are equal to any in Europe; yet I never hear their names mentioned in their lecture-rooms here, or see them referred to in the books of the Europeans; whilst we, on the contrary, are constantly paying tributes of courtesy wherever they are due, and sometimes where they are not.

It is all well enough to take a look at their old ruins and castles and leaning towers; to admire their painting and statues; to appreciate their pretty gardens and groves, and artificial fountains and cascades; to climb up their church-steeples and arches of triumph; and lastly, to enjoy with one's whole soul, all the beauties of nature — the magnificent scenery, such as it is presented around Zurich and the rest of Switzerland, with the creation of which neither kings nor people nor governments have had anything to do. But to institute a comparison of all this with our own great country would be simply and emphatically ridiculous.

Let us not be blind to our own defects; our little sprinkling — to draw it mildly — of party corruption; perhaps our inferior police-system; our careless railroad management; our — our — well, that is about all; I cannot think of anything else in which we stand behind aught that I have thus far seen in Europe. This I do know, that if any citizen of the United States becomes a little demoralized — a trifle dissatisfied with matters and things at home — let him come abroad here, and — how it happens I am not prepared to say — but a short time will suffice to bring him to his senses.

Notwithstanding all which, I shall not soon forget this elysian retreat of Zurich, or the felicitous home that may be enjoyed at the Hotel Baur au Lac.

LETTER IX.

SWITZERLAND.

UP THE LAKE.—OVER THE ALBIS TO ZUG.—A LITTLE DASH AT HAYMAKING.—THE SIHL RIVER.—AN INCIDENT.—THE ROSSBERG.—THE RIGI MOUNTAIN.—A SUNSET AND SUN-RISE.—A FAMILY SNOWED UP ON THE MOUNTAIN EVERY YEAR.—LUCERNE.—THE GREAT ORGAN.—FLUELEN.—ALT-DORF, THE HOME OF TELL.—THE ST. GOTTHARD PASS.—SNOWBALLING.—GRAND SCENERY.—BACK TO LUCERNE.

INTERLAKEN, SWITZERLAND, *June*, 1867.

ON board the pretty little lake steamer Concordia, I left Zurich, in Switzerland, and proceeded to Horgen, about nine miles up, and on the southern shore of the lake.

From here I journeyed afoot over the Albis chain of mountains to Zug, a distance of about sixteen miles; nor, in view of the beautiful scenery, the healthful recreation, and the cheerful incidents associated with this trip, did I have the least occasion to regret the small amount of labor and fatigue incurred thereby.

From the top of the Albis Mountains, the prospect, embracing Zurich, the entire lake, with the numerous villas that adorn its gradually sloping green shores, interspersed here and there with beautiful vineyards, groaning under the promise of a rich harvest, was one that the eye loved to dwell upon; nor would it be satiated with a single enjoyment, but ever and anon I would rest me at full length upon the green sward, and feast upon the luxury spread out before me, to say nothing of sundry bits of bread and cheese, by way of dessert. About one third of my journey extended along, and in plain view of the river Sihl, that runs dancing and skipping playfully through crags and ravines, with every imaginable inducement for the lively and wily trout, until it empties itself into the lake at Zurich. Here, too, I beheld the first really fine Swiss barn, of which I had heard so much, and which, up to this time, I had looked for in vain, so that I almost began to suspect them to be a mythical institution.

The farmers were busily employed at haymaking, and they looked so cheerful and happy withal, and their dwellings so refreshing and attractive, that I resolved to abide a day or two with one of these families, and participate with its members a short paroxysm of rural pleasure and fatigue. With this object I singled out a lovely and enticing home, close by the river side; and after a little difficulty in satisfying its inmates that I was not, after all, a travelling vagabond, I was received in their midst, and remained "in clover" for the following two days. The first of these I gambolled in the field, armed with a rake, as blithely as my untrained nerves would let me. And there were pretty assistants, with short frocks and blue checkered bodices; plump, red cheeks, and brawny, bare arms, with laughing eyes dancing merrily in their orbits, and a deluge of hair tucked up snugly about their heads. These pretty charmers cast an obliviousness over all that was tiresome in the day, though the sport of it made the great beads of perspiration start upon our brows. It is true this was a little romantic, considering all things, but I needed no tonic to promote an appetite, nor bitters to help digest that which I ate for supper. Upon the whole, should I live many years amid the home-circle of my own loved ones, it is not likely that I will soon forget the day when I was haymaking in Switzerland.

On the second day, with the rod and fly, I meandered up the stream, "enticing the finny tribe to engulph in their dentriculated mouths a barbed hook upon whose point was affixed a dainty allurement." This was attended by a little vexation; for the 'tarnal things would not bite in conformity with my ideas of the Swiss law of nature; though with perseverance, and by dexterously following up every nibble that came along, I managed, toward sundown, to return to mine host, Herr Burkli, with a right presentable mess of trout. On the third day, for the temptation to abide there during the period of another diurnal revolution was irresistible, I lent my feeble aid in pitching and tramping hay upon the wagon and on the mow, during the process of hauling it from the fields by the help of a very philosophical and sedate-looking yoke of oxen. When all the space allotted for hay in the capacious barn was thoroughly crammed, we stacked the remainder in a contiguous field, an operation that afforded us any quantity of practical joking, and all manner of genuine fun. Down we packed it — about a dozen of us, men and women — tugging and sweltering away — clipping it from one place, and filling up another; bouncing about like great india-rubber harlequins, tumbling over and getting all tangled up with one another, pinching, by mistake, blue marks into the aforesaid brawny arms and rosy cheeks, our commingled voices producing a grand confusion,—an incoherent medley of boisterous merriment. Up *it* went, the great round pillar of hay, till it was as high as any house; and deviating a little from its perpendicular, it looked for all the world like a cheap imitation of the leaning tower of Pisa. Oh! but it was a privilege, after that, to partake of the frugal evening fare that was spread over the spotless cloth of linen, on the long, plain table that stood on the thatched portico of the cottage for the occasion. How delicious was the new-drawn milk! you felt that the least change in the magic laboratory of the body would convert every draught of it into structure of new and bounding vitality. It was muscle and nerve in a rich state of solution, which, in flowing along the avenues of the system, precipitated the requisite materials here and there, even as the failing parts required them.

And the well-baked bread of rye—the blessed staff of life—tasted never so sweetly invigorating as at that memorable repast. Dainty pastries, and elaborate compound dishes there were none, but the bread and milk, some golden cheese with numerous oily cells, some generous slices of cold roasted mutton, an accompaniment of potatoes and leek, and lastly, an abundance of blushing cherries, constituted the entire meal; but, nevertheless, in the estimation of its partakers, seasoned as it was by the balmy evening breeze, loaded with the delightful aroma of the new-mown hay, this was a banquet worthy of the gods.

The following morning I departed, not without feelings of regret, from that excellent family, and continued my travel through the still beauteous country that lay before me. Having passed a number of statues of the Virgin Mary, and representations of the Crucifixion, I inquired of a countryman whom I passed whether the Catholic religion was prevalent in that section. He answered me, "Yes, sir, it prevails this side of yonder bridge that you crossed some time ago."

Here was a line of demarcation, a solution of a knotty question, that was exceedingly graphic and tangible. Preachers have defined "the Church," and authors of great concordances and commentaries expounded it, without ever letting the world into the secret, that all the difference between two denominations is a geographical one, of rivers and bridges, over which it is the easiest matter in the world to pass from one side to the other, from Protestant to Catholic, and *vice versâ*. Was not this a sage, to be sure! And his countenance was expressive of such a thorough conviction that it is impossible for persons with either of the two persuasions just mentioned to exist on the wrong side of that bridge, that if I had catechized him, "What is the difference between Protestantism and Catholicism?" I believe in my heart he would have answered me, "The river Sihl, sir!" And I had walked over the bed of this river, wading from right to left, back and forth, catching trout on both sides of the median line, without prejudice or partiality, and without ever dreaming how seriously inconstant and vacillating I was on such a solemn subject. I have related this incident as an illustration of the abrupt manner in which not only religious faith, but dialect, dress, habits, and customs of life take a change, not simply in different nations, but in sections of the same nation; so that in a day the traveller may encounter quite a number of these changes without getting outside of the jurisdiction of a single prince.

Arrived at Zug, I sauntered through the puzzle of streets which distinguish that rather antiquated-looking place; and the principal object that there engaged my attention was a band of wandering minstrels that went tooting through the town, and heralded a tight-rope and other gymnastic performances that were to take place in the evening.

There were five of them, playing respectively on drum, fife, cymbals, clarionet, and bugle; and at every street-corner a halt was made, when they outraged the great vault of heaven with the loudest and most deafening noise that ever tore time and tune into tatters and shreds. Every man of them was another Jem Baggs, of the wildest description, who evidently knew "the value of peace and quietness," and having the advantage over the people, could not think of "moving" for any trifling consideration. He of the drum, almost hidden from view behind that large wooden cylinder, would pound away at its leather head with such an earnest industry that every thump he gave it seemed to split the air, and smote upon one's auricle like the blasting of a rock in some deep mountain chasm.

After every painful paroxysm from this violent

quintette had subsided into a humming sound, that was still undulating in the air, like that of a blue-bottle fly in a paper pill-box, then the head man issued his proclamation of the forthcoming performance, in a stentorian voice scarcely less penetrating than the shrill notes of his own cracked and rusty bugle. I will warrant me that every citizen of the good old town knew what was to be in the evening. Whether they all flocked to the performance, as they did to the street-doors of their houses to hear these terrible minstrels play, it is not in my power to place upon record, as I did not remain to see.

I took a small steamer that plies on the pretty lake bearing the name of the town just mentioned, and which, though only about eight miles long and two wide, has, nevertheless, places over fifteen hundred feet in depth, and is inhabited by some of the finest and largest fish that may be found in any of the Swiss lakes. Proceeding in a southerly direction, we landed at Aart, a small town, at the foot of the mountain Rigi, and near the famous Rossberg, the summit of which, in 1806, being of a calcareous geological structure, and saturated with the unusually protracted rains in the spring of that year, precipitated itself down into the beautiful valley beneath, covering three villages, and burying alive some five hundred human beings; filling up, also, with its enormous debris, the one third of Lake Lorberg.

Here I undertook the steep ascent of the Rigi afoot; and after nearly four hours of uninterrupted and toilsome walking, had the satisfaction of gaining the summit just in time to witness what is termed, by those who are posted, a very fine sunset. On the following morning, too, at a few minutes past three o'clock, there were people gathered to the number of more than a hundred — people from all parts of the world, and for the most part entire strangers to each other, but who, cold and shivering, though bundled up in their shawls and bed-blankets, united here in one common worship to the sun. And I would love dearly to describe the scene, when he arose in all his morning majesty before our enraptured vision; but it would need an angel and an eagle's quill, dipped in alternate liquids of flame and diamond and amber, to depict the glory of that heavenly light, as its effulgent beams appeared in lanceolet points, darting high into the azure firmament; then spreading far and in all directions along the horizon, and gilding with radiant splendor the snow-crowned Alps, that here extend as far as the eye can reach; and among which the echoing notes of the Alpine horn, greeting the new-born day, joyously reverberate "from peak to peak, the rattling crags among," long after they have ceased to issue from the instrument. From this summit, a distance of thirty miles can be seen on a clear day, in every direction of the compass; and the panorama that is presented of the long chain of Alps is not equalled from any other accessible point. The number of pilgrims who ascend the Rigi every season for the purpose of enjoying the view it affords, is very great. But hundreds who make the tiresome journey are sorely disappointed in the end thereof; for clear days — when there is no fog or cloud around this mountain top — are the exception, and not the rule. This feeling of disappointment is graphically set forth in two verses which one of this class inscribed in the strangers' register that is kept in the hotel on the top, yclept the Rigi Kulm:

> "Seven up-hill, weary miles we sped,
>   The setting sun to see;
> Sullen and grim he went to bed,
>   Sullen and grim went we.
>
> "Seven sleepless hours we tossed, and then,
>   The rising sun to see,
> Sullen and grim we rose again,
>   Sullen and grim rose he."

The hotel is a fine structure, and of sufficient capacity to accommodate several hundred visitors. All the timber and material of which it is formed, as well as the vast quantity of provisions that is consumed, when thronged with guests during the summer months, were and are carried up on the backs of pack-mules, as no team can possibly ascend. It is not practicable to descend this mountain in the winter; though I am told of two individuals who suffer themselves to be snowed-up on its top every winter, in order to take care of the hotel and of the cattle. They abide there in perfect solitude during four months of the year, effectually imprisoned on that cold, dreary peak, with no society but that of the eagles and the stars. And, astonishing to relate, these two persons are actually man and wife! They must be either exceedingly fond of each other, or woefully put out with the rest of mankind. Before winter sets in, they are provided with all the stores and necessaries of life to support them comfortably until the following spring; but what either would do in the case of sickness or death of the other it is impossible to conjecture.

> "O Solitude! where are the charms
> That sages have seen in thy face?
> Better dwell in the midst of alarms,
> Than reign" on this very high place!

I descended on the side of the mountain overlooking the lake of the Four Cantons, and arrived, after two and a half hours of labor, more telling on limb and muscle than the climbing up had been, at the little town of Weggis, whence, with a steamer, I proceeded to Lucerne. This is a city most delightfully situated, facing from the north the most interesting of all the Swiss lakes, with the towering, cloud-capped Pilatus to the right, and the majestic Rigi to the left. Both of these mountains appear in close proximity, and stand there like colossal giants, holding a jealous guard over the city — awful in appearance, and monstrous in proportion — as though they might be the great-great-grand-parents of the Pillars of Hercules.

But of the town itself there is not a great deal to be said, except of the truly beautiful and romantically situated Lion Monument, erected, or rather chiselled, into the side of a rock, to the memory of the Swiss Guard who stood and suffered in defence of the king at the commencement of the Revolution in France; except also of the great organ in the Stiftskirche, said to be the largest in the world — save what my American friend calls "our Boston Blower" — and which does, in reality, produce a monstrous deal of noise; too much, in fact, to enable a body to distinguish the music. Thus I heard what at first I took to be the Anvil Chorus from Trovatore, with about a dozen anvils, half a dozen of cymbals, fifty clarionets, and a hundred trombones thrown in promiscuously; when I was agreeably surprised to find out that it was Old Hundred, and not the Anvil Chorus after all. I had never heard that solemn, time-honored air produced in such an exceedingly lively and boisterous manner before; and an English friend at my side suggested, it was " Jolly nice for Hold Und red, wasn't it, now?"

Socially, I cannot say much in favor of Lucerne. Being a central point for travellers in Switzerland, and especially patronized by the English aristocracy, the people, generally, have been spoiled, and manifest a ravenous eagerness for "the lucre" that detracts gravely from the charm of the reputed virtue and simplicity of the Swiss populace. And, with all this, the landlords of hotels receive you with such an air of insufferable condescension — as though in accepting your napoleons and sovereigns they were doing you a particular favor; yet I am free to confess that I cannot see it in that light.

On the steamer Gotthard I made a voyage over the entire length of this lake, a distance of some thirty miles, to Fluelen, situated at its extreme southern point. The latter portion of this voyage, that between Brunnen and Fluelen, is particularly interesting on account of the picturesque grandeur of the scenery that here environs the lake on both sides. Here, also, is pointed out to the stranger the Tellscapelle, a small chapel, erected over the great flat stone on which Tell sprang from the boat when Gesler was taking him a prisoner to his castle at Küssnacht. From Fluelen I proceeded a short distance, per omnibus, to Altdorf, where the famous trial of Tell, shooting an apple from his son's head, occurred; or, at least, is said to have transpired. A statue of Tell is situated on the spot where he should have stood on that eventful occasion, and a fountain on the place where, it is said, the boy was stationed—the two being a hundred and fifty feet apart. Formerly a linden tree, against which the boy stood, occupied the place of the fountain.

A short distance from here is Bürgeln, the home and birth-place of Tell. On the site of the house where he was born, is built a small chapel to his honor and memory, the interior walls of which are embellished with imperfect, highly colored paintings descriptive of the historical incidents of the era in which Tell lived; and with oddly worded, old-fashioned, proverbial rhymes, in which the grotesque and sublime are jumbled together with a reckless disregard of style, propriety, and even sense. On the outside the chapel is embowered with rose-bushes that were in full bloom at the time of my visit, contributing greatly to the effectiveness of the scene.

I now commenced a pilgrimage through the St. Gotthard Pass, that brought me in view of scenery more replete with awful sublimity, and the fulness of God's majesty in His works, than any I had ever beheld. Upward and onward led the road, until in the region of almost perpetual snow, and yet the tops of the mountains appeared as far away as ever. Winding along the gorges, I frequently seemed to be, as it were, in a kettle, of which overhanging rocks, looming high into the clouds, constituted the sides, and whence I could see no farther than about a hundred yards in any direction, except skyward. Sometimes, close by the road, over its uneven, stone-strewn bed, shot with the swiftness of an arrow on the wing, the torrent which constitutes the river Reuss; then pitching down into the abyss, from crag to crag, leaping in wild madness over the rocks, rushing onward, dashing forward, boiling, seething, and foaming, as it were in a wild rage — blindly, like a suicidal element that gloried in its own destruction — furious, like a harpooned whale, precipitating itself upon every obstacle, and spirting a white column of spray into the clouds. Around an angle of rocks it would be heard as in the distance, like the muttering of low thunder; then it would suddenly appear again, rushing along with a rattling noise, like that of a tornado in a forest of dry leaves.

Near Antermatt this river is spanned for the eighth time by a bridge that is here called the Devil's Bridge. The new structure has not been many years in existence; but the old one still remains by its side, and somewhat lower down in the ravine. Here was the scene of a terrible conflict between the French and Austrians, on the 14th of August, 1799; though it is difficult to conceive how a battle was possible, between any number of opposing forces, in a place like this.

From a short distance above the bridge to an

equally short space below, the river takes a fall of several hundred feet — not in one pitch, but by regular gradation, as it were, rushing down a long granite staircase. The fall from its source to Andermatt is two thousand feet, and from thence to Fluelen three thousand feet more. Here the road, by many zig-zag turns, ascends Mount Gotthard proper. It was three more hours' walk to the Hospice on the top; but, as there was quite a company of us from America, England, and France, that had gathered in the hotel at Andermatt, we enjoyed ourselves hugely, as though we were a parcel of real brothers and sisters (for there were ladies among us) and not at all like casually met strangers.

There was a large drawing-room, that contained a piano — not exactly like Steinway's best; still it would yield a sound, and was in tolerable good tune. To this my American friend seated himself, and played the Star Spangled Banner with an emotion that indicated his whole soul to be in his fingers just at that time; and what American heart is there that would not bound with rapture at the eloquence of that music, situated as we were then? The following morning the whole company proceeded in joyful procession up the mountain to the Hospice. There arrived, we were in the midst of the regions of snow, that lay in places to the depth of six or eight feet.

Can anything exceed the novelty of a snow-balling battle in mid-summer? Now I'll warrant me, that there is not a plucky, high-spirited fellow in the whole of our good country who would not look upon it as one of the proudest epochs of his life to indulge in such a set-to, and feel the reactionary tingle in his hands, after laboring thus in the snow during the genial period of the dog-days. It was while our gleeful company was at the Hospice of St. Gotthard, that some one proposed a pitched battle at snow-balls; which was received with a shout of approbation. Directly we were divided into two belligerent parties, with four gentlemen and two ladies on each side, and the manner in which we pelted away at each other was a caution to old folks, I promise you. My American friend said that it was the darlingest shindig he had participated in for many a long day; and he hammered away with the cold missiles and a hearty good-will at his antagonists, laughing and shouting in German, English, and French alternately, sprawling on the snow, leaping over deep crevasses — dodging the icy pellets from every direction, and cutting the most ludicrous gyrations in the air. Oh! but he was jolly, was my American friend; and whenever he succeeded in planting a sockdolager plump into the bread-basket of the fat Englishman, or the lean Frenchman, who were of the party, then his delight knew no bounds; and he would laugh you, up there upon the mountain height, with such a joyous, merry peal, that would call up the echoes from those Alpine caverns for miles and miles around.

At length, however, our social company dispersed themselves again as suddenly and unceremoniously as they had met. The most of them went over on the other side into Italy; and a few, myself among the number, retraced our steps to Andermatt, where we remained over night; and thence took the diligence to Fluelen, and from there the steamboat back to Lucerne.

LETTER X.

SWITZERLAND.—BERNE.

THE CITY OF BÄREN, OR BERNE.—DERIVATION OF ITS NAME.—BEAR PEN.—THE PREDILICTION OF THE CITIZENS FOR BRUIN—ASCENT OF A GLACIER OF THE ALPS.—AN ALPINE GROTTO.—STORM UPON THE ALPS.—A NIGHT SPENT IN A CHAMOIS-HUNTER'S HUT—THE DESCENT.

GENEVA, SWITZERLAND, *June*, 1867.

IN the first of these letters allusion was made to a bear, who was a deck-passenger on our steamer; and in the second to the bears of the Jardin des Plantes, Paris; so that I almost feel ashamed to approach the subject again, for fear of being suspected of being as fond of it as Davy Crockett was; or of having rubbed bear's grease into my head until it "struck in," and affected the brain. But I have recently strayed into such a nest of these animals as would put Wall Street to the blush, even on the days when the bears are in the palmiest ascendency over the Bulls; so that I am bound to ventilate the theme once more, sincerely hoping that the indulgent reader will *bear* with me throughout the effort.

The ursine family, then, that now engages our attention is the entire city of Bären. Modern people call it Berne; but that is an unpardonable mutilation of the name – a degeneration of Bären, which is the German word for bears. The way in which this city came by such a name was as follows: In its incipient state, when it was yet a nameless village, Duke Berthold von Zähringen, attended by a number of his courtiers, entered upon an extensive chase, in what was all about here a vast and mountainous wilderness and publicly proclaimed that the name of the animal that was first slain should thenceforward be that of the newly founded village. The first victim being a bear, he was carried forth in great pomp and circumstance; and the theretofore humble *flecken* was triumphantly baptized, and denominated Bären. From that time to the present day the bear has been the coat-of-arms, the symbolical representative, the pet, and the idol of the people who inhabit this place. I say, the idol; for I do not believe that heathens ever worshipped bulls or snakes, fire or water, wooden images or golden calves, with half the zeal and adoration that is here lavished upon these interesting and gentle quadrupeds.

At the western end of the town is situated a handsome pen, (I wish I knew a prettier, more romantic name for it—but I do n't,) which is about twelve feet deep, of a circular form, perhaps forty feet in diameter, walled up with fine granite stone from the bottom of the pit to some three feet above the ground outside, and forming a parapet over which persons can gaze into the interior of the rotunda, to admire the gambols of the playful creatures within. This domicile being divided into two compartments by a central wall, is occupied by two separate families of bears. I saw the parental members of these families; but on inquiry about their tender off-shoots — their little responsibilities, (great respect is necessary in every allusion to the bears,) I was informed that the cubs — I mean the dear little bear-babies — were in the (n)*ursery*, an adjoining apartment; and found, indeed, that they reversed the maxim appertaining to little boys and girls, in this — that they were *heard*, and not *seen*. These bears are enormously wealthy; for no rich man, who hopes for a name beyond the grave, would think of dying without remembering the bears in his will; and his respectability in the public estimation will be in proportion to the amount he settles upon them. Thinking this a novel method of creating a charity-fund, I inquired whether any of this money was ever distributed among the poor. "No, indeed," said my informant, with a much injured look. "These bears are emblematical of our own prosperity; and we do n't want them to be poor, miserable, poverty-stricken devils!" Sure enough! how ridiculous that I did not see this point at first!

As to the diet upon which these "emblems" subsist, it is composed, principally, of bread and honey, and many other dainty and delectable morsels. I have not heard that they indulge in wine and cigars, though doubt not that in that case they would be furnished with the choicest brands. But I suspect that, in this particular matter, their order of intelligence is a little in advance of our own — being well aware that such naughty habits would *b' ruinous* to their constitutions. It is interesting to observe the high degree of domestic happiness that these bears enjoy, and the serene composure and well-to-do contentment depicted on their expressive countenances.

Reposing upon its gluteii muscles, (whoever is not familiar with this phrase will please refer to Gray's Anatomy — not Elegy — or Youatt on the Horse,) I have seen the biggest and the handsomest take another more delicate and sickly looking bear upon its lap in the most soothing and sympathizing manner, hugging it to its bosom, and caressing it with a tenderness more touching to behold than — to endure. Their playfulness exceeds the sportive dalliance of little kittens, though it does not appear to be of a nature suitable to any member of the human family; for, several years ago, an English captain, in hopes of having a little recreative sport with them, jumped into the pen, and commenced poking fun at them, in the shape of an umbrella, whereupon, apparently overjoyed at such an unusual visit, one of the bears took the captain to his hairy embrace so long and so fervently that the poor fellow died.

From dawn to dusk hundreds of people are to be seen at the "*Graben*," looking after the bears; for they are the pets and property of all; and every citizen feels his own individual interest and pride in them; so that probably no person who is not sick abed, ever lets a day pass by without paying these municipal treasures a visit.

You pass along the streets, and bears in stone and bronze will attract your attention everywhere; monuments and fountains and public places are ornamented with them; the shop-windows temptingly exhibit them in every variety; carved in wood and ivory, you have them perched on the corners of toilet and fancy boxes; you grasp them in the handles of knives and forks and brushes; you see them in groups of all descriptions of character—as musicians and ballet-dancers, with fiddles and umbrellas and fans; with spectacles on the nose; a bear in the pulpit of a miniature church is represented as preaching to a congregation of bears; and a very saleable article is a set of chess-men, all bears, distinguishable from each other by their different attitudes, and the queen from the king, by having a young bear in her arms. You go into the houses, and pictures of bears adorn the walls of almost every room; while the mantle-pieces look fearful with representations of them in marble, soapstone, and plaster of Paris. Embroidered, in a crouching attitude, into the canopy that overhangs your bed, they appear ready to spring upon you with the awakening day. You eat beautiful models of them in butter, blanc-mange, and gelatine. Worked in raised worsted, on comfortable chairs, you sit down upon them, with a very uncomfortable misgiving of a growl, accompanied by the unpleasant sensation of an imaginary bite. In conclusion, the town-clock contains a mechanism similar to that at Strasburg, by which, whenever it strikes the hour, a procession of bears is made to march in a circle around the seated figure of an old man with an hour-glass in his hand, to whom every bear, in passing, bestows a friendly nod of the head; which, considering the source, I look upon as an exceedingly civil and well-behaved proceeding. And now — *sic transit historia ursi.*

I believe that every man fills, in his career through life, at one time or other, a situation which ever after looms up before his soul as the great and particular event of his entire existence; tied up within the meshes of his memory, the Gordian knot that he can never separate or cut — the Rubicon of experience, that never becomes diminutive in the distance of the other side. This situation, as far as it relates to the individuality of the writer, has recently transpired.

At Grindelwald, about fifteen miles from Interlaken, are situated two glaciers, the upper one filling up the gorge between the Wetterhorn and Mettenberg mountains, and the lower one that between the Mettenberg and the Eiger. Into the latter of these glaciers a grotto, very similar to the drift or gangway of a coal mine, has been driven to a distance of about three hundred feet. At the extreme end of this is a space some fifteen feet square, called the "chamber of ice," or, sometimes, the "ice-chapel." Lamps are suspended at regular intervals along the gangway, and the chamber itself is more brilliantly illuminated with a number of others; the effect of these lights upon the intervening wall of ice being one indescribably beautiful, rendering it of an amber color, and the crystals, in apparently globular masses of limpid clearness, sufficiently translucent to enable one to distinguish the shadowy outlines of an object on the opposite side, though the wall is at least a yard in thickness. In the chamber were seated two women, singing, for a consideration of ten cents, "Komm heraus, komm heraus, du Schweitzer Bub," and other Swiss airs, accompanying their voices with a zither. They were rather pretty, not to say that they were absolutely charming, with an arch playfulness about their eyes and lips that indicated two palpitating hearts exceedingly out of place in the chilly atmosphere of that icy vault. (Does any one ask whose hearts were they? and insinuate something about my American friend and *his* friend? Get out, now! you ought to know better.) But with the prettiness alluded to, and attired in the gay and picturesque costume of the country, they rendered the *tout ensemble* somewhat interesting and romantic; and my American friend, with a degree of impudence most assuredly acquired in Europe, threatened to steal from one of these songstresses a kiss, remarking knavishly, that such would be the only thing necessary to complete the romance of the occasion. But, like another Mentor, I restrained him with a word of admonition; and it was well, for just then a young peasant entered, who, methought, glanced with more than a brother's interest at the fair young damsel, and who might, in the event of my friend carrying out his threat, have converted this beautiful grotto of ice into a horrible boxing-mill — something that would have detracted very materially from the charm of the adventure.

Arrived again outside, I ascended, accompanied by a guide, the Mettenberg to the distance of over four thousand feet; and attained, after three hours' climbing, along a fearfully dangerous and precipitous pathway, the height where the glacier is almost level, and constitutes what is called the sea of ice, three miles long and two wide. Here it was that occurred the peculiar impressiveness before alluded to; for while thus placed, midway upon this sea of ice, the sky darkened, the clouds gathered over our heads, the winds began to blow with sudden and fearful violence, and the rain to fall in sheets upon us; the thunderbolts were scattered about, as if it were

> "That in such gaps as desolation work'd,
> There the hot shaft should blast whatever therein lurk'd."

An immediate return down the mountain pass was not to be thought of, as the storm would have hurled us irresistibly into the abyss below; so we fled for refuge into a little hut, inhabited by a goatherd, that was situated on the mountain side, near the very edge of the ice-lake; but the hut looked in imminent danger of being blown down itself, so that the feeling of shelter it afforded was scarcely one of safety, and certainly none of comfort. Oh! it was terrible, that moment! To see the swollen cataracts gushing like great rivers down the rocky precipices, to hear, like a thunder-clap, the crash of the avalanche, and witness it shooting down the gorge, presenting the appearance of a great column of animated snow; to hear the wild howling of the wind, and the heavy splashing of the rain, interspersed with the terrified bleating of the goats that clamber in great numbers to the mountain sides, like flies to a wall; to feel yourself alone, battling with the great storm-king, in his own domain, at an altitude far from the fixed foundation of men's ordinary dwelling places; when

> "The loud hills shake with their mountain mirth,
> As if they did rejoice o'er a young earthquake's birth,"

is a situation of awfulness and sublimity that cannot

be surpassed; the terrors of a storm at sea cannot be more fearful in their nature than those of a hurricane upon the Alps. The fury of this storm continued about an hour, after which it gradually subsided; and then my guide and myself, accompanied by the goatherd who occupied the hut, which, after all, had proved itself a great friend to us, undertook the descent of the mountain by the way we had come. This path was crossed by numerous little rivulets, over which, at ordinary times, it is easy enough to step without much risk of wetting the soles of one's shoes; but now, the first of them that we reached presented the formidable character of a mighty torrent, arching itself over the narrow footway, and tumbling with furious velocity, and a great roaring noise, madly into the chasm, at least five hundred feet below; washing away, too, and carrying with its impetuous tide a shower of stones from the still higher regions above us, so that it was utterly impossible to proceed farther. We therefore retraced our steps to the hut, and as it was already eight o'clock, and growing dark, no alternative was left us but to remain there all night.

The hut was not very inviting, and the major part of it was partitioned off for the goats, of whom there were at least twenty or thirty, all having little bells attached to their necks; the constant tinkling of which, interspersed occasionally with the dull sound of two heads butting each other, was not calculated to vary the monotony of the situation to any great extent. Nor was the aroma that emanated from the goats and pervaded our apartment like that which Lubin prepares for the fair sex, or I could advise him how to obtain a double-distilled extract, strong enough to perfume all the pocket handkerchiefs and waterfalls in creation. We had a supper composed of goat's milk and *kirschwasser*,— the latter is an article that the strongest whiskey need not be ashamed of,— and I am not certain but that we repeated this supper, or at least the latter half of it, sundry more times during the night. As a curious fact in philosophy, I would mention that as the kirschwasser *descended* in the barometrical bottle that contained it, *our spirits rose*, though the prospect appeared to grow *foggier* all the time; and had our barometer continued to descend, which it did not, until morning, I doubt not but that our condition on a lofty mountain would have been reduced to one simply *a little elevated.*

In the absence of anything resembling a bed, and in the presence of our neighbors with the bells, sleep, of course, was not to be dreamed of; so I resigned myself with mute attention to the wonderful accounts of hair-breadth escapes, of being snowed-up on the Alps, of living the dear knows how long on roots and the bark of trees, which our host, who is also a chamois hunter, recited of himself with great gusto. In this he was seconded by the guide, who was not a whit behind in adventurous experiences; and between the two, a life upon the mountains was pretty thoroughly canvassed and discussed, with all its merits highly praised, and its little imperfections but lightly touched upon, throughout the dreary livelong hours of that night. Be it freely confessed, however, that, notwithstanding the glorious colors and fascinations with which they embellished such a life, I would prefer not to pass the remainder of my days in its rapturous enjoyments.

In the morning, at daybreak, we sallied forth once more; and crossing the ice to the opposite side — the side resting against the Eiger mountain — we began our descent with the help of ropes and pronged staves, mutually aiding each other; and partly over the glacier, partly down the mountain side, we arrived at length at its foot in the village of Grindelwald, where we learned that a party of men had started out with lanterns in search for us late in the night, but found the roads impassable on account of the mountain torrents and avalanches, which defeated their kind intentions toward us.

One of our trio, who passed the night on yonder peak, a good deal nearer to the moon than he had ever been before, was almost cured of any further desire for Alpine investigation; whether it is likely that this one was either Peter Joch, the guide; Ulrich Schlunegger, the chamois hunter; or the subscriber, is a subject left open for conjecture.

LETTER XI.

SWITZERLAND.—LAKE BRIENZ.

VISIT TO THE GIESBACH WATERFALL.— THE STAUBBACH CASCADE.—INTERLAKEN.—GENEVA.—THE TURNER-FEST. TRIP TO CHAMOUNY, AND ASCENT OF THE ALPS.— OVER THE TÊTE NOIR PASS, TO MARTIGNY.— THE CASTLE OF CHILLON.—DOWN THE LAKE OF GENEVA.—RETURN TO ZURICH.—INTERESTING INCIDENT.— EN ROUTE TO MUNICH.

MUNICH, *June*, 1867.

HAVING returned in safety after the adventurous visit to the Grindelwald glaciers, I proceeded on a steamboat over Lake Brienz, to the Giesbach Waterfall, which is undoubtedly one of the finest examples of that character in the whole world. It is a stream of water about the size of Norwegian Creek, in Pottsville, after a pretty smart rain. It has its source from the great Scheideck Mountain, whence it here falls, in a series of pitches that follow each other in rapid succession, a distance of probably six hundred feet. Under one of these distinct shutes, about midway from the commencement of the fall, a bridge is constructed, over which one may pass and look through the sheet of water and spray into the valley beneath. At night, during the summer season, the proprietor of the hotel here situated is in the habit of illuminating these falls with

Bengal fire, and the effect thereof is eminently grand. Another very beautiful cascade is the Staubbach, at Lauterbrunnen, about nine miles from Interlaken. This is a small rivulet flowing from Alpine springs at a very high altitude, and precipitates itself from a perpendicular rock the enormous distance of nine hundred and twenty-five feet. If there is the lightest breeze in the atmosphere, this sheet of water becomes so scattered before reaching the ground, that it has the appearance of a column of dust, (hence its name *Staub*bach, or Dust-Spring,) and settles upon the earth, moistening a large surface, like a heavy dew. During sunshine it resembles a long veil, whose light and gauzy texture waving to and fro, assuming a variety of shapes by its constantly changing folds, and reflecting a bewildering succession of prismatic colors, produces a result of peculiar and inimitable beauty.

Interlaken is a very fashionable resort; and just now the season is in its zenith of bustle and excitement. It is a kind of breathing-place — a lovely situation to pause and reflect in, for the hundreds, I might say thousands, of the worshippers of God's glorious architecture who are engaged in what is technically termed "doing" Switzerland. There are sixteen hotels, every one of which is capable of accommodating about two hundred guests; yet I am told that the influx of visitors is so great that the establishment of additional boarding-places is in immediate contemplation.

The Bernoise highlands present from this point a panorama of indescribable magnitude and grandeur, in the centre of which the towering Jungfrau, veiled in perpetual snow, constitutes the chiefest object of man's wonder and admiration.

Leaving Interlaken, I passed through Berne to Lausanne, and thence to the beautiful city of Geneva. There, where the azure current of the Rhone sweeps with an arrow's swiftness from the bosom of Lake Leman.

Geneva, with its fine houses, wide and cleanly thoroughfares, pretty gardens and pleasure-grounds, numerous fountains, magnificent bridges, and — shall I say it? — handsome women; yes; for their faultless figures, fair and spotless complexion, regular and well-defined lineaments, speaking eyes, cheerful expression of countenances, graceful elasticity of movement, deserve that tribute of homage and admiration due to everything that is beautiful in art or nature; and where the two — the artistic and the natural — are united so intimately as in the Genevese ladies — I beg their pardon! but — Geneva, with its unknown grave of Calvin; its aged, gray-grown, almost tottering homes of Voltaire and

> "The self-torturing sophist, wild Rousseau —
> The apostle of affliction; he who threw
> Enchantment over passion, and from woe
> Wrung overwhelming eloquence —"

aye, yes, Geneva, the charming inter-Alpine metropolis, whose windows glitter brilliantly with Time's monitors, in the shape of anchor-escapement and thirteen-jewelled watches.

The day of my arrival was that of the beginning

of the Turner-Fest, or Fête Gymnastique, which is an annual period of festivity and great jubilee, continuing five successive days, on which occasion all the Turner, or Gymnastic associations of the different cantons of Switzerland come together in one of the principal cities, and indulge in reciprocal trials of strength and gymnastic exercises on a great field prepared for the occasion, and decorated with flags, wreaths, and flowers. Indeed, as far as I could see, every house in the city exhibited more or less bunting from roofs and windows—a display of patriotism that reminded me much of our own cities, after some brilliant victory had been achieved, during our late war; nor were they unmindful here of our own banner; for the Stars and Stripes floated from at least one window of every hotel—a circumstance that, I strongly suspect, was occasioned more by a love for our monetary impressions of the American eagle, than any emblematical admiration that might attach itself to that glorious old bird.

Thus it may be said, that Geneva came under my observation clothed in its gaudiest holiday attire; and were it not for the marring circumstance of great cannon firing, processions, with the loud accompaniment of brass bands, boisterous hilarity, speeches, bonfires, and illuminations which characterized the commencement of this fête on the Sabbath day, my impression of the city would be an exceedingly pleasant and satisfactory one.

On my way hither I had formed the acquaintance of a worthy gentleman from Pittsburg, Pa., who had just returned from an extensive tour through Syria and the Holy Land, and with whom I now proceeded in a diligence to Chamouny, to see the great giant of the Alps, Mont Blanc, and its associate chain of mountains. This was my second introduction to that European institution, a diligence—a great lumbering concern, like a menagerie wagon, two and a half stories high, and drawn by six powerful horses. On this occasion the caravan contained nineteen passengers—eight who occupied the interior, six who were above these, in the second story, covered by an awning, and five others, who were perched still higher up, in the front part of the vehicle, just behind the driver. These five were my Pittsburg friend and myself, besides two gentlemen and a lady from Australia. The distance from Geneva to Chamouny is forty-two miles, which we made by frequent relays in twelve hours.

On the following day, together with my four companions of the high position on the diligence, I started on another pilgrimage afoot up the Montanvert, the summit of which—an altitude of nearly six thousand feet, we attained after three hours' walk. We then crossed the sea of ice lying between it and the Chapeau, a mountain on the opposite side, and descended by what is known as the Mauvais Pas, or dangerous path, which led along the ledges of the rock, where these were so perpendicular, and the footholds so narrow, that spikes were driven into the sides, to which an iron railing was attached for a distance of some hundred and fifty yards, whereby one could hold and steady oneself in the descent. At the foot of the glacier is another crystal grotto, or ice-tunnel, similar to that at Grindelwald; into this we made a short excursion, and afterward ascended the Flegère, another high mountain, lying immediately back of the small town, and constituting one of the towering sides of the great natural kettle known as the Valley of Chamounix. From here we had a view of Mont Blanc such as it is equalled from no other point. The huge and rugged snow-covered excrescence of earth lay before us in all its nakedness; from its base to the glittering white summit, with not a cloud to mar the awe-inspiring prospect, looming up into the sky like a giant medium between earth and heaven; and if it were the only one by which the chosen might pass from the former to the latter, I should say that the way, though not very narrow, is indeed difficult to wander, and "few there are who go thereon." They say that such mountains bear about the same proportionate relation to the general rotundity of the earth, as that of an orange is characterized by the little pimples and roughness on its surface. It may be so—at least, I am not prepared to argue against the time-honored geographical dogma; but in that case, here were some pimples, now, that made the old face of Nature very wrinkled indeed; and I marvel much how our sublunary globe can avoid making some very ugly lurches, when such protuberances get on the down-hill side of the revolving mass. The following day we started out afoot for Martigny, over the Téte Noir pass — a distance of twenty-four miles. But after six miles of walking, I looked upon discretion as the better part of valor, and bestrode a frisky mule, whereon I also loaded the satchels and surplus accoutrements of my two friends, and rode triumphantly along, forcibly impressed with the recollection of all the pictures I had ever seen of Napoleon crossing the Alps. Arrived at the top of the mountain, however, I sent the mule back in disgrace, as he had not been of much comfort to me, and there was that about me that was sorely bruised. The Tête Noir is a ledge of rocks, high up, on whose face the sun never shines, and is black and mouldy and wet with the never-ceasing trickling of water down its side.

At Martigny we took the cars and proceeded to Villeneuve, at the head of the Lake of Geneva, where we took lodging at the Hotel Byron, formerly the residence of the poet. This is one of the loveliest spots I ever beheld; and I wonder not that Byron could write poetry, with all the associations that surrounded and inspired him here.

> "Lake Leman woos me with her crystal face,
> The mirror where the stars and mountains view
> The stillness of their aspect in each trace
> Its clear depth yields of their far height and hue."

Here it was where much of Childe Harold, and the whole of the Prisoner of Chillon was located, imbuing the untamed poet with a portion of that dreamy, misanthropical melancholy, which made of him a wreck amid all his flowery imagery.

> "Is it not better, then, to be alone,
> And love earth only for its earthly sake?
> By the blue rushing of the arrowy Rhone,
> Or the pure bosom of its nursing lake."

The castle of Chillon is in a well-preserved condition, and one of the finest relics of the Feudal period. Many a thing " of quaint and curious lore " is shown in connection with it, but especially the old prison vaults, with seven stone pillars, to which the prisoners were chained. Then there is the Knights' Hall, where the heraldry of the Duke of Savoy were wont to gather at the festive board; and it had a spacious medieval air about it, that it needed but a slight inflation of the mind to realize, as it were, the heavy-booted tread of the myrmidons, the clash and clangor of arms, the Babylonic commingling of loud voices, the boisterous song, the clinking of the wine-cups, and the general " sound of revelry by night." The joists and rafters were relieved from presenting a positive barn-like bareness by a number of yellow and tattered banners, interspersed with antique weapons, helmets, and coats-of-mail; and here and there some uncouth fresco was still dimly visible through the dingy, time-darkened surface of the compact stucco on the walls. There, too, was the terrible Hall of Justice, (?) and the stairway, down which the condemned were obliged to descend blindfolded, to a watery grave; three steps they would pass in safety; but the fourth would plunge them into the lake, which is here eight hundred feet in depth. It was here where the Reformer, Bonévard, was chained to one of the stone pillars before mentioned, during a period of seven years, by the then reigning duke; and released at last by the united Bernese and Genevese forces. A track in the stone floor around the pillar is pointed out as having been occasioned by his footsteps. After his release, the good man lived many years in Geneva, and was amply cared for by its citizens.

From here we sailed down the beautiful lake, over its entire length of about fifty miles, and arrived again at Geneva, where on the following day we separated — Mr. Miller, the gentleman from Pittsburg, before mentioned, taking the straight route for Paris, and I that to Neufchâtel.

On this line the railroad passes by some of the loveliest scenery I have ever beheld, by the shores of Lake Neufchâtel, and frequently through the midst of luxurious and far-reaching vineyards.

At Bienne it was necessary to change cars; and up to this point the language of the railroad officials had been French, and I had been painfully impressed with a snubbishness and want of courtesy that I had not heretofore witnessed in any parts of France. But here we came under German management, and the difference of pleasanter cars, together with the extreme attentiveness and politeness of the officials, came upon us with a suddenness of contrast that was both curious and agreeable.

At length, after nearly five weeks' rambling through Switzerland, I returned again to Zurich, (where I had left a portion of my baggage,) and to the almost home-comforts of the Baur au Lac hotel. Here I found ex-Governor Curtin, just on the point of leaving for a tour among the mountains. Here I also formed the acquaintance of a gentleman who had been travelling during the two weeks previously, with Hon. James H. Campbell; and it appears that I had just arrived at the head of Lake Geneva, (where Mr. Campbell had resided two weeks,) about a day after his departure. With this gentleman, Rev. Mr. Blake, from Massachusetts, I afterward continued my travels, during a short period, in company.

Shortly before our departure from Zurich, my American friend had a little colloquial adventure, the narration of which may not be altogether out of place. Seated at the window, with his chin resting in the hollow of his hand, he was gazing wistfully into the serene distance without, and lost in a revery whose burden was the dear ones beyond the surging waters of the broad Atlantic; when he was suddenly aroused by a light tap at his chamber-door.

"*Herein!*" called he in a distinct voice; when presently the door opened, and there stood before him the timid figure of a young girl, of interesting and thoughtful mien; with traces of care, beyond that generally allotted to one of her years, that cast a tempering shade over her otherwise personal attractiveness. Then, with faltering German accents, she said what in substance was about as follows:—

"O, sir! I hope you will excuse my boldness; but I would like — if it is possible — to go with you to America."

"Go with me to America!" said my friend, perfectly dumbfounded at such an unaccountable appeal from so amiable an apparition.

"Why, my good child, what in the world possesses you with such an idea? and how do you know that I am an American?"

"I heard you say so to the gentleman in the bookstore to-day, when I took some work there that he had given me to do."

"But why do you wish to go to America?"

"Because I have a sister who went there with her husband five years ago; since which time I have lost both my parents, and am so lonely now without my sister." Here the poor girl's voice faltered still more, and her eyes were swimming in tears.

"Have you no other relations here?" said my American friend, becoming more interested in the case.

"Yes, sir; but they are all poor, and have a hard time to get along for themselves. Besides, they are unkind to me, and expect me to work more for them than I am able to do."

"What kind of work do you do?"

"I make fancy card-cases and toy-boxes of paper, sir."

"But that should pay you pretty well, my child."

"Ah! no, sir; I cannot earn more than a franc a day, and it costs me nearly all of that for a bare living."

"I should think so, indeed! You have not mentioned your name, Miss; perhaps"—

"My name is Rosina, at your service, sir."

"But do you not know that it requires considerable money to go to America?"

"Oh! yes, sir; my dear parents left me enough to defray the necessary expenses; and I only desire to place myself under the protection of some kind gentleman who would take the trouble to have a guardian care over me, during so long and perilous a journey.

You said at the bookstore, sir, that you had a wife and children at home, and spoke of them with so much feeling, that I felt sure you would not be unkind; and therefore I took heart to approach you in this abrupt manner."

Here was an artless and confiding creature, to be sure! My American friend now explained to her, how it was impossible to comply with her request, as he did not contemplate leaving Europe for some months to come. But he gave her good advice how to proceed; answered her many inquiries fairly and explicitly; and above all, cautioned her not to be too zealous in her lookout for a guardian gentleman. I could see that he was greatly moved by the simple story and manners of this young Swiss girl; and it is but natural to hope that she may attain the fulfilment of her desire, and arrive in safety, to be cheered with brighter prospects and a sister's presence in that land of promise and of plenty.

We left Zurich for Schaffhausen, to view the Rhine Falls in that vicinity. In these I was agreeably surprised; for instead of finding the dull and uninteresting "small affair," which a number of persons had pronounced it to be, I found it a grand and tumultuous cataract — the "hell of waters," as Mr. Murray calls it; and the associate situation is of the most romantic character imaginable, of Nature tamed down from extreme wildness by agricultural industry and art. From the old city of Schaffhausen we went by railway to Constanz, the city where the martyr Huss was burned at the stake. The place where this terrible deed was done is pointed out to strangers; but the train of thought which it recalls is of such a horrifying and revolting nature that I hastened onward. Here the river Rhine flows out of Lake Constance, or the Boden See, as it is called in Germany, and we took a steamboat and passed over its entire length. It is the largest of the Swiss lakes, being about sixty miles long and ten wide. On the water we had a fine view of the Senis chain of Alps, and of a magnificent sunset, that far exceeded in beauty and effectiveness any that I had seen on the ocean. At Lindau the entrance is guarded by a colossal statue of white granite, representing a lion, the principal figure in the coat of arms of Bavaria, which kingdom we now approached. In the city is a fine statue in bronze of Maximilian, father of the present King of Bavaria. There is also here, as the most noteworthy object of curiosity, a portion of a wall built by the Romans, it is said, fifteen years before the birth of Christ.

We now took the train for Munich, and passed in a few hours from view of the Bayern Hochalpen mountains, over a ground of interminable flatness in every direction, as far as the eye can reach. Indeed, it is in every respect, except character of soil, similar to our western prairies. Trees are but thinly scattered, and nothing like a forest is at all visible. The farms are in a high state of cultivation; and I am told that the people throughout the country are, generally speaking, in very comfortable circumstances. At Augsburg we stopped a short time, and then passed on to Munich.

LETTER XII.

MUNICH. — MUSIC.

MUNICH.—PASSION OF THE PEOPLE FOR MUSIC.—GOSSIP ABOUT THE KING.—ART GALLERIES.—DISTINGUISHED PORTRAITS.—VISIT TO THE BRONZE FOUNDRY.—A MONUMENTAL COLONNADE.—BEER.—STUTTGART.—ITS PALACES AND OTHER BUILDINGS.—CARLSRUHE.—BADEN-BADEN.—THE ARCHDUKE'S CASTLE.—THE CONVERSATION HALL.—GAMING.

HEIDELBERG, *July*, 1867.

ON entering Munich, almost the first object that greeted my attention was a cavalry regiment returning from parade, headed by a corps of buglers, consisting of at least thirty instruments, who performed one of Strauss' waltzes, in a manner that appeared to fill the very horses with sprightliness and elasticity, as they stepped along, one might say, in a measure, keeping time to the music. It was evident that I had arrived in the land where instrumental music is a passion, and where people in straitened circumstances, if it needs must be, can play away their dinner-hour on a flute or violin, leaving the poor stomach none the wiser for the little deception. For the sound of piano-music was floating toward me on the waves of the atmosphere from every direction all the time I was in the city, except that which is appropriated for sleep. The King himself is a warm admirer of the divine art, and performs very creditably on a number of instruments. Recently the prima donna of the royal opera of Munich, Fräulein Mallinger, for whom the people have an adoration bordering on frenzy, had an offer of twenty thousand thalers for a season, from the King of Prussia, to sing at Berlin; but the King of Bavaria immediately offered her the same amount to stay where she is; and as he is just turned twenty-one years of age, and said to be the handsomest monarch of Europe, the odds were greatly in his favor, Bismarck and all to the contrary notwithstanding. They say, indeed, that the King's intended bride, a sister to the Empress of Austria, is a little jealous of this pretty opera singer; and recently, when she was having her portrait taken, together with her royal lover, at a photograph gallery, the young actress — incidentally or designedly, as the case may be — entered the establishment, whereupon the King proceeded to shake hands with her, and treated her with uncommon civility; seeing which, the Princess that is to be the Queen was immediately seized with a fit of the pouts, ordered her carriage and departed. Now, the story does not say that the King hurried after her, entreating her for mercy's sake to pause and gather the fragments of his broken heart; but certain it is that they are reconciled; for I saw them ride out together on horseback, attended only by a single valet, who rode dreamily behind, beyond a whispering distance of the lovers, and they certainly looked too exuberantly happy to leave any doubt on my mind as to the felicitous nature of their feelings. On the same evening, however, I saw him again —

without the Princess — at the opera, witnessing the representation of Richard Wagner's Lohengrin; and it appeared to me that the prima donna tried very hard to please his Majesty, as she seemed to see none other, and he frequently stepped forward in his box, to bestow his gracious applause. He is a good-looking young fellow, certainly; and my American friend says of him, "He sings like a martingale, and dances like pop-corn on a hot stove." Dear me! what more can you expect from a king?*

There are two very fine art-galleries in Munich, containing a large number of excellent and valuable paintings, many of which were formerly in the gallery of Düsseldorf; among which are the Last Judgment and the Condemnation of the Wicked, two strong, impressive, and highly finished paintings by Rubens. In view, however, of the numerous works purporting to be executed by Rubens, Murillo, Raphael, Van Dyck, and others, I could not help thinking how wonderfully industrious these artists must have been, to have done all the work that is attributed to them, and which now adorns so many of the galleries of Europe. They were nearly as productive of pictures as the Champagne country is at the present day, of the delicious beverage which the world enjoys so much. The most attractive paintings of Munich are those which constitute the Gallery of Beauty in the King's palace, consisting, originally, of thirty-seven portraits of the handsomest women of Bavaria during the reign of King Louis, the grandfather of

---

* Since this was written, the marriage-contract has *not* been entered into.

the present monarch. They are, certainly, very beautiful creations; and if they do not flatter the ladies whom they represent, then the court of Louis must have presented a very gay and charming spectacle. One of these portraits, that of the celebrated Lola Montes, was removed a few years ago; leaving but thirty-six in the gallery at present.

A very interesting place to visit, in Munich, is the Bronze Foundry — the largest establishment of the kind, I believe, in existence; where bronze statues and all descriptions of monuments are cast and finished, and sent to all parts of the world. I here saw the model in plaster-of-paris, made by Story, the American sculptor, for some years past at Rome, of the bronze doors in the Capitol at Washington; also that of the colossal equestrian statue of Washington at Richmond, Va. They were working at the time of my visit at a magnificent statue of Edward Everett, which is nearly completed, and intended to be erected at Boston. There was also a very fine piece representing two figures — the one Abraham Lincoln, the other a slave. Mr. Lincoln is in a standing posture, extending his left hand over the head of the kneeling slave, as if in the act of calling a blessing upon him; his right hand rests upon a shield, which is supported by the Emancipation Proclamation and a pile of books, representing the laws — signifying that the act was one based upon justice and the common law. The model of this design was also executed by Story.

Here were models of Henry Clay, Daniel Webster, Chief Justice Marshall, and many others of the great men of our country. Need I add, that a feeling of peculiar interest was awakened by the sight of these figures, recalling the familiar outlines of men whose "names that were not born to die" are household words with us, so far away from home — away, beyond the great waters of a mighty ocean — away, where kings and potentates hold their oppressive rule. It seems to me, as though I could love Munich more, for being the guardian of these precious treasures — for holding within her limits the images of our republican lawmakers and benefactors.

Situated at one of the extremities of the city is a monumental colonnade, built after the Grecian style of architecture, and constituting a gallery, where busts of all the great men of Bavaria are erected to the honor and perpetuation of their names. Immediately in front of this is the colossal statue of Bavaria, represented as a female, standing erect, with a wreath in her extended left hand, and the right resting on the mane of a crouching lion by her side. It is of bronze, and the largest in the world. The granite pedestal upon which the figure is erected is thirty-six, and the statue itself sixty feet high. Some idea may be formed of the enormous proportions of this production of art, when it is stated, that a stairway runs up inside of it, by which I was enabled to ascend, and walk about in the lady's head on — what I hope to be excused in calling — the cribriform plate of the ethmoid bone. The folds of her hair form seats, interiorly, that could not be covered by a couple of ordinary-sized carriage cushions. Yet as viewed from without, this work presents an artistic perfection of outlines; the proportions are correct and symmetrical; the posé of the lady is elegant and graceful; and the folds of her drapery are delineated with a naturalness that is charming. Assuredly the city of Munich can pride itself upon the singular fact of having the greatest and tallest specimen of the fair sex — though she is cold, (except when the sun shines on her,) hollow-hearted, and monstrously brazen.

The greatest institution, however, in this fair city — greater even than her statue of Bavaria — is beer, and the drinking of beer is the proudest privilege of the Munichian.

I have seen the teams going down the street, before my own home in America, in long processions, groaning under the weight of Yuengling's beer, and wondered where, in the name of Gambrinus, it all went to; I have seen the stream of thirsty pilgrims pass to and from, and heard the subterranean music of Max Leimmer's mysterious elysium, and wondered whether the liquid happiness that he taps out there would be eternal; but all this dwindles away into the utmost obliviousness when I stand in the august presence of this great DRINK, as it presents itself in Munich. Shade of the great Falstaff—and ye ghosts of Bardolph and Peto, I would seek you here; for if an element of "sack" is congenial to your repose, then surely *this* is the haven of your flightiest aspirations! A man that is in anger — say but "Beer" to him, and — he smiles; say it to the poor man, and he is rich; to the rich man, and he is happy. Ask for information about beer,—How is it made? whence come the best barley and hops, and what are the best means of cultivating both? who makes the most delicious beer? and how many gallons can a body drink without dissolving or bursting asunder? and there is hardly a man, woman, or child in Munich, but what can give you every possible instruction on the subject.

Music and Beer are the enthroned monarchs here, before whom Louis II. does as much homage as the veriest vassal of the kingdom. It was a mistake in nature that Meyer*beer* was not born of these people; and that *Beer*have was the product of any other community, is the greatest puzzle of the century. I have been in the Hof-Brauhaus, where no beer is sold except what is drank upon the premises. They have no casks, but provide the establishment with about a thousand pewter quart-pots; one of which it is necessary to secure, rinse it out in a tank of the several running fountains provided for the purpose, and then crowd your way to a tapster, get it filled, go to one of the numerous tables, and drink it leisurely. I have seen at least five hundred persons drinking beer at one time in this place, which is nothing more nor less than a yard, shedded over; and sometimes the ground floor becomes so saturated with the slops from the pots that are spilled upon it, that it forms a kind of quagmire, in which it is impossible to preserve clean shoes.

A gentleman told me in all seriousness, that if I had any business to transact, I should attend to it before nine o'clock in the morning; because after that time everybody would be engaged in drinking beer for the rest of the day! . . . . . . It was twilight; and I stood leaning over the balustrade of a bridge, gazing long and lovingly into the gurgling water below, that carried me back to the days of my boyhood, when it was my peculiar pleasure to spout:

> "On Linden, when the sun was low,
> All bloodless lay the untrodden snow,
> And dark as winter was the flow
> Of Iser rolling rapidly."

Can it be that this is the stream which inflated my youthful imagination, and that should roll down its thick volume of water with boisterous commotion, as it did

> "When the drum beat at dead of night?"

What can have become of all the water of the "Iser rolling rapidly?" I appealed to my American friend, who, with native sagacity, immediately answered: "They made beer of it." And now

> "Wave, Munich, all thy banners wave,
> And charge with all thy" — breweries!

The next city to which I proceeded was Stuttgardt. Going thither, I happened to go into a car containing four Austrians, and one Prussian gentleman. It conveyed an agreeable impression to witness the good feeling and extreme cordiality which characterized their deportment toward each other, of these two kinds of people, who but last year were involved in such a terrible conflict, and which presented a strong contrast to the vindictive bitterness of *our* rebels, who, though thrashed and doubled up completely, still persist in spitting out their contemptible defiance in the most ridiculous manner.

From Stuttgardt I took a walk of two miles to the beautiful palaces of Rosenstein and Wilhelma, the former of Grecian and the latter of Moorish architecture. The way thither leads from the King's residence in the city through a continuous avenue of trees, whose branches, uniting above, form a beautiful archway along the entire distance. The spaces between the trees on both sides of the road are filled with contiguous lines of rose-bushes, that were in full bloom, of every variety and color.

Stuttgardt contains many beautiful and attractive buildings, and has the finest railway depot that I have thus far seen. It is a perfect palace, both in beauty of architecture and in spacious proportions, constructed of chiselled granite and iron, and roofed over with thick glass, that admits light to every part of the building.

In the principal square is a fine statue of Schiller, and in another square I saw a column about ninety feet high, surmounted by a bronze figure of Concordia. On my way from Stuttgardt, I asked a lady in the car what their king's name was, whereupon she blushed, looked a little confused, and said she really did not know; that they had other things to think about that concerned them more nearly than the name of the king.

I next arrived at Carlsruhe, where I remained but a few hours; but saw enough during that short period to be greatly pleased with this truly beautiful city. It is built something on the plan of the city of Washington, the streets radiating outward from a central point — the Archducal residence — like the ribs of a fan; and these again are intersected by semicircular streets, the first being called the Inner Circle, the next the Second Circle, and so on. In the Carl Friedrich Street are situated a large number of statues and monuments; of which the most noteworthy is a brown sandstone pyramid (modelled after the Egyptian pyramids) which incloses the remains of the founder of the city, and the stump of a tree against which he leaned for support when he was tired and exhausted, after having roamed about all day, looking up a site for his intended city; and hence the name Carlsruhe, or Charles' Rest.

I now arrested my journey at a place that I cannot pass over without an extended notice, due to its character as one of the most fashionable summer resorts in Continental Europe; and one, too, wherein gambling is carried on to an extent that is absolutely frightful. This is the city of Baden-Baden, in the archduchy of the same name. Situated at the entrance to the Black Forest, as it were in a kettle of hills, abounding with stately trees, between which a stream of water as clear as crystal threads its way in serpentine irregularity, appearing from the heights like a broad ribbon of silver when the sun shines upon it; favored, too, with a great number of mineral and saline springs, some of which have the high temperature of a hundred and fifty degrees Fahrenheit, and whose medicinal properties are highly extolled in the treatment of many chronic affections, this city has advantages of local attractiveness that are rarely found in similar numbers and proximity with each other. Among the antique places of interest are the old castle, or rather the ruins of it, situated on the top of a hill, and which was formerly the seat of the margraves; the "new" Castle, which, however, scarcely deserves that title, it having been built as long ago as the thirteenth century; and the ruins of Castle Eberstein, which, tradition says, the Emperor Otto I., not being able to take by storm, endeavored to capture by strategy, to which purpose he invited its incumbent to a tournament and dance at Speyer, intending to attack the stronghold during his absence. The Emperor's daughter, smitten with the young Count, informed him of her father's scheme, during the dance, when, hastening home, he barely arrived in time to save his castle. The tradition very properly terminates with the marriage of the Count and the Emperor's daughter, who, it is said, had their cup of happiness flowing over ever after. I was shown all through the new Castle, at present occupied by the reigning Archduke, and found it retaining all the attributes of feudal grandeur, and as gorgeously furnished as any of the imperial palaces I had seen in or near Paris.

Returning to the city, we will find in the west-end thereof situated the sanitary and gaming establishments, which together constitute the principal feature of the place. The waters of the different springs are variable in quality and temperature, and all exert a very salutary influence. The city has a number of intelligent physicians, who are well conversant with the availability of the waters for the manifold derangements that the human system is liable to undergo. As a general rule, the expense of medical advice here, as in all German cities, is not great. I knew a gentleman — a wretched dyspeptic and hypochondriac — who bored a doctor in his office with the same story of his infirmities, nearly half an hour every day for six weeks; yet the kind doctor never winced, never appeared annoyed or ill-humored, and at length when he presented his bill, it only amounted to fifty florins, equal to about twenty dollars. Such urbanity of disposition, and devotion to the profession deserve the gratitude of the world.

The Pump-Room, containing an overflowing fountain of hot mineral water, of which it is the custom for everybody, sick or well, to drink large quantities every morning before breakfast, on general principles, is fronted by a large colonnade, whose wall is embellished with some of the finest frescos I have yet seen; representing legendary traditions of the Black Forest. The one delineating the mermaids of the Mummelsee is a production of rare qualities.

But the edifice which is, *par excellence*, the attractive feature of Baden, is the Conversation Hall, a large and beautiful building, magnificently fitted up, and comprising spacious apartments for social intercourse, dining, concert, and gaming purposes. In front of this building is a kiosk or pagoda, for the musicians, that alone cost seventy thousand francs in its construction, and might serve for a fairy palace or a beautiful bower in dreamland. Here every morning at seven o'clock, about forty of the best musicians greet the new-born day with the morning hymn, whilst hundreds of promenaders, composed of all characters, classes, and nationalities, from the —

> "Gay, licentious, proud,
> Whom pleasure, power, and affluence surround,"

to the weak and decrepid invalid, who hopes to find here some amelioration of his physical sufferings, may be seen strolling up and down the shaded avenues, attired in careless negligé. In the afternoon, however, the scene is changed into one of bewildering enchantment. Crowds of people are seated around hundreds of small tables; valets and waiters are flitting about like eccentric rockets, shot off on all manner of irregular errands; high words in shrill tones from this end, and merry laughter from that, are intermingled with the clatter of knives and forks, the clear jingle of glasses, and the popping of corks from champagne-bottles — and thus the epicurean part of the scene goes on. But the regular concert of the day has also commenced. Strains of music, now soft and mellow and low, as though heard afar off, filling the soul with a dreamy luxuriousness, the very sensuality of sound,— and now swelling up by regular gradation into a melodious acme, culminating in a volume of wild and over-running harmony, that sends vibration and a thrill through every nerve of the body. And now the untoiletted figures of the morning are converted into pedestrian broadcloth and kid gloves, silks and satins, and bonnets and ribbons and tucks, ringlets and flowers and paint.

Let us enter the building, and listen to the music there — the clink of gold and silver that brings alternate agony and joy to those who are under its baneful fascination. The doors are all open; you cross no obstruction; no questions asked; no fees to pay. As you enter the apartment with a timid and palpitating heart — as though guilty of a wickedness from which you could never recover — you see God's glorious and heaven-born sunlight pervading this abode, even as it does those of less social darkness. Everything that surrounds you is calculated to separate your mind from the importance of money. The most lavish expenditures glare at you from every point. The gorgeous draperies of the windows; the rich frescos of the ceilings; the fine paintings, in frames of shining gold, that decorate the walls, and mostly represent figures and scenes of luxurious and seductive import; the sofas and chairs covered with crimson satin; and, lastly, the long table spread with green cloth, whereon great stacks of gold and silver coin, bright and shining, are scattered about in such profusion, as though they were the chippings of a tin-shop. On the table are two fields marked off with intersecting lines, into smaller squares and spaces, and figures up to thirty-six in number. On the centre of the table is the *roulette*, or wheel; and around it a throng of players and spectators, among both of whom there is always a goodly number of females. The persons who conduct the play on the part of the proprietors are called *croupiers*, and are seated at both sides of the table, like marble figures, except the slight movement of their pliant wrists, as they rake in the specie from all parts of the green field by means of little wooden hoes with long, slender handles. They abide the issue of every play with stolid indifference, being well aware that the odds are constantly in their favor, whilst their poor deluded victims shell out "the rhino" with facial jerks and grimaces, as though a tooth was sacrificed with every wrench of the *croupier's* wrist. Sometimes, however, a freak of chance appears to shower a golden harvest over one of the outside players; but even then they are generally so intoxicated with their good fortune that they persist in the play until the ill-gotten gains have again been swept from them. It is interesting to watch the physiognomies of those engaged at play. Some of them are old veterans at the fascinating deviltry, and stake large amounts when they can do it; but when straitened down to small change, this must be risked, too, as bait for the great bulk that went ahead. Sometimes the last dollar brings back thousands; and then dozens of new players will be drawn into the vortex by such fortunate examples.

More frequently the last dollar goes after the rest; and then watches and jewelry are sold, and disappear after the last dollar; money is borrowed on the security of estates, and these go after the jewelry; clothes are sold from their backs, and fade away after the estates; then comes borrowing on personal honor, begging and stealing — and the terrible finale is of frequent occurrence — that the desperate victim rushes from this hell of excitement and blows out his brain with a pretty little silver-mounted pistol that he borrows for the occasion. But it is wonderful how some persons hold out for years and years — persons who are not reputed to be rich, yet are apparently losing as constantly as they are playing. In such cases it is supposed the devil has a hand in the matter, and you feel like giving them a wide berth in the street. Worst of all of this description, are some old women that are to be met with at these tables every day. An old countess, eighty years of age if she was an hour, was at her place constantly from the opening of the play to the last minute. She was a deliberate, silent, sinister-looking, wrinkled beldame, and I am sure she could not jump over a broom, for other reasons than old age. Many of the participators in this feast of madness, on the other hand, are young adventurers, who may be safely said to indulge in this sort of thing but once in their lifetime, when it either " makes or breaks " them — and these have but a limited control over their expressions. As illustrations of the different characters, I saw an antiquated dame, embellished most unbecomingly with ribbons and flowers, dismiss her twenty-franc pieces one after the other, her fingers all the while twitching, and her feet beating a tattoo on the floor, as if she was operating on a sewing-machine, and every stitch she made was a trifle out of pocket. A young fellow with unexceptionable moustache, and encased in exquisite gârments, deposited a roll of a thousand francs upon one of the figures of the table, and a minute after he raked in thirty-six thousand, exchanged them for bills, which he stuck in his pocket, then turned on his heels and walked off. Another man lost, in the course of two hours, seventy-four thousand francs, then retired, lit a cigar, and rambled along the woods with a countenance as serene and unconcerned as that of a sleeping infant. The Prince of Wales — who is also the prince of good fellows — has been sojourning here some weeks;

and he visits the Roulette daily, squanders, for the fashion of it, a couple of thousand francs with good-natured indifference, "just"—as he says—"to help the thing along."

A young girl had won, in rapid succession, to the amount of twenty thousand, and was all smiling and joyous with her success, not able in the least to suppress her triumphant feelings; but she continued playing, and her "fickle fortune" taking a turn, she lost not only everything she had won, but laid down her last napoleon as if she was parting for ever from her lover, with tears in her eyes and distraction depicted in every lineament of her face.

It is remarkable that the passion for gaming appears stronger in women than in men, which is probably owing to the circumstance that they procure money through their operations on the opposite sex, and are strangers to the cares and anxieties with which it is generally acquired by these. Though between their lovers and this expensive taste for gaming, the women who resort here have an exciting time of it. Many of them are of the grisettes of Paris, and of the *demi-monde* of other large cities, and have journeyed hither under the guardian wings of paramours, who too frequently are truant to relations of a stronger tie, in order to enjoy a short season of stolen and unlawful pleasure.

The excesses of luxury and extravagance that are indulged in by these fair beings, whose name is frailty, are quite astounding to people of circumscribed ideas on such matters. I have seen them defying their ill fortune at Rouge-et-Noir with arch raillery; holding their pretty little kid-encased hands over their shoulders for fresh supplies, to the swains behind their chairs, who are "backers" in the true sense — the lovely face, half turned around and upward — that twinkle of the eyes — that playful smile about the lips, with "*J'ai toujours de malheur, mon cher; mais maintenant je vais finir d'un grand coup.*" It is enough: the swain passes with a bland, excruciating smile, the monetary exactions of love into the pretty trap, and away it goes, to be followed by another and another similar drainage in precisely the same manner. All the while the dulcet cadence of the tinkling gold goes on, and men and women are tortured with hopes and fears, as it shuffles and shifts into or for ever out of their possession.

In conclusion, if any person expects to behold me returning to mine home arrayed in white cashmere vest, with heavy chain and ponderous seals, a flashing gem upon my bosom, and tilting hat upon my head, let me kindly suggest to him to be prepared for disappointment.

LETTER XIII.

HEIDELBERG.—FOURTH OF JULY.

HEIDELBERG.—FOURTH OF JULY.—THE AMERICAN FLAG. MANHEIM AND ITS SURROUNDINGS.—VISIT TO WORMS.—DRIVE TO BENSHEIM.—RELIGIOUS MEETING IN THE WOODS.

COLOGNE, *July*, 1867.

IT was the Fourth of July, and I was at Heidelberg. No flags nor festal trimmings; no gala-day attires; no stalls with spruce beer and ginger-cakes and candies; no music, wherein the drum and fife do double duty; no processions of gayly uniformed volunteers, or handsome firemen, whose shirts rival the lily and the rose, and whose shining belts are only excelled by the dazzling splendor of the polished and be-wreathed and be-ribboned "apparatus;" no firecrackers or double-headed dutchmen — not to be too certain of the latter — by day; no pin-wheels, and rockets, and Roman candles by night; no hurrahs; no loud and boisterous hilarity; no grandiloquent orations on the "great and glorious" occasion; but a quiet, warm, and ordinary summer day, just as any other working-day in the month of July might be. I arose betimes, and ascending the mountain against which Heidelberg appears to lean to keep itself straight, I felt like greeting the rising sun with a shout like a Choctaw war-whoop. I would have given worlds — had worlds been mine to give away —

for a few salvos of the eloquent cannon without whose welcoming voice it almost seemed impossible for the sun to rise on Independence Day.

Meanwhile, having arrived at the famous castle, I wandered about among its ivy-clad ruins, wrapt in wonder and amazement, that those colossal walls, of twenty feet in thickness should have fared so badly during war-times as they have. It is the grandest remnant of a feudal stronghold throughout all Germany, and affords a theme for sober reflection in the contrast which it presents, as a monument of the instability of art, with the perpetual rejuvenescence of Nature, as shown by the old ivy that has garlanded these walls for hundreds of years. But the subject has two sides, like every other proposition, and this old castle encloses an awful evidence of the fallibility of nature — at least of human nature — in the shape of a huge cask or tun, capable of holding fifty thousand gallons, that has thrice been filled with wine, and as many times exhausted, to slake the perennial thirst of this same human nature. Walking along the terrace situated to the right of the ruin, I arrived at a point from whence I recognized at a glance the subject of a painting in the possession of a friend at home, and which I unhesitatingly aver to be one of the most faithful reproductions of a grand and beautiful scene that I ever beheld. If the painting were mine, now that I have seen the original of its subject, and the sharp tooth of necessity was making itself felt, I might be tempted to hunger and thirst a trifle rather than part with so precious a piece of art.

After dreamily wandering about a long while in

the beautiful grove that constitutes the Stückgarten, at the rear of the castle, and forms, among other uses, a botanical school of trees for the benefit of the students who attend the celebrated university of Heidelberg; and after having visited also the Molkenkur further up, on the brow of the mountain, and the Kaiserstuhl on its top, which presents a lovely and far-reaching prospect, embracing the spires of Strasburg and Worms, the beautiful valleys of the Neckar and the Rhine, the sombre outlines of the Black Forest and the Odenwald, I descended again into the town; and while walking along the street that runs parallel with and near the promenade called the Anlage, my attention was attracted by a beautiful American flag floating luxuriantly in the breeze from an extended staff on the balcony of what was, apparently, a private residence. A young gentleman was leaning over the railing of the balcony; and addressing him in English, I said, in a random way, not knowing but that it might be the residence of our Consul, "What does that flag represent?" To which he instantly replied, in the good Yankee vernacular, "It represents *me;* I'm an American, and to-day is the Fourth of July." "Hurrah!" said my American friend, who of course was along with me; "wait a bit, young man; I will be with you in a jiffy." Saying which, we joined the personage addressed, who is from Wilkesbarre, Pa., and who greeted us with great cordiality, appearing as highly delighted as ourselves at an opportunity for passing the remainder of the day not in utter exclusiveness. We soon began to "celebrate;" and although our party was small, it was none the less patriotic, and none the less thorough in the little details of the celebration. My American friend especially was very happy; and on adjourning, in the afternoon, to the Prince Carl Hotel, distinguished for the talented manner in which its worthy host caters to the gustatory wants of the most fastidiously epicurean guests, the sun had not yet finished its declining course, when he propounded the voluntary assertion, that "Longfellow is the gr-gr-greatest po-po-poet that ever lived; because he was— hic—aware of the—hic—remarkable fact that—hic!

> "At Bacherach on the Rhine,
> At Hochheim on the Main,
> At Würzburg on the Stein,
> Grow the three best kinds of wine.'"

Aside from the castle, and the peculiar phase of life exhibited by its belligerent students, there is but little to be said of Heidelberg. It is prettily situated, has a few handsome churches and public buildings, a university frequented by some eight hundred students; but has nothing else to distinguish it from the generality of towns.

A half hour's ride on the railroad brought me to Manheim, situated at the head of navigation on the river Rhine. This city is laid out in a hundred squares, with the precision of a chess-board, and is in that respect the handsomest town that I have visited. It has a fine theatre; the same in which Schiller himself directed the performance of some of his best dramas, as the "Robbers," and "Fiesco." On the square fronting the theatre are situated three excellent monumental statues in bronze, the centre one representing Schiller, and those on the sides two eminent delineators of his plays on the stage. Manheim is quite a commercial town, and among other things with which I have seen the boats at the wharf loaded, was coal, or rather coal-dirt, brought from the Ruhr district of Prussia. I inquired, of an official, what this stuff sold at, and what it was used for. He mentioned a fabulous price, and said it was burned in stoves for heating purposes. I told him where, probably, great quantities of such material might be had for nothing; whereupon his face brightened with prospective happiness, as though he had a great notion to go and get some. If he should ever call on the proprietors of the great coal-banks at St. Clair, I hope those gentlemen will give him all the black dust that he yearns for, and not stickle with him about the price.

There is abundance of fruit in this country; and of the different species, the cherry especially is very large and succulent. I have seen plenty of them nearly the size of walnuts. It is a pleasure to walk through the market square of any of these German cities in the morning, and see the numerous baskets loaded with cherries, gooseberries, whortleberries, raspberries, apricots, pears, &c., and sold by women from the different parts of the country, attired in all manner and fashion of costumes.

The animated scenes of bustle, and indiscriminate chatter between the throngs of buyers and sellers, are truly amusing, and afford an excellent repast for the philosophical student of human nature. Not content, however, with this kind of repast, I approached, one day, near noon-time, a fair vendress of gooseberries, for which I feel an innate gustatory infirmity, (I mean for the berries, not the vendress,) and these having an appearance exceedingly big and luscious, I requested the fair peasant-girl to mete me out an equivalent quantity for six kreuzers; but when I found that my demand involved the possession of a half-peck basket, my acquisitiveness was reduced to two kreuzer's worth — two kreuzers constitute about a penny and a half of our money — and the result was such a quantity, that I luxuriated in gooseberries till I was incapacitated from participating of any other food until supper. I mention this little matter, because it stands prominent in my mind as the cheapest dinner I ever ate in my life.

Let me not be understood to imply that this "swinging around the circle" in Europe is unattended by expense. Ah! no. The pocket that in the morning was musical with the jingle of guilders and kreuzers, will show a lack of *principal* and be devoid of *interest* in the evening, with no two metallic surfaces to rub against each other a doleful dirge to the departed ducats. Landlords and clerks, servants and porters; little ragged boys, and little ditto girls, who, as Byron says, "offer flowers for nothing, but expect presents of shiny bits of silver in return;" railroad officials; baggage smashers and guides, all act upon your "pecuniary resources" like a screen with gaping interstices, and in constant agitation. You arrive at a hotel, register your name, and signify that you hail from U. S. A.; in an instant everybody in town knows it, and — prepares to fleece you.

I have recently been, methinks a little prematurely, the *prey* of Worms, to say nothing about the *diet*. That is, to couch the subject in a ditty, and give it in explicit terms, I've paid my footing through the city which people designate as Worms. Yet, truth to say, I shall take with me from this venerable town some of the pleasantest reminiscences that have thus far followed up my European trail. For here I enjoyed the privilege, the first time since I quitted the shores of America, of entering the domestic circle of a private family, even as one of its own members; of sitting down by the frugal meal prepared by the skilful hands of a busy, bustling, happy little housewife, with the smiling faces of pretty children around me, beaming as so many blessings upon the occasion. It was an "oasis in a desert" of hotels — a gurgling spring of refreshing water in a monotonous wilderness (if the figure is allowed) of dry bread.

And then the old cathedral. How grand and awe-inspiring it presents itself before the view! How close and massive it appeared before my chamber-window of the Alten Kaiser Hotel! It seemed to fill up all out-doors, and created space appeared to shrink up close around this structure, like the mantle of night upon a Parian statue. Its half dozen towers, whose walls are eight feet thick, have been a citadel in times of war, and the church a refuge for the people when the surrounding city was burned to ashes. Ancient, and grand, and venerable it looks, with the grass growing in many places out of the crevices between the stones. Its tolling bells convey their solemn notes far up and down the Rhine, mingling with the distant peals from other churches bordering on the Odenwald, in the lovely villages of Eppenheim, Lambertheim, and Bensheim; reverberating from the castles of Starkenburg and Auerbach; passing, still, in faint melody over the head of the Melibochus. I wandered along the streets whence Luther came when he entered Worms, to appear before the Diet of April, 1521, in order to defend his doctrine in the presence of Charles V., six electors, and a numerous assembly of ecclesiastical judges. At Pfiffigheim the wonderful and monstrously large tree, about eight feet in diameter, which is known by the name of Luther's tree, presented itself to my admiring gaze. Tradition says, that here the great Protestant founder was preaching to a multitude of people one day, and during his discourse he thrust a stick into the earth, saying: "As surely as this stick will grow and become a tree, so surely are these things true that I say unto you." The present tree of such immense proportions is said to be the result. Tradition is a little at fault, however, in not conveying the explicit knowledge whether the stick had a root to it, or whether it was a real, whittled, polished, and varnished walking-cane.

An object of interest to the antiquarian at Worms, is the synagogue, which is said to date its existence as far back as 588 B. C., to the time of the first destruction of Jerusalem by the Babylonians. The Jewish community, worshipping here, is said to be one of the oldest in Germany. Attached to the most ancient portion of the building is the chapel of Raschi, who was the first and most learned expounder of the Thora, and taught in this chapel in the ninth century.

At one time the population of Worms was over sixty thousand. Now it is but eleven thousand; but the city is richer at present than it was then. There is great business activity in it, and its commercial products consist of wine, grain, tobacco, and leather. Opulent patent-leather manufacturers reside here in stately palaces; and one, who is said to be the possessor of several million florins, has one of the finest botanical gardens I have ever seen. His hot-houses contain a variety of rare palms and many tropical plants. Attached to his garden is a pleasure-room, dedicated to reading, smoking, card-playing, and the dear knows what. Then there is a billiard as well as a bowling-room, got up in gorgeous style. The garden is bordered on one side by the highest portion of the town wall still remaining; the top of which serves as a promenade, and affords a good view of the surrounding landscape. The city is entirely encircled by an avenue of linden and poplar trees, which during the blossoming season convey a delicious fragrance to the neighboring atmosphere. Here, too, the sweet songsters of the air, the lovely nightingales, still pour forth their enchanting music, that touches the heart as with a wand of love and kindness, as the mellow warblings come gushing through one's open windows at the break of day.

> "Schmelzend flöted Philomele
> Tief im dunkeln Pappelhain;
> Liebe haucht aus ihrer Seele,
> Klage kann ihr Lied nicht sein."

> "Think every morning when the sun peeps through
> The dim leaf-latticed windows of the grove,
> How jubilant the happy birds renew
> Their old, melodious madrigals of love!
> And when you think of this, remember, too,
> 'Tis always morning somewhere, and above
> The awakening continents from shore to shore,
> Somewhere the birds are singing evermore."

With several members of the family before alluded to, with whom I resided during my week's stay at Worms, I took a drive to Bensheim, across the Rhine, about ten miles distant. It was at sunrise of a beautiful Sabbath morning that we drove over the bridge of boats which here spans the proud river of many legends. Our conveyance was an elegant barouche, drawn by a proud span of Norman bays, and the equipage was altogether one of the finest I had seen in Europe, outside of Paris. The excursion of that day will always remain prominent as one of the most delightful reminiscences of this period of my life.

Our journey extended over a vast plain of fields in the highest state of cultivation. One crop of hay had been harvested, and a second was near at hand, from as rich, tall, and blooming grass as could be wished for. The grain was almost ready for the sickle, and the ripening fruit on the trees bordering the roadsides, glittered under the first streaks of the rising sun, like pretty toys and sugar-plums on illuminated Christmas-trees. How balmy and sweet-scented was the atmosphere from all this thrifty vegetation! Here and there we crossed a little stream of water, hedged in on both sides, and wending its tortuous course through the little valleys of the wavy plain for miles without getting out of the range of sight. Toward the end of our journey, and when the warmth of a midsummer day was already beginning to manifest itself, our road suddenly brought us through a forest for the space of nearly a mile. The trees were tall veterans, that had withstood unharmed the storms and blasts of many years; their far-reaching branches, compactly clothed in deep-dyed foliage, sheltered us so effectually from the sun, that it was almost chilly to anybody not warmed up with enthusiasm at the beautiful surroundings.

My American friend burst out with the exclamation: "What a splendid place this would be for a Camp-meeting!" And then, as if his words had wrought an act of enchantment, we suddenly arrived upon a collection of good and pious people, who were actually having a bush-meeting for the good of their souls, and possibly a little for the enjoyment of their senses. There were no seats or tents or pulpit or any other evidence of even a temporary habitation; but the meeting was on its feet, in a migratory condition, ready at a moment's notice to transpose itself to any other spot at the first warning shake of the finger of authority. It looked very much as if it wanted to be persecuted, like the ancestral flocks in the early days of Christianity; but there was no evidence of its being gratified in this respect. The worship consisted principally of solemn singing of the old orthodox Lutheran hymns, interspersed with short, sententious prayers, and occasional words of exhortation from the most anointed among their number. On our way back in the evening, as we were passing this place again, and found that the meeting had dispersed, my American friend surprised us all with the exclamation: "Have any of you ever taken

A DRIVE TO A CAMP-MEETING?"

"Have you ever, my friend," (addressing himself especially to me,) " assisted, not in the French, but in any sense, at a genuine, old-fashioned, Pennsylvania camp-meeting? Not one of those monster assemblages of devout Christians who congregate by thousands under hundreds of canvas tents and slab-board edifices, in the far-off wilds of the uncivilized West; but a nice, cosy, comfortable gathering of some thirty or forty muslin tabernacles of the righteous, all in a ring or quadrangle, the pulpit — that holiest of the holy — included, it being the only ligneous structure of the entire circle; and whereon, seated upon an imperishable, unyielding bench, are always to be seen, when not at breakfast, dinner, or supper, (and *such* breakfasts, dinners, and suppers!) the never-deviating number of ten — that's the figure; I never found it otherwise in my life — ten Teutonic-looking, brown-haired, no-whiskered, strong-featured, shad-belly coated ministers of the Gospel. Such a camp-meeting as you can only find — and it's a great comfort that you *can* find them, even at this day — during the month of August, when people who don't know better go to Newport, Cape May, Saratoga, Niagara, and all the other equally stupid places, such as you can find, I repeat, scattered all over the sylvan groves of the good, old, fertile Keystone State, where people live in that happy condition that always follows the consciousness of serving God "with all their might."

"And then again — for a thing is not done at all if not rightly done — if you have been to such a camp-meeting, then *how* did you go, my dear fellow? tell me that! Were you sitting in a solid country buggy, with a horse in front, trotting over the turnpike of —— like the very dickens?

"And had you a beautiful young country girl, full of heart and sense, and wild as the old Scratch himself, seated upon your right knee, with the reins in her right hand, driving Billy, whilst the left encircled your neck, and the little plump hand attached to the arm caught hold miscellaneously of all prominent places in its vicinity, such as your nose, ears, or whiskers? And did her rosy little mouth every now and then come in collision with your own, and the two 'jintly' produce a concussion like the report of a little pocket-pistol, perhaps accidentally, perhaps to make the horse run faster, but more, perhaps, the natural ebullition of your wild hearts that were boiling over with too much of something — I don't know what? Say, were you ever at such a camp-meeting, my boy; and did you go in such a way? No? Bless my soul! But hold! What a thing it is to arrive at last — horse, buggy, sweetheart, and all — at the woods! You heard the shouting and hallelujahs two miles distant already — quite different from the solemn affair we just passed, I assure you. You drive in, among and between the trees. The branches brush the flies from the horse's back, and he neighs in gratitude as he approaches the hallowed precinct.

They brush — the branches, not the flies — along the rosy cheeks of your sweetheart, who screams; but laughs out loudly directly, to find herself not hurt, and her cheeks more rosy than ever.

"They brush your hat off, and get entangled with your hair, till you're in danger of the fate of Absalom; but your horse is no Bucephalus, and has a generous instinct worthy of his genus. He stops; you disengage your hair from the pesky branches, squeeze your hat over your head down to the eyebrows, and renew your course between the trees and through the woods more cautiously than before. The foliage sweeps the dust from your buggy. The dry twigs and leaves rustle and snap, and fly off in all directions from under its wheels, startling a timid squirrel who runs up the tallest tree, and still looks doubtfully down upon you, as if he expected to see you come driving up the tree — horse, buggy, sweetheart, and all; — startling, also, a woodpecker, who stops hammering for worms, hides behind a cluster of leaves, and eyes you not less suspiciously than the squirrel, till you have passed. And then, at last, those temporary habitations of unbleached muslin are seen like patches of sky glimmering through the woods — now lost to sight again — and now again you are full in front of them. You alight and unbridle the animal; tie him to a tree, and take a silent and revengeful satisfaction on observing his ferocious attack upon all the young *birch* twigs within his reach. You take Rose — her name may be Lily, or anything else, for that matter — around the waist, and she bounds from the vehicle like a thing of air.

You link her arm in yours, and march her through the narrow entrance into the consecrated sphere, down the aisle between the rudely constructed benches, and find yourselves seated among the saints or gentiles, as the case may be, listening to the sermon. Listening? Likely you are; but vastly more likely you are eating candies, and exchanging love-mottoes with Rose. After the sermon, you wait half an hour to see the rush of sinners that want to be converted, and listen to their clamorous prayers, wofully commingled with the equally clamorous rejoicing, 'shouting,' and clapping of hands of the sinners who *are* converted. And then you leave Rose with a friend of hers, and go off with Charley, a friend of yours, to stroll about the woods a while. But wherefore stroll about the woods, eh? Oho! you want me to keep mum! Well, I am good-natured, and to oblige you, I will;—only I hope that that isn't you, nor that companion of yours, Charley, who are rushing out of the adjoining cornfield, each with one of Klinger's watermelons under the arm, toward your buggy.

"It is night, and I cannot distinguish the features in the darkness—they may belong to others; at least, I hope so; for I have no hesitation in saying that it's very wrong to go to camp-meeting for the purpose of stealing watermelons. Mercy me! it *is* you, after all; for there I see you coming from the benches with Rose hanging to your arm, whilst you are chuckling all the while and telling her what a capture you have made, and what a treat you have in store for her. You seat her in your buggy; pull a great big jack-knife out of your pocket, cut her a nice, large slice of the juicy fruit, and are just cutting another for yourself, when suddenly she bursts out laughing — oh, how wickedly! — slaps you on the cheek and cries out: 'My goodness gracious me! how could you be so stupid? Why *it's a pumpkin!*' and laughs like mad again, whilst you hang your head and felt never so sheepish in all your life. Verily, sin is often attended by its own punishment. But you have some comfort in the reflection that Charley feels sheepish too; so you and Charley make the best of a bad bargain, and laugh at yourselves more boisterously than the girls, if not more heartily, whilst you get ready to start for home.

"Leading the horses, you glide carefully, like conscience-stricken (as you are) spectres, through the woods; for it is near midnight now, and the pale moon, not more than two hours in the ascendant, casts a long shadow of your "establishment" to your right, which sneaks along in noiseless stealth, contrasting greatly with the sound caused by the *real* horse and buggy, made doubly loud and awful in the solemn stillness of the night.

"You reach the open road at last; and away you drive, past woods and fields and solitary habitations; startling the fowls perched upon the trees and roosting on the fences of farm-yards, as you whirl along. Away you drive, rumbling over bridges that span small creeks and runs, startling the little sun-fish and other small fry that have taken their night quarters upon the pebble-stoned bottom underneath. Your friend Charley and his sweetheart are before you. His friend Aleck and his sweetheart are behind you. And all three of you, with your three sweethearts, are singing something lively in camp-meeting style, making the night-air resound again as you pass along. Away you drive, like a treble elopement, with the three brides' three fathers, the sheriff and a whole army of constables after you; but you care not for the pursuit, singing and shouting and laughing as you fly along. Away you drive; not heeding the delicious fragrance that the gentle night zephyrs waft over you from yon orchard pregnant with mellow fruit, startling again the little birds in their nests among the apples, peaches, and plums, and making the plaintive air of the whippoorwill hovering overhead more plaintive still. Away and away you drive; rattling over the broken stones of the new-made road at the entrance of the little village where you live. Aleck has left you to drive down a little street that contains six houses, a cider-press, and a little shoemaker shop. Charley is just turning down another little street that has lots enough to build twenty houses on. And you are trundling on a hundred yards further, if not more, to that beautiful two-story white house, which is Rose's home. You alight from the buggy; help Rose to do the same; give her a good-night kiss at parting under the door, and off you go, another hundred yards, to your own home. There arrived, you unhitch your good, faithful, darling Billy; you almost feel like taking him around the neck to hug him for affording you so much happiness with Rose; then lead him to his bed of straw; and retire to your chamber — not to sleep, but to dream of Rose, and camp-meeting, and pumpkins all jumbled up together."

As my American friend thus wound up this lengthy and rhapsodical apostrophe, which had evidently carried him away to other days, we observed that our German friends were sound asleep. They did not understand a word of what had been so enthusiastically declaimed; and this rattle of English words had acted like a gentle lullaby to their drowsy senses.

Crossing the bridge homeward over the Rhine, the noisy tramp of the horses, with the gentle soughing of the night-wind and the splashing of the water against the boats, was sufficient to waken them; and rubbing his eyes after a little yawn, my cousin from Worms said: "*Mein Gott! das war aber interessant!*"

LETTER XIV.

MAYENCE — FORTIFICATIONS.

MAYENCE—ITS FORTIFICATIONS.—FRANKFURT—NOTABLE HOUSES.—IMPERIAL HALL—WIESBADEN.-A MARVELLOUS SPRING.—THE CURSAAL.—VISIT TO THE CASTLE OF JOHANNISBERG.—DOWN THE RHINE.—SCENERY, CASTLES ETC.—COLOGNE.—CATHEDRAL—INTERESTING FEATURES OF THE CITY.—CASSEL.—UNIVERSITY OF GŒTTINGEN—ARRIVAL AT NORDHEIM.

NORDHEIM, HANOVER, *July*, 1867.

IN travelling through Europe it is melancholy to observe what a vast amount of time, talent, labor, and money are expended upon the great purpose of warfare among men. Soldiers in gaudy uniforms circulate with swaggering strides, making the day picturesque, and the night loud with songs of revelry. Millions of rifles that were constructed for the fell purpose of taking human life, have been suddenly discovered to be inefficient, condemned untried, and reappear in the arsenals of nations as more worthy weapons in the form of needle-guns. Men's ingenuity, art, and science are all ingloriously prostituted in the construction of deadly missiles. There seems to be a jealous rivalry between doctors devising new ways and means to save life, on the one hand, and artisans that rack their inventive talents for more cunning measures to destroy it, on the other. Instead of erecting more asylums, school-houses, and universities, men barricade themselves from their fellow-men by great bastions and fortifications;—and of this kind of perverted labor the city of Mayence on the Rhine may be cited as an illustrious example.

This town is surrounded with walls and trenches and citadels to a degree that, if its houses were built of mother-of-pearl, with diamond windows; and its streets paved with bricks of gold, running over with milk and honey, it could not well be better protected than it is from the rapacious covetousness of an invidious foe. Instead of this it is simply, a very respectable old town, that might be a great deal larger, and airier, and better off, but for the ugly stone belt that cramps it up in such narrow limits, and acts as a stricture on its vitality.—Yet, not content with its present capacity for resistance, Prussia — since her abandonment of Luxemburg — is making this place stronger, if possible, and more impregnable than ever. Whatever be the strategic advantages of this encasement of a people, in this era of great guns and destructive columbiads, may be known to wiser heads, but is extremely problematical to the subscriber.

About the principal things of interest to be seen at Mayence are some old impressions by the inventors of the art of printing, Guttenberg and his associates, dating from the year 1459 to 1462. What a great discovery that was! And yet, what would Guttenberg say, could he visit this sublunary sphere, and see some of the great cylindrical presses of the present time, and watch the act of enchantment that creates the literature of our day. These old relics of printing, isolated from the world by the grim walls, bristling with cannonry, that surround them — what a paradox they present! My American friend says, "The one is the type of barbarism, and the other the barbarism of type."

An hour's ride on the railroad brought me to Frankfurt, which has every appearance of an opulent and prosperous city, containing many houses built on the style of the palatial residences of New York and Philadelphia.

The quaint old house wherein Gœthe was born, is situated here in one of the narrower streets called the Hirschgraben, and is kept in its primitive state by the city. The room in which the great German poet was accustomed to write is still preserved — so they say — as it was in his own time, containing the same furniture that it did then. As a curious contrast to this, one may visit the original house of the Rothschild family, in the Judengasse, and were the maternal parent insisted upon residing to the time of her death; though her sons where almost wielding the financial destinies of nations. The house has a very ordinary appearance, and is on the narrow, repulsive-looking street from which the Jews, in former times, were not permitted to issue after sunset, or on Sundays and holidays. They have outlived this tyrannical oppression, however, and are now the occupants of some of the handsomest villas of the suburbs.

The place of the greatest historical interest, in Frankfurt, is the Imperial Hall in the Rœmer; where the princes of Germany were wont to dine with their newly elected Emperor. The walls are embellished with life-sized portraits of these Emperors, successively, from Charlemagne the first, to Francis the second, the last Roman Emperor of the German nation. One of the finest ornaments of the city is the magnificent marble stair-case that leads from the labyrinthine basement of the old building to this grand Hall of the Emperors. Another is a galvano-plastic monumental group, representing Guttenberg, Faust, and Schöffer, which is situated in a conspicuously open place in the city. There are also two superb statues of Gœthe and Schiller. The principal business-street, the Zeil, has quite an American aspect; and the suburban promenades are exceedingly fine.

The citizens of Frankfurt are rather dejected under the new Prussian regime, and give up their cherished idea of a free city with quite a touching reluctance. Besides which, the heavy ransom-tax which the wary Bismarck laid on these good people has greatly increased the longitude of their faces, and, in fact, changed the latitude of the entire place. At least, so it would seem from a remark which I caught from the lips of a charming young lady, who being told that the weather appeared to be very cool and dismal in her beautiful Frankfurt, replied : "Ah, sir, our climate has been dreadfully chilled since we belong to the *Northern* Confederation."

From hence I proceeded to the charming watering-place, Wiesbaden; though *watering*-place is a name probably less pertinent than *gambling*-place would be; for it is equal in this respect to Baden-Baden. Among others who here placed their fortunes on the hazard of a wheel, was a young South Carolinian, who had crossed the ocean on the same steamer with myself.

I believe the young scape-grace lost seriously, for he had an air of extreme financial dilapidation.

There is a spring here marvellous for the high temperature of its water, gushing in a thick current from the earth, at 158° Fahrenheit. It is rather palatable to drink, and has a taste not altogether unlike that of thin, highly salted beef-tea. Great confidence is placed in its restorative virtues, for invalids affected with rheumatism or dyspepsia, and as an element for bathing it is, probably, inferior to none other for its tonic effect upon the general system. There are bathing-establishments in almost all the principal hotels, to which the water from the hot spring is conducted through pipes. To these the decrepit in limb may be seen carried by the score on litters and hand-carriages every day during the proper season.

The Cursaal is the principal place of resort, and that, too, where the gaming goes on. It is fitted up in the most gorgeous style, and surrounded with promenades, fountains, arbors, and walks, that constitute in all a very pleasant retreat. If any of my readers should ever visit Wiesbaden, I would recommend them to procure their meals at any place in the pretty town (and they will be bountifully and satisfactorily served) but *not* in the restaurant which is connected with the Cursaal, unless they derive peculiar enjoyment from being most shamefully and outrageously swindled.

A truly beautiful work of art is the Greek Chapel on the Neroberg, which was erected by the Duke of Nassau as a mausoleum to his first wife, a Russian princess. The interior is entirely of marble, and in a pentagonal recess is a magnificent monument to the Duchess. The recumbent effigy is of the purest white marble, and rests on a sarcophagus, at the side of which are statuettes of the twelve apostles. Divine service of the Greek form is held here every Sunday, but the public is not admitted.

Not being very far from the castle of Johannisberg, and having often wondered why the wine of that estate is so greatly lionized, and stands conspicuous with such a wonderful difference of price over all the other wines named on the lists of the hotels, I was curious enough to visit that place, explore its subterranean mysteries, and sip the daintiest morsel from a goblet of the genuine Nectar. Now, although it is commonly supposed that the great Prince Metternich, who is the lawful owner of this new Parnassus, is so churlish and ungracious as to withhold his luscious liquids from all but a few, select, patrician throats, whose hydrometric talent he esteems; and interdicts all plebeian footsteps from this sacred soil, let me gently whisper into the public ear, that by means of that all-potent agent which in our good Republic we recognize as Dollars and Cents, backed up with German eloquence, such as my American friend has always at command, it is quite possible to "reconstruct" the good old butler who guards these precious vaults — yea, they will open almost as readily as the cave of the Forty Thieves to a blithe word — and a silver key. Seated upon a keg, with a small libation to Bacchus in close proximity, I soon discovered that the atmosphere of that cavernous abode was about as strong and spirituous as the meat in a mince-pie. My American friend, by whose opinion I am always guided in such matters, snuffed in the air, sipped at the goblet, smacked his lips, closed his left eye, and looked learnedly with the right at the spider-webs on the ceiling, then delivered himself of the following Jack Bunsbyan opinion: "Either I don't know the difference between one kind of sour grape-juice and another, or else the dear good-natured public is most egregiously humbugged, and I strongly suspect the latter." Satisfied on this point, we returned to Mayence, and thence took passage on a boat down the Rhine for Cologne.

At Bingen I tried very hard to see what there was " sweet" about it, in the poetic sense; but the effort was fruitless; and the only interesting thing that I could discover was the Mouse Tower, with its wonderful legend of Bishop Hatto all exploded by some soulless, unromantic writer of recent date, and the rock of Ehrenfels. Further down is the really beautiful castle of Rhinestein, which is a striking ornament in this naturally picturesque region. The castle contains a richly decorated Knights' Hall, in the style of the middle ages, and all the apartments with their contents are in perfect keeping with the predominant idea. Then follow a succession of castles, ruins, churches, and small villages, to Bacherach, the curious Pfalz, and Obernesel, whose old wall, relieved from monotonous uniformity by battlements, gates, and turrets, presents a fine scenic effect. According to ancient tradition, there resided "once upon a time" at Schönberg (an extensive castle situated here) seven beautiful young ladies, whose charms had excited many a bloody fray among their noble suitors; and to punish them for their cruelty and coquetry, the haughty maidens were cast into the Rhine by a stern fairy, and transformed into seven rocks. There is no manner of doubt about this story, for I saw the rocks myself. — Moral: Young ladies, don't be charming; secondly, don't flirt; lastly, if you *are* charming, and *can't help* flirting, don't go near the water, and keep away from the inexorable fairies.

In the descent down this wonderful river follows hence the Lurelei, an immense and projecting ledge of rocks, that look as though they meant to hurl themselves into the stream some dark night and dam it up. At this place there is an echo that repeats itself some sixteen times. In passing, the officer of the boat ordered a gun to be fired, which is a customary performance, I believe, with every boat that passes, for the benefit of tourists. Directly the shot was fired, it was answered by the echoes, like the successive musket-firing along a long picket-line, the last shot being faintly heard in the far-off distance behind the bend of the river.

Next we came to St. Goar. This is a small town in which, the guide-book tells us, it was at one time the custom, whenever a traveller came by that way, to seize upon him, and thrust his head into an instrument of torture, a species of collar, of which the interior was decorated with raised work, consisting of carpet-tacks or something of that sort. In this felicitous condition he was kept till he paid a fine, which they levied according to the presumed capacities of his purse. If there were any on board of our boat who had any misgivings about the comfort of their necks being interfered with in passing this awful place, they did not say so, and it is, therefore, not in the power of the writer to record the circumstance.

We soon arrived at the ruins of the two castles, Sternberg and Liebenstein, where two brothers lived at one time, (it is said by the authority above quoted,) and were constantly at loggerheads with each other, through the wily machinations of a beautiful Greek girl, who, it seems, played the deuce with both their hearts. History only records that both parties died in due course of time — a very common event — and the point of the story is, it must be confessed, a little in the clouds.

Königstuhl, the beautiful castle of Stolzenfels, the majestic Ehrenbreitstein, and the city of Coblentz are successively passed; and then, after more towns and castles and ruins, the old Drachenfels, the grandest ruin of them all, makes its appearance. Grim and jagged, like a weather-beaten sentinel of the old guard of the seven hills, it stands there, menacing and weird, defying the thunderbolts of Heaven, and frowning over the rugged surface of its parent earth.

Next comes the city of Bonn, with its beautiful environs, but otherwise of no great interest to the tourist, save for its excellent university and numerous students.

From Bonn the Rhine flows through a country monotonous and level, and we reach, in a short time, the city of Cologne; the crane on the unfinished tower of whose renowned cathedral has been visible for miles, long before anything else of Cologne could be seen ; first like a dim speck in the horizon, then like a short diagonal rent in the blue sky, and lastly like the ominous-looking crooked thing that it is and has been these three hundred years and more.

The great predominant feature, and that which casts a smallness upon everything else by comparison, is this Cathedral. To describe it with any degree of justice would require much space, and I will only say, that it is large enough to have built in its interior, in the principal nave, six ordinary-sized churches, steeples and all; that it was commenced nearly five centuries ago, but was for a long time abandoned, and appropriated in war-times to profane uses ; that if it will ever be finished, its steeple will be higher than any other in existence—some forty feet higher than that of Strasburg ; that its architecture is altogether peculiar in style, and the plan must have been an inspiration to the genius who projected it ; that I plucked a moss-rose that had grown spontaneously on the top of one of its unfinished towers, where the seeds must have been carried by the birds ; that a great number of laborers and artisans were working at this colossal job, singing in concert all the while some charming melody ; that it is not nearly finished, but such as it is it constitutes (with the exception, I am told, of the Cathedral at Milan, and which I cannot comprehend to be possible) the most beautiful fragment that was ever dedicated to Divine worship.

About a mile from the city are the geological and botanical gardens, both very superior in their way, and a great deal more complete than I had any expectation of finding such institutions here. The Museum, in the city, is a very elegant building, and contains a great number of old and modern paintings, besides a gathering of interesting antiquities, chiefest among which are some very ancient manuscripts on parchment, illustrated with quaint-looking pictures — by hand, of course. In the gallery the principal attraction consists in the old Cologne school of paintings, by Meister Wilhelm and his followers. The new synagogue is a rich affair, glittering with copious gilding, fine frescoes, carved woodwork, a splendid window with painted glass, and in the interior is a candelabrum of solid silver that weighs one hundred and eighty-six pounds. At one time Cologne had about two hundred places of public worship, and was justly called the city of churches. Since the first French revolution that number has been reduced to about twenty-five.

Not the least interesting feature of this city are the Cologne-water establishments; and there is a great rivalry between the two houses, Jean Maria Farina and Maria Clementina, though they are both of the same family. The latter is in the ascendancy just now, having recently received the best prize awarded at the Paris Exposition.

Leaving Cologne, I also parted company with the Rhine, and in doing so I must fain acknowledge that I was somewhat disappointed with my journey down that river. Perhaps I had set my expectations too high, which is an error so aptly committed. Its scenery is not as grand and picturesque as that which borders the shores for the most part of our own beautiful Hudson, and if it were not for the, to an American, almost unknown, prospect of continuous vineyards, on all manner of shaggy and precipitous slopes, and the legendary and historical interest that clusters around its many medieval castles, I would scarcely recognize any excuse for the extravagant laudations that poets and enraptured tourists have devoted to this river. I cannot even bear testimony to the "limpid clearness" that I have read of as characterizing its water; for on the five or six occasions that I have seen it since the end of May, it was always nearly, if not quite, as muddy as the Mississippi. Great credit is claimed for the boats that navigate this stream, and they are said to be constructed somewhat in imitation of our palatial river steamers, but resemble the latter about as much as a common mud-scow resembles a New York and Brooklyn ferry-boat.

Passing through Marburg and Giessen, both flourishing towns, and the seats of noted universities, I arrived at Cassel, the former capital of Kur Hessen, but at present a dependency of Prussia. The great centralization-point of all strangers here is the waterworks of the Wilhelm's Höhe. These exceed in character and extent those of Versailles, near Paris, and with the surrounding associations of scenery and the noble palace, constitute, upon the whole, a very superior affair. Like nearly all the European cities and towns, Cassel is encircled with shady retreats and enticing promenades. The old abandoned castle outside of the city, that, doubtless, had its origin some centuries ago, and is a stately wreck of by-gone magnificence, appears almost conscious of ancestral glory, and recognizes no adversity in its very straitened circumstances of to-day. Statues in brown stone of the old Roman kings and classics adorn its walls and parapets, and throw upon the otherwise naked aspect of the building a somewhat sinister and sardonic cast; and the mockery is completed by a long line of tall well-trimmed spruce-trees, planted in ground that was confined in what appeared to be medium-sized dry-goods boxes, that stand guard, as it were, around the dismantled residence, to prevent the statues from carrying it away. I felt an involuntary sympathy with these poor trees, as suffering terribly from corns; and if a pinched-up footing can ever induce such a thing in the vegetable creation, then I am sure that my diagnosis was correct. Strolling through the streets of the city, I came across a sign, outside of a barber-shop, that appeared sufficiently amusing to be worthy of mention. It denoted that within was an "Amerikanische Kopfwäscherei mit Champu,"—Anglicized: *American Headwashery with Shampoo.* I might have subjected my head to a cleansing operation, with probably some advantage, but that sign was too much. It filled me with terror, and reminded me of Midshipman Easy's father, with the machine for developing phrenological bumps.

Again on the railway - again drawn forward by the great motor, steam, I soon arrived in the lovely city of Göttingen, whose scholastic institution was associated with the dreams of my boyhood. To me Oxford and Cambridge, Yale and Harvard were second-rate affairs. The only place where one might become truly learned was at the University of Göttingen. Oh! to be a student there, with a red cap, a ribbon across my vest, and a long pipe! Duels with rapiers, a scar upon the cheek, to remain there a proud relic through the whole of life! What bliss! Oh! what blissful dreams, never to be realized!

Now I approach my native town — the dear little Northeim, from which I was carried when an infant. From under the cobwebs of time just enough of the romance of an ardent nature peers forth, to cause a little palpitation, and awake a reflective feeling of pleasure not unmixed with a shade of sadness. From afar off the only steeple of the town is visible. It belongs to the old church that has stood there more than four hundred years. To approach that sacred edifice is an impulse not to be resisted. The door yields, and in a moment the earnest man, with bowed head and deep veneration, stands at that altar where as an infant he was held over the baptismal font. Were it not better to drink of the waters of Lethe, and forget all of the interval between these two occasions? God knows! God only knows!

LETTER XV.

A TOWN IN GERMANY.

A GERMAN TOWN.— RURAL LIFE.— THE DWELLINGS.— A DIGNIFIED GAME OF NINE-PINS.— MY AMERICAN FRIEND ROLLS, AND PRODUCES A "PUMPE."— A FINE SULPHUR SPRING.— A DANCING HALL.— THE DELIRIOUS WALTZ.— LIFE AT THE BRUNNEN AND IN THE TOWN.— CLOSE OF THE DAY AT THE "HOTEL SONNE."

BERLIN, *July*, 1867.

WOULD the reader know aught of a German town not metropolitan in character, and of German life in its more rural aspect? Then let his fancy wander to that new portion of Prussian territory, where the rivers Leine and Rhume form a junction at right angles, the former running through the highly cultured valley from the direction of Göttingen, and the latter winding its course through the undulating ground from the Hartz mountains; and, though of small and placid appearance generally, yet will it swell up occasionally after fall and winter freshets, and inundate wide portions of the more level countries through which it flows. Receding back from these rivers in the angle of their confluence, on a plateau of the least elevation, and skirting the foot of the gently rising Wicter mountains, is the town whereof we write, with a steady population of about five thousand souls. The style of architecture is very unlike any generally adopted in our own country, the houses consisting principally of skeletons of heavy frame scantling and joists, the interspaces of which are walled up with bricks of an inferior character, or stones, and the surface plastered over with lime-and-sand mortar. The frame-work of the windows, doors, cornices, and wood-work generally are heavy and clumsy, and the roofs composed of ponderous guttered tiles manufactured from potter's clay. Many of the older houses are built in such a way that each succeeding story from below upward, protrudes forward from one to two feet farther into the street than the story immediately beneath, so that the upper portions of houses on opposite sides of a narrow street almost approach each other. Nor is their interior arrangement as well and practical as our own. There is a want of taste, of symmetrical division, of the proper adaptation of space, and the proportionment of halls and staircases. As yet I have seen nothing like an elegant door-knob; but in their places are uncouth levers by which the latch is raised, that resemble the handles with which our engineers open the steam-valves of a locomotive. Carpets, as a covering for halls, stairs, parlors, or chambers, are unknown, and the nearest approach to anything of the kind is occasionally a rug by the side of a bed or sofa. The stoves are horrid, monstrous, misshapen contrivances, the very looks of which are enough to chill a body to the marrow. The furniture is solid and durable, excellent in quality, and often very richly upholstered; but there is also a want of elegance and lightness in the pieces; though exceptional secretaries, bureaus, and clocks may be seen that are very ingenious mechanisms. Rosewood, walnut, or mahogany veneerings are rarely met with; but in their stead, ashwood — constituting, when polished, furniture of a bright yellow — beech, ebony, &c. The pianos in general use are of the upright, cabinet form, and considerably inferior to our American manufacture. In corroboration of this I need only say that the best prizes at the Paris Exposition were awarded to Chickering and Steinway of the United States. The above general description of dwellings is not peculiar to the town under our immediate observation; but may be taken, with exceptional instances of large and modernized cities, for all Europe.

To return to the subject: Let us commence at the Mühlengate, and outside of the old walls that only partially remain, promenade all around the town by the beautiful gardens that are intersected by hedges of box, currant, sweet-brier, or other bushy vegetation; for the citizens, instead of having gardens attached to their houses, have them thus outside of the town. We arrive at the Höckelheimer gate, pass into and traverse the place through the Breite Strasse, which is its principal street, say, "*Guten morgen-morgen*," and take off our hat to everybody we meet; then enter at "*Vetter Eduard's*," take a *happen* bread and a *betten metwurst*, then we stroll leisurely past the brewery,—it is not finished, or we would not talk so lightly about passing *it*,—we make our exit through the Obere gate, and meander along till we get to the Brunnen.

The Brunnen constitutes the capitolium of social life for miles around. The gay students from Göttingen, the young Prussian dragoons from Northeim, and the blonde peasant girls from Hamstett and Osterode all converge here in one brilliant focus. The seat for all festive occasions, *Schützenfeste*, target practice, May-day frolics, and games of all kinds among the young folks, is here at the Brunnen,—while the staid old pillars of the town congregate in semi-weekly rejuvenescence, under the shed of the old bowling-alley, that rejoices in this glorious situation, and indulge in a dignified game of nine-pins, or the ten-pins of our own country. Carefully the Herr Bürgermeister gathers up his coat-tail in his left hand, poises the bowling-ball in his right, and rolls it with swift velocity toward the pins. It strikes, and reduces five of them *hors-du-combat*, one is a "wackeler," but three stand firm like the cedars of Lebanon. The Herr Bürgermeister has one of the kindliest faces imaginable, illuminated by an eminently Grecian and the least bit florid nose; turning its beaming light upon his associates, he resumes the recital of a difficult law case, involving somebody's pig and somebody else's dog, which he adjudicated in the morning to the perfect satisfaction of all parties concerned. Up starts his prime minister the Herr Syndicus; seizes the ball as he would a feather, and hurls it at the pins as if his soul was rioting in the very sweetness of revenge. Powerless to skedaddle, the poor pins await their doom, the square is broken, and they topple over in centrifugal directions. "*Alle neune!*" resounds through the entire camp, (which is equivalent to the Irishman's cry of, "A ten-strike, be jabers!" or the Young American, "Set 'em up!")

and the Herr Syndicus, caressing his gray whiskers, proceeds toward his seat with tragic strides, like Forrest in the Gladiator, and orders himself a sandwich and a glass of wine, while his serene countenance is lit up with a quiet expression of the most perfect complacency. The Herr Inspector follows next, and in succession several Herren Senatoren, Assessor, Kaufmänner, &c., who all direct their artillery against the forlorn hope at the other end of the alley, creating havoc and confusion with every *bowl'd* attack.

Now it is the turn of my American friend. Surely, he will do credit to his great country, and startle these good people with the precision of his projectile powers. Deliberately he turns up the cuff of his right coat-sleeve, dips the points of his fingers into the basin of water, takes up the largest ball, and revolves it on the palm of his upraised hand-like the man in the circus, glances knowingly along the orbit over which the balanced globe is to make its speedy revolutions, makes a pendulum of his right arm, and then — one! two! three! lets fly the deadly missile, and produces a — "*pumpe.*" N. B. — When the ball rolls sideway off the alley, it is called a *pumpe*. When any of the above-named veterans makes one of these, it is always "*das verdammte Malheur;*" but my American friend turned the matter off with a joke, saying: "*Am Brunnen ist's ja ganz natürlich dass man Pumpen macht.*"

The Brunnen itself is a cold spring of water, whose healing qualities are extolled far and wide. There is a bathing establishment, where the Herr Stabsarzt sets the example of taking fifty sulphur baths every summer. Close by the running fountain that throws a perpendicular jet of water about twenty feet high, is the *Tanz Halle*, where the young people move in the airy circle of the delirious waltz. The cotillon is entirely ignored; but during a whole afternoon and evening these male and female corpora may be seen revolving on their axes, and around each other, and in the prescribed orbit, with astronomical precision. They revolve in an atmosphere of their own, that sweeps along like a hot simoon, bathing its whole universe in scalding vapor. Oh! but it takes the Germans to waltz! How instinctively their feet preserve the magic of the harmonious three-quarter time! One, two, three; one, two, three, and they "swing around the circle." Behold the prim young soldier in sky-blue uniform, his arm encircling the waist of his beauteous vivandiere, while his own waist is nearly cut in twain by the tightly drawn zone of polished leather. Thus conjoined, for a while they march along, keeping step to the music, gracefulness in every movement, flexibility and elasticity in every pace; happiness sits triumphantly enthroned upon their foreheads. Suddenly they are seized as by a spasm; they sway tunefully backward and forward several times, then away they plunge into the rotary vortex, and whirl along, like two corks in a gutter after a heavy shower. The gauzy lawn that at first floated airily over those sylph-like shoulders, now clings to them with glutinous perspiration, and gives an unromantic prominence to the clavicular arches; the fair complexion that but now eclipsed the lily and the lilac has become bronzed and turgid with deoxydized blood; the Minervan head that recently preserved such an arch and buoyant equilibrium on its own, now droops wearily on the shoulder of the gallant swain. How languishing and love-sick — how spiritless and sentimental — how completely collapsed they appear — but oh, how gloriously they waltz! Such is life at the Brunnen; such it is also at the Bergmühle, on the other side of the beautiful Rhume. But we will follow it once more in the every-day routine which it exhibits among these people.

It is four o'clock in the morning, when you are suddenly awakened by a trumpet-blast that makes you quiver in every nerve; you are paralyzed with the apprehensions of a Millerite. Visions of which Rubens might have felt proud when he painted the resurrection of the dead, flit before your dreamy soul; you start out of bed — a fit figure for such a picture — and rush for the window, expecting fearfully to behold the dread messenger himself, trumpet and all; when lo! it is only the cowherd, who blows his great trombonic horn, that people who have cows may rise, let them out of their stables, and place them under his pastoral charge. A little abashed at your *cowardly* misgivings, you return quietly to bed again; and just when you have attained once more that condition of delicious somnolence which is a kind of compromise — a Mason and Dixon's line between sleep and wakefulness — you are again recalled to a state of painful sensibility, not unmixed with a sprinkling of ire and a word or two of no prayerful etymology, by a quartette of buglers who march lazily down the street, tooting all the while the "stable call," for the dragoons to get up and "curry their horses, and give them some water and fodder and hay; or if they won't do it, the Colonel will know it, and then there will be the old Harry to pay." In explanation of this it should be said, that many of the soldiers are permitted to have their night-quarters among the families of the town, and are not confined to the barracks, consequently it is necessary to sound the *reveille* through every street, that no ear may escape its blasted invitation. The sun has already risen some twenty degrees in the celestial vault; you also have had your rising process graded by the two disturbances above narrated; you now *go through the third degree, and rise for good.*

After this, the first thing to be done is to send for the barber. In two minutes he appears all breathless before you, bids you good morning, spreads out his shaving materials, lathers your face, gallops his razor fearfully over the turnpikes of your chin and cheeks, and before he has fully recovered his breath, he is through with the operation, and ready to trot off to the house of his next customer. In the regular order of things coffee now makes its appearance, but with no other edible accompaniment than a small roll. This dispatched, the avocations of the day are commenced and continued until nine o'clock, when a more substantial breakfast is indulged in. On this occasion, among other things, may always be found a dish of the nutrimental specialty of the town you happen to be in, and for which said town is noted all over Europe. Thus you have goose-liver patés at Strasburg; world-famed sausages at Bologna;

Leckerle ginger-bread at Basel; Göttinger metwurst; Northeimer knapwurst; Brounschweiger schinken, &c. *ad infinitum*. The nomenclature of cheese is without limit. It hails from every direction, retains its local name, and no two kinds are supposed to be exactly alike. It may be had from the consistency of thick cream, through the unctuous Mainzer hand-cheese and the loud Limburger, that sends such savory messages over the olfactory telegraphic nerves, to the firm and yellow Schweitzer, though interspersed with numerous oleaginous cells.

Strange to say, people spin and speculate, barter and sell, labor and toil and suffer, to get their daily bread here, even like at other places — the artisan at his shop; the tiller of soil in his field; the merchant among his traffic; and the usurer over his pelf. In the market-place, too, the contestants for bread and butter present a motley gathering — the farmer in a blue frock and tight knee-breeches, with pipe in his mouth, and pliant pole, wherewith to goad his oxen, in his hand; the market woman squatting upon a low seat, with her basket of produce before her, gazing wistfully for customers, and now and then adjusting the flapping wings of the enormous head-dress that sits upon her vertex like an ominous bat. The fair embroideress for a moment quits her Berlin work to buy here her scanty meal; and the ruddy housewife trips merrily along from stall to stall, until her basket is well stored with provisions for her flock. Officials flit about with hurried pace, whilst boys and girls enliven the scene with sportive play, and speak German with remarkable fluency for such young people as they are. Dinner and coffee at three, and supper past, the evening is spent in various ways.

You see the bright lights twinkling through the darkness away over at the Bergmühle, and in the surrounding stillness of the night you hear the music and shuffling of waltzing feet, songs and revelry and the clink of glasses, and they all constitute that untranslatable state of things which the Germans calls *Gemüthlichkeit*.

It is moonlight, and like a true philosopher, you take an evening stroll, with a zealous thirst for observation. Lovely maidens there are sitting on the door-sills, knitting stockings, by the "bright silver light of the moon," with unblushing faces; or if their cheeks are crimsoned, it is because that color is always there, or perhaps because some daring youth is whispering to the not unwilling ears those precious dictations of the heart, which we all call sentimentalism in others, but are sure at some time in our lives to cherish with the liveliest sense of propriety. In the back-ground, behind the open door, are the parents, settled down into a quiet composure after the fatigues and cares of the day, interchanging periodical remarks whose chief merit, the young folks think, is in their brevity, whilst pater familias labors so earnestly at his great, long porcelain pipe, that ever and anon the fire in it blazes up, and illuminates the situation to the great discomfiture of the lovers. Pass we along, and observe those two gentlemen leaning far out of the second-story windows of their respective houses, on opposite sides of the street, holding a neighborly conversation through the evening air; long pipes again in full blast, and swinging to and fro like pendulums of old-fashioned clocks. Their conversation is interrupted by yonder squad of juvenile troubadours that is passing along the street, pouring out, as it were into every house, a good-night blessing with their delightful minstrelsy.

Let us finally go to the Hotel Sonne, and behold once more our friends of the nine-pin alley. Solemnly these dignitaries are seated around a table. Every one has his glass of hot grog — a vulgar concession, but nevertheless the truth — at which he sips leisurely during the whole of the evening. A spasmodic conversation on all subjects is the rule. Politics are lightly touched upon, but the news of the day freely discussed. Anecdotes and jokes and mirth prevail. Lütje Fricke is happy; the Assessor loquacious; Preusse good-hearted and blunt; and the Bürgermeister running over with the milk of human kindness. *Hoch auf, meine Herren! Es lebe Deutschland!*

LETTER XVI.

BERLIN.

GROWTH OF BERLIN.—MILITARY SPIRIT OF PRUSSIA.—THE KING & BISMARCK.—THEIR VISIT TO NAPOLEON.—UNTER DEN LINDEN.—NATIONAL LIBRARY.—MUSEUMS AND UNIVERSITY.—THE HOUSE OF ALEX. VON HUMBOLDT.—BLUCHER'S MONUMENT.—THE ORPHEUM.—ZOOLOGICAL AND BOTANICAL GARDENS.—THE RIVER SPREE.—A BEAUTIFUL FOREST.

BERLIN, *August*, 1867.

CITY of the Prussians, thy star is in the ascendant! From the small hamlet which fishermen founded in the thirteenth century on the sandy shores of the Spree, (a stream scarcely worthy of the name of river,) and which prior to the advent of King Frederick the First, still remained a town of very ordinary pretensions, Berlin has at length risen into a great and populous metropolis, and is the head and centre of a powerful nation. Whilst I am seated in one of the quiet cells of this great honeycomb of houses, above the noise of the din, the labor, the confusion, and the hurrying to and fro of the bees and drones that constitute its motion and machinery and life, I hear the rattle of cannonry which, but for its regular periodicity, might be easily mistaken for distant thunder. It is occasioned by the artillerymen, who, six miles beyond the city limits, are practising with some new invention, more terrible and destructive and death-dealing than any of its predecessors. For while all the nations of Europe are busied with the imitative labor of reconstructing their musketry to the character of that which last year taught them such a bitter lesson, Prussia is quietly occupying herself with some still more effective means of thrashing, in a future conflict, any nation less educated and less cringing under the yoke of bigotry than herself. The military spirit of Prussia is something entirely unequalled in the annals of nations. From the highest prince of the realm to the lowliest peasant's son, every one that does not suffer from sickness or malformation must devote a portion of his life to the service of his country in the army. Here is no paying of forfeit money; no buying of substitutes; no favors from the medical examiner, (this is just put in by way of rounding off the sentence,) no getting out of the scrape on any pretext whatsoever; but every man, when he attains that "stage of life" which Shakespeare and the Prussian laws dedicate to the soldier, must shoulder arms and march; though he be never so "full of round oaths" when he looks "into the grim cannon's jaws."

Although the nation has for its King a respectable-looking elderly gentleman, who has probably quite as good a head as heads run in the general crop of the human family, (I beg the human family's pardon; I mean of *royal* heads,) yet the King's king is Bismarck, who is, besides, the genius of the nation, and the ruling politician of Europe, and who does not practice Talleyrand's theory of "using words to conceal his thoughts." Doubtless the shrewd Italian minister, Cavour, was of great service to him as an illustrious example, and he was not too mole-eyed or thick-headed to profit by the lesson which that genius conferred upon Europe.

Bismarck, by virtue of his high position and great popularity, has become haughty, if not altogether overbearing; yet there are times when he can unbend, and acquit himself with great geniality and good-nature; and he never fails to respond in this spirit to the approaches of his boon companions in early life. He was at that period, during several years, a student at the university of Göttingen, and I am told that when, last year, Hanover came under his conquering King's jurisdiction, and he had occasion to visit the seat of his youthful educational career, he was moved with a very kindly leniency toward the people of that classic city, and disposed to promote their comfort to the utmost extent within his power. At Northeim, too, situated but a short distance from Göttingen, where many of his frolicsome student-tricks were perpetrated, he is yet held in lively recollection by the old citizens. The principal hotel there is still kept by the same individual that presided over it in Bismarck's time; and when last year he saw this landlord, who had, meanwhile, become monstrously corpulent, he walked up to him, took him familiarly by the hand, and exclaimed, "*Was Thausand! Ei das bist du ja, du alter Sonne. Potz Donnerwetter, wie bist du so dicke geworden!*"

Bismarck scarcely ever leaves the society of the King, least of all on important occasions. After the

Luxemburg question was settled, and there was a reaction of sufficient royal friendship (a peculiar species of the article) to enable the King to visit Paris and be the guest of Napoleon, like all the other kings and princes, he was very careful to accompany his sovereign. When, afterward, at parting, Napoleon condescended to shake hands with the wary minister — which astonished all the editors of France — it was the recognition of an intellectual presence not inferior to his own.

For some time past, the King has been at Ems, and has recently gone to Wiesbaden, where the Count joined him, ostensibly for the purpose of conferring with him on matters of domestic import, but in all probability for the purpose of keeping him under his overshadowing observation, and from the commission of any social or political indiscretion; for he advocates the total abolishment of all these gambling concerns; whereas the King heretofore generally encouraged them, and has been known, on occasions when the "Rouge-et-Noir" banks at Wiesbaden and Homburg were "swamped," to replenish their treasury from his own purse. And he has had his way thus far in all other things, Bismarck will have it also in this, and the days of public gaming upon Prussian territory are already numbered.

The bright side of Berlin is undoubtedly on the street called "Unter den Linden," that runs from the Brandenburger gate to the royal castle. One may not easily find elsewhere, on an equal area of ground, so many and such magnificent buildings as here. Commencing at the grand castle, second only to the

Tuileries at Paris, we cross over the bridge that is adorned on both sides with eight groups of marble figures, more than life-size, representing tableaux in warfare; Victoria teaching the youth in heroic lore; Minerva instructing the young warrior in the use of arms; Victoria crowning the warrior; Victoria raising the wounded hero; Pallas challenging him to renewed conflict; Pallas sheltering and protecting him in battle; Iris leading the wounded victor to Olympus. Such are these groups, that stand out like great white cardinal letters in the war-alphabet of the rising generation of Prussia.

We next pass the two splendid museums, and, in succession, the arsenal, the royal guard-house, the university, the Acadamie on the one side, and on the other side the palace of the Crown Prince, the opera-house, the Hedwig's-church, the library, and the King's residence, that may all be seen from one point of observation; whilst the gendarme-market, two large churches with magnificent cupolas, the capacious theatre, and an array of fine residences are in the immediate vicinity. The focus to which the rays of Berlin life converge, is Unter den Linden, in the neighborhood of the opera-house. Here the people walk about in their finest embellishments, or trundle along in their superbest equipages, while the shop-windows offer their temptations to the passers-by, even as on Centre Street, in Pottsville, or the Boulevards, in Paris.

The library is one of the characteristic institutions of this nation. It contains nearly seven hundred thousand volumes, on all subjects of science, art, history, and literature, and is accessible to all free of charge. The large reading-room is open from nine o'clock in the morning until four in the afternoon; or the readers may take books to their own homes by paying a nominal sum of about twenty cents a year. Here, too, are many relics of curious interest to the visitors, among which is one of the first seven Latin Bibles printed by Gutenberg, in 1450; some of Luther's translations in manuscript, and the Hebrew Bible which he used in this work; manuscript writings of Virgil, and other ancient poets; and of Gœthe, (whose entire Faust is here in manuscript,) Schiller, Humboldt, and many other modern classics. Many specimens of the Koran are also exhibited, and some beautiful printing in Chinese on silk; also very ancient writing in Greek, more than two thousand years old, on parchment, leather, palm-leaves, papyrus, bark, and stones. Here, also, as a scientific relic, are preserved the two bronze hemispheres upon which Otto von Guerike made some of his first experiments with an exhausting air-pump; and who, when accused of being leagued with the Evil One, demonstrated to his sovereign his discovery by adjusting the well-fitting edges of these hemispheres in cohesive union, then, having exhausted the air from the interior of the hollow globe, hitched eight mules to each hemisphere; but they could not be pulled asunder; and thus it was that he disproved his collusion with the devil. If every inventor of the present day had to acquit himself in a similar manner of this relationship, what a demand for mules there would be!

Remarkable for the many objects of interest they

enclose are the two museums of this city. They contain an extensive collection of antiquarian curiosities; several series of mythological frescoes, that fail not to refreshen one's interest in the poetic lore of the gods and goddesses of old; galleries of paintings and sculpture, both of which contain gems of the highest order, among the latter of which, especially, are a copy of the Venus di Medicis, and a Hebe, by Canova, the two finest creations from stone that I have thus far seen, excepting, indeed, loveliest of all, that inspiration of art which is in the Roman baths at Potsdam, the Hebe and Ganymede, by Hentschel. This is a work so chaste in execution, so pure, simple, yet noble in design, that it is utterly impossible to conceive an adequate idea without seeing it. You cannot but gaze upon these figures with ardor, with wrapt enthusiasm, and hold your breath for fear you might disturb them. You feel as if it were a desecration of the Divine power to make such things as these from out the cold material of marble.

It is impossible, in the limited space at my command, to enumerate anything more in detail of these interesting museums, and we must pass on. The university, attended by an aggregate number of two thousand students of divinity, law, philosophy, and medicine, is a temple dedicated to science, that is truly worthy of its exalted purpose; for no edifice of man's creation should be more beautiful and imposing than that wherein is educated and developed the intellect of our youth, the divine spark by which only we resemble the Creator. An object of interest to all admirers of great minds must ever be the house wherein Alexander Von Humboldt dwelt during the latter seventeen years of his life. In universal knowledge, as far as it is permitted our finite understandings to comprehend things in the heavens, upon the earth, and within the earth, Humboldt certainly was the most learned man that ever lived. In the Royal Library above alluded to, I have seen the entire collection of works that he has written, on all scientific subjects, in Latin, German, and French—for he wrote with equal readiness in each of these languages — and it is almost incredible that one mind should grasp, and one man's lifetime suffice, for the whole of that stupendous work. Yet Nature dealt kindly with him; and his physical organization, under the healthful influence of his peaceful, temperate, and philosophical soul, was permitted to preserve its harmonious movement unto a ripe old age — when no taint of disorganized flesh destroyed him; but, having finished all his labors, he went to sleep in his chair one day, and quietly breathed his last.

Among the many monumental statues that embellish Unter den Linden, the most noteworthy is, probably, that of the old hero of Waterloo, Blücher. With drawn sabre, and his left foot resting on a cannon, he looks like a veteran, every inch of him. The Prussians have a peculiar fondness for the memory of this chieftain; and if the truth were known, which two names in the history of their country stand uppermost in public estimation, it is quite probable that "der alte Fritze," (King Frederick II.,) and "der alte Blücher" would carry off the prize.

Now let us ambulate leisurely to the other side of

Berlin, and in the Old Jacob's Street we will enter an establishment that is honored with the titulary distinction of Orpheum. This is a large garden, covered and almost enclosed with glass. Within it are alcoves and fountains, palm-trees, bananas, and other tropical plants. Scattered about among the foliage, in artistic effectiveness, and pendant in wreaths of all manner of devices, are some four thousand gas-jets, enclosed by glass globes of different colors, whilst from a balcony a band of the ablest musicians captivate the senses with strains of delicious sweetness. Alas! this is a nursery for exotics in more senses than one; for here the merryblades and the camelias mingle in the bewildering dance denominated "cancan," in which the display of gaudy dresses, pretty feet and ankles, and great bushy, tow-colored ringlets is quite electrifying, and apparently galvanized some of the old weather-beaten hearts that I saw there into a momentary spasm of new life again.

Pass we now outside of the city, and follow the serpentine course of the river Spree, as it skirts the northern boundary of the Thiergarten-wald, and flows lazily along, the dear only knows where to. In some of its convolutions, however, it has been widened and deepened into a species of canal, wherein it is absolutely possible to ride very short distances on light canoes. Into one of these my American friend seated himself the other day, avowing, with frantic looks, that he "*must* have a little frolic in one of those dolphins," and this was the first and only *spree* he was on since he left "Columbia's happy shore." Turning to the left we enter the Zoölogical Garden, which is a very Noah's ark for the completeness of its selections from animated nature. An elephant flourishes here who seems the solemnest patriarch of his kind, and answers with a distinct neigh whenever his keeper asks him a question. Two grizzly bears dwell here that would make Seth Kinman's heart jump in very ecstasy, and his fingers itch to exercise the trigger of that famous rifle of his. In other respects the menagerie is very similar to that of Paris.

We now bisect the whole of the woods called the Thiergarten, and take a look through the Botanical Garden, which is one of the most extensive of its kind in Europe, having no less than eighteen large hot-houses, in which, and in the open gardens, some sixteen thousand kinds of plants are cultivated. Finally, let us return into the innermost depth of the woods, to the "Great Star," a place from which numerous roads diverge in various directions. We take that which extends to the Brandenburger gate of the city, and walk quietly toward it.

It is a beautiful forest, though only about a mile square, composed of oak, beech, ash, birch, and linden trees, very thickly planted, but without a particle of underbrush, and upon ground as level as a prairie. It is just the place where you would expect to meet a posse of wood-nymphs at almost every turn, and where, without in the least startling your nerves, King Oberon, with the little silver horn around his neck, and the silver wand in his hand, might descend through the foliage in his golden chariot, drawn by doves and butterflies, stretch out his wand and create a castle of pearls, emeralds, and rubies for you, then disappear. The darkness of night has come over the place; but it is intersected with numerous excellent roads, on every one of which is a double row of lamps with burning gas-jets, which sparkle through the green vestiture of trees, appear and disappear as you pass along, that it seems indeed like an enchanted region wherein you wander.

O, lovely forest! if your leaves were all eyes and ears and tongues, what stories you could tell, of timid confessions that are whispered in your hearing; of raptures that thrill the children of men under your ambrosial shadow! What a code of ethics you could weave from the woof and web of thoughts that escape into your trackless waste! Let the students of books enter the libraries of men, flutter among their leaves, and read; but let me, O bower of Nature, seek refuge in your shady retreats and THINK! Let me, panting, draw new life and inspiration from the oxygen of your expiring foliage!

LETTER XVII.

MY AMERICAN FRIEND TAKES A RAMBLE THROUGH THE STREETS OF BERLIN.— GAZES IN THE SHOP-WINDOWS AND SEES SOMETHING.— FINDS OUT AN ADDRESS AND GOES IN PURSUIT OF IT.— WHAT HAPPENS THERE.— AN ACCIDENT.— DOES A LITTLE DOCTORING.— MAKES THE ACQUAINTANCE OF A PRUSSIAN SOLDIER.— SOME MILITARY TALK.—DESCRIPTION OF THE BATTLE OF LANGENSALZA.

BERLIN, *August*, 1867.

THE other day my feelings were greatly exercised, not to say harrowed, by the conduct of my American friend. Having ascertained that I should be employed the greater part of the forenoon in writing, he determined to take a stroll, and speculate on the current of human events that would present themselves to his philosophic view on the streets and by-ways of Berlin.

Now, we had always been as inseparable as mind and body of the same individual; and how he could have the hardihood to venture on such an undertaking must be forever a mystery to all who understood the bonds of unity between us. Indeed, it is unintelligible to myself even now; and were I called upon to solemnly affirm or swear, that I in the body, remained at home, occupied with the aforesaid writing, whilst he in the body wandered forth, I should stand upon a demurrer at all hazards, as being in some doubt of my own identity. One thing, however, is incontrovertible, namely, that he *did* sally out; and whether I followed him in the flesh, or simply in the spirit, can be of no earthly consequence to the reader, who is only asked to accept this record of M. A. F.'s experience on that day in good faith of the latter's individual responsibility.

He had just turned a corner from Unter den Linden, and was proceeding leisurely down Friederich's Street, which is lined on both sides by a dazzling galaxy of shop-windows.

When we see a person, in whatever city we may reside, loitering along the streets, and looking curiously into the shop-windows, it is human nature to set that down as an evidence of social greenness, and to our minds the idea is inseparable from a tall, lank, straight, and yellow-haired individual, clothed in long, swallow-tailed coat, too short in the sleeves, and in nether garments too short in the extremities. Yet, reader, to be candid now, have you never caught yourself in other cities bigger than your own — or perhaps not even that — doing this same thing that you deprecate as countrified in others? The truth is, there is much wisdom to be gathered from this roadside display of tradesmen's goods; for there is evidenced therein not only the productiveness of a people, but their skill, taste, ingenuity, and enterprise; and in these are the essential elements of whatever degree of prosperity they enjoy.

My American friend, then, without any disparagement of his fine sense of 'cuteness be it said, was gazing into the shop-windows of Friederich's Street, and admiring the manifold objects therein exhibited, and intended to respond to the wants and vanities of never-satisfied mankind. The particular productions that attracted his special attention, were some beautiful samplers of embroidery in zephyr work, displayed in the window of one by the name of Levi, and among these he espied a pattern, though not worked out, which quite suited his fancy. The figure it represented was a copy of Correggio's Repentant Magdalene, of which he determined to purchase, if possible, a finished piece. Accordingly he entered the store, and made known his request; but was told that they had no completed sampler of that kind on hand, and that there was but one lady in their employment who could do any degree of justice to that figure on canvas, not with pallet and brush, but with needle and zephyr. "Would they be kind enough to give him the address of that lady?" "Certainly, *mein Herr*, with great *Vergnügen*."

The needle-work artisans of Berlin are noted throughout the world for this kind of manufacture; and in Berlin, those who work for the house of Levi are distinguished for the peculiar excellence and finish of their samplers. He was therefore anxious to procure a fine specimen of this beautiful workmanship, by, if possible, the most accomplished hands of Berlin. To this end he purchased the pattern before named, and proceeded forthwith to carry it to the lady whose address he had obtained.

She lived on the second floor of a plain, unassuming, but comfortable and sufficiently spacious residence in Charlotten Street. The chambers in question were pointed out to him by the housemaid, who also acted as portress; and on tapping lightly at the door, he was told by a sweet voice from within, to come "*herein.*"

Entering the apartment, he found it occupied by three individuals. One of these was a very pretty maiden, blonde and blue-eyed, with joyful smiles dancing playfully about her pleasant countenance, like the first fitful rays of the rising sun upon the morning dew. Attired in neat and tasteful simplicity, hers was of that "beauty unadorned" which is ever "adorned the most." She was seated upon an ottoman, and occupied with a piece of satin embroidery.

Another lady, who was apparently her sister, and some half dozen years her senior,— also very fair to look upon, but with something of a more matronly comeliness,— was seated at a sewing-machine, which M. A. F. soon discovered to be one of American manufacture.

The third personage was a bright, curly-haired child — a little boy some four or five years old, who shrank up close to his mamma, the elder lady, with a half-frightened expression on his face, evidently occasioned by the presence of a stranger. The latter, whose knowledge of German was limited, needed all his address to go through the form of his self-introduction; but he had acquitted himself right cleverly, and was about stating the object of his visit, when the elder lady, upon rising to receive him, by some inadvertent movement gave the large fly-wheel of her sewing-machine a sudden turn; whereupon the child startled them all by the painful utterance of a piercing scream. His little hand, that had been resting in one of the inter-radial spaces of the wheel, was, by the quick turn of the latter, violently jammed against a fixed portion of the machine, and the alert eye of my American friend (who, it will be recollected, was a doctor) immediately discovered that the child's wrist was broken by the accident. Upon realizing this fact, the ladies were thrown into great consternation, taking the child by turns in their arms, and mingling with his frightened and distressful cries their sobs and lamentations.

They had become quite oblivious of the presence of their visitor, when he recalled their attention to himself, by explaining his professional calling, and assuring them that with their permission he would take the proper steps to remedy the injured arm at once, as it was important to replace the fractured edges in apposition with as little delay as possible, in order to obviate to a great extent the swelling and inflammation that must otherwise follow. This permission being readily granted, he sent the younger lady out for some plaster-of-paris, or gypsum, whilst he readjusted the displaced parts, and kept them so until her return. Then, after slaking the plaster-of-paris, he moulded it around the child's wrist and forearm, making a cast which upon drying formed a firm and solid casing in which a re-displacement was impossible.

After the little fellow had his arm thus fixed and placed in a broad silken sling suspended from his neck, he still looked dubiously at the white mass that confined it, and which seemed like the arm of a statue that had been knocked off for his amusement by some Italian vender; but he appeared quite comfortable again, and ceased crying at once.

This unforeseen, though sad occurrence, had the effect of setting aside in a measure the feeling of strangeness between the ladies and their visitor; and placed them in something of that familiar relation which is so soon established between doctors and their patients. Directly they were lost in the labyrinth of a friendly conversation, in which he however learned, that it was not possible to execute the Repentant Magdalene for him in the short time that he proposed remaining in Berlin. So he expressed himself satisfied with a less elaborate production, and on leaving, promised to step in again next day, to see how his little patient would be getting on.

On his visit of the following day, my friend was made acquainted with the child's father, who is an orderly sergeant in the Prussian army. He was a tall and rather fine-looking young man, and met my friend with a profusion of thanks for his attentions of the previous day.

"Let me rather express my sincere regrets to you, sir, for having been unwittingly the cause of the accident to your little boy," said M. A. F. in return.

"If you was the innocent cause," replied the soldier, "you have made us forget it by your kindness, and the prompt manner in which you have repaired the injury."

"How, then, did my little friend rest throughout the night?" asked the self-installed surgeon, while his fingers were playing among the curls of his now quite reconciled young patient.

"Oh comparatively well, sir," responded the mother. "I feared that the weight of that cast around his arm would embarrass him much more than it does. He slept quite sweetly all night."

Without going further into the details of this preliminary conversation, we may simply state, that it soon drifted into a military vein

The sergeant was dressed in a full uniform of blue that was well fitting, and appeared new enough to have just arrived from the tailor's; and he wore on his left breast, suspended by black and white ribbons, (the Prussian colors,) a bright shining medal.

"I should suppose," said my friend, glancing significantly at the medal, "that you have seen some active service; may I ask where it was?"

Apparently pleased at the inquiry, the young sergeant replied, "At Langensalza, sir, in our battle with the Hanoverians. I had the honor to contribute the humble service for which I was rewarded with this distinction."

"Ah," said his wife, her eyes beaming with love and pride at the husband whom she evidently considered the bravest of the brave; "but why do you not tell the gentleman by what act of gallantry it was that you earned it?"

"If there are any special circumstances connected with the matter," said his visitor, "and you have no particular reasons for withholding them, I should be pleased and thankful to hear you relate them."

"It wasn't much, sir; the story is soon told. I simply picked up a bombshell, before it exploded, and threw it into a stream of water that was running near by. That is all," was the modest reply.

"Yes," retorted his wife, "that was all, and there was great courage in the act; but he did not do it for a joke either, did you, Carl? He might have run *away* from the bombshell rather than *toward* it; but his presence of mind saw a useful purpose, that made him forget all about his own safety — all about his loving wife and child at home." She was evidently quite full of the subject; and winding her arm around his waist, continued, "The shell fell almost under a powder-caisson, and if it had exploded there, the destruction would have been terrible."

"Besides, Carl," added the sister, "don't you know that Generals Falkenstein and Manteufel were standing close by, in consultation with each other, and if they had been killed, we would certainly have lost the battle. So his Majesty may well make you a *Feldwebel*, (orderly sergeant,) and hang a medal upon your breast."

"My brave friend," now exclaimed M. A. F., grasping him warmly by the hand, "I am proud of your acquaintance; you ought to have been at our own great battle of Gettysburg, so you ought."

"I have read of that battle, and learned that you got along right well without me," good-humoredly rejoined the sergeant.

"Will you not give me some further account of the conflict at Langensalza?" asked my friend; "I have heard that the Hanoverians fought bravely there, with their blind king in their midst."

"Like tigers, sir," was the reply; "oh! we had a foe worthy of our steel, I can assure you. I saw with my own eyes how they broke up one of our Prussian infantry squares. A cavalry lieutenant, whose name I have since learned was Von Einen, rode up against the solid phalanx, then spurred his horse until he reared over the bristling bayonets, and bounded almost into the centre of the square, scattering it to the right and left. It is true, that horse and rider went headlong into death, but the sight of it was horribly sublime."

Having now fully worked himself into the spirit of his subject, the sergeant went on with it, his face glowing with enthusiasm.

"Oh, sir, you should have seen what a glorious and gallant fight it was! I do not say it from egotism, or because I was there myself; for my praise of the Hanoverians is as great as of the Prussians; I love them as warmly for their daring heroism as I do my own comrades in arms. Their cavalry is unsurpassed all the world over. The battle raged over undulating ground, the centre of which was traversed by a stream that is generally small and shallow, but was now swollen by the June freshets to a depth in some places that horses were obliged to swim in crossing it. Our infantry swooped down like birds of prey upon the enemy, from the rising ground to the right and left of the town of Langensalza; that of the enemy rushed like infuriated fiends down the slopes of the greater hills on the opposite side of the creek. Both forces met and fought by long lines in and across the water. Our artillery was chiefly planted on a conical knoll of ground, called *Judenhügel* (Jews' Hill), theirs on the opposite eminence; and the two blazed at each other over and through and aside of the *Badewäldchen* (Bathing-grove), and were doing a terrific carnage also among the regiments of cavalry and infantry that were engaged all over the two descending slopes. At Kallenberg's Mill, a little back from the foot of the hill, it was where I performed that little action of which my wife is so proud, now that it is over, but which she would not have thanked me for when it occurred. The place was considered at the time comparatively safe; Generals Falkenstein and Manteufel were anxiously conversing, apparently heedless of what occurred around them. I, who was then but a private soldier, was about to assist a comrade to carry ammunition to our company from the caisson before named. The shell fell, burrowed a deep hole, and ploughed along the ground a distance of about fifty yards, when it ceased rolling, and lay motionless a few feet from where my comrade and myself were standing; but the little spiral column of smoke was still curling upward from its fuse as it lay there. I instantly sprang forward, seized the terrible missile, raised it with difficulty above my head, and hurled it as far into the mill-stream as I could. General Falkenstein, who was about seventy years of age, saw the act, and had me brought before him. 'I will say to you what Marshall Blücher said to me at Waterloo: "*Du bist ein braver Junge;*"— come to me when the battle is over, and I will make you a *Feldwebel.*' Those were the words the General spoke to me; you can imagine how proud I have ever felt of them.

" It was then that the Hanoverian hordes swarmed forward in fearful carnage against our ranks — then that the struggle in and across the water was the deadliest, and the fire the hottest. There was a bridge spanning the river, that was contested like another bridge of Lodi. Wounded horses were plunging about madly in the water, and the dead and dying soldiers floating down upon it by scores. Indeed, you must allow me to repeat, sir, that it was a glorious battle — that battle of Langensalza."

"Eventually the Hanoverians capitulated, did they not?" asked my friend.

"Yes, sir, on the first day, the 27th of June, they fought us steadily, hopeful of success — and against great odds too — odds of greater numbers, and our superior needle-guns; but the next day fresh reinforcements came to our aid, and the enemy was overwhelmed from all sides; escape was hopeless, and he surrendered at discretion."

"Did the King of Hanover continue in the field to the end?"

"Yes, the poor, blind, but infatuated King commanded to the end. Riding along between the Crown Prince and a general officer, these gentlemen led him by reins fastened to the bridle-bit of his horse. He was bitterly opposed to the surrender, and entreated his officers to continue the struggle until he at least should be killed; but they in turn opposed this, and justly so, as utterly at variance, not only with humanity, but the laws of civilized warfare. So he was obliged to succumb, though he lamented greatly at the downfall of what he was pleased to call his 'beloved *Guelphen Haus.*'"

LETTER XVIII.

TRAVELLING.—THE WIND-MILLS.

CITY OF LEIPZIG.—HAHNEMANN'S MONUMENT.—GŒTHE'S FAUST, AND AUERBACH'S CELLAR.— THE BOOK-TRADE, AND UNIVERSITY OF LEIPZIG. — DRESDEN.— TREASURES AND WORKS OF ART.—THE GREEN VAULTS.—KAUFMAN'S ACOUSTIC CABINET.—THE SCHUTZENFEST OF THE VOGEL-WIESE.—A TRIP UP THE ELBE TO KONIGSTEIN.—VISIT TO THE BATTLE-FIELD OF SADOWA.

VIENNA, *August*, 1867.

MY American friend has been suddenly seized with a passion for wind-mills, of which he counted no less than seventy-eight on our way from Berlin to Leipzig. He says: "Behold their wild, weird, and threatening appearance! How beautifully they relieve the monotony of these sandy and fenceless fields! Is it a wonder that the valiant Don Quixote was tempted to break his knightly lance on one of them? And yet they throw their great, long arms around in such an agonizing manner, as if their internal grinding caused them excruciating pain. Oh, why can we not keep apace with Europe, and have wind-mills too?"

The city of Leipzig was made memorable by the great battle which Napoleon fought there against twice his number of the allied forces, in the year 1813, and which precipitated in one great lurch the downward tendency of that destiny whose child he had so oft and fondly proclaimed himself to be.

Standing by the stone which marks the place he occupied during the whole time of that great struggle, and gazing over the vast plains in every direction, now pregnant with vegetation that bends under the yellow burden of its ripening nouriture, I could not help wondering what were the thoughts and emotions of that one man, on whom alone rested the whole responsibility of a half million human beings killing and butchering each other, whilst he was quietly gazing on, and directing the manner of the frightful carnage. Now, over the whole ground where the defiant walls and bastions of Leipzig once stood, are a series of flower-beds, arbors of overhanging vines and trees intersected with walks, forming an agreeable promenade that entirely encircles the city.

Occasional places of this promenade are embellished with monumental statues, among which I was gratified to find one of Dr. Samuel Hahnemann, the founder of Homœopathy. It is truly a noble piece of art, and exhibits the learned Doctor in a sitting posture, an open book in his left hand, a pen in the right, and on his naturally fine and open countenance is depicted a well-drawn expression of thoughtful meditation. The statue is in the centre of a flowerbed of roses, geraniums, daffodils, and honey-suckles, the latter creeping along an iron railing which surrounds the monument. Whatever may be said by the opponents of Homœopathy against Hahnemann's theory, one thing is certain, that its application on himself had a very salubrious effect; for the good man lived to the respectable age of nearly ninety years — something that doctors can rarely be accused of.

The reader who is familiar with Gœthe's "Faust" will recollect that some of its scenes were transacted in Auerbach's cellar in Leipzig, and of course, to leave the city without bestowing a hasty visit on this famous place, was not to be thought of. This dingy old cellar, with a dank, subterranean smell, with arched ceiling and massive walls, covered interiorly with faded frescos, illustrating the friendly intercourse between Doctor Faustus and the devil, really enjoys the air of a place where one might have a civil little conversation with his Satanic Majesty right cosily. An old German book, containing the original legend of Doctor Faustus, is chained to the wall, and said to be the one which Gœthe used in the elaboration of his great drama. Another old book, containing the "chronicles of Leipzig," really has a paragraph in it stating, that on a certain occasion, "Doctor Faustus, by the aid and assistance of the Evil One, did wickedly ride out of Auerbach's cellar, a-straddle of a barrel of wine." Even the old barrel — *mirabile dictu!* — upon which this feat was performed, is still here in an astonishingly well-preserved condition! Goodness! what things a body sees when one travels!

The book-trade of Leipzig is the largest on the Continent, and the city is, beside this, noted for its general commercial character. On three different occasions of the year there is a market called the "Messe," when the influx of strangers from all parts of Europe, and even from America, is so great sometimes as to double the aggregate population; and the amount of business transacted during these periods is enormous. The University is one of the best in Europe, and generally attended by upward of fifteen hundred students, among whom there are always quite a number from the United States.

We now come to Dresden, of which lovely city my reminiscences are too agreeable ever to be forgotten. It has been called by a distinguished poet the Florence of Germany, and whatever Florence may be I have not yet realized, but certain it is that Dresden contains the elements to satisfy the profoundest philosopher, as well as the most fastidious idealist, and yields enjoyment of the most diversified description to all.

The chief attraction of this city, as evidenced by the daily crowds of visitors, is doubtless the "Green Vaults," wherein are stored treasures and works of art from precious materials of incalculable wealth. Figures and groups carved from ivory and mother-of-pearl; vases and statuettes and all manner of things from gold and silver; necklaces and tiaras, swords and royal badges, and insignias of all kinds, that dazzle the eye with their profusion of large and resplendent diamonds and rubies. Among these is the diamond necklace belonging to Queen Amelia, (of Saxony,) which is said to be unequalled by that of any other queen or empress in Europe; a stone of onyx valued at 48,000 thalers; and a work made by Dinglinger, which represents the throne and court of the Great Mogul of Delhi. The open and richly furnished pavilion is at the end of a garden; the whole is of solid silver, and about two yards square. The Mogul himself is seated on a golden throne, and in the pavilion, and scattered about the garden, are a hundred and thirty-two figures of solid gold, being men with camels loaded with the tribute exacted by their sovereign. After examining, during an hour, the curiosities and brilliants displayed in these chambers, one's eyes feel quite relieved to escape again to their habitual observation of common objects.

The Art Gallery at Dresden contains many of the most highly treasured productions of the old masters, chiefest of which is Raphael's Madonna di St. Sisto, brought here at a cost of sixty thousand thalers! It is honored with a room by itself, in which hundreds of people may be seen daily, with "eyes in fine frenzy rolling," gazing upon this picture as if it was their daily bread, and they had to live upon the sight of it. Some of the other paintings of greatest note are the Repentant Magdalene, by Corregio; another similar subject, by Battoni; the St. Cicilie, by Carlo Dolce; the Children of Charles the First, by Van Dyck; a Venus and Cupid, by Guido Reni; and another by Titian; and, of course, the usual number by Rubens, whose horrible naturalness in delineating flesh and blood I am quite tired of.

A place of great interest in this city is Kaufman's Acoustic Cabinet of self-playing musical instruments, of which there are a great variety, from that of a little artificial bird, no larger than a humming-bird, that jumps out of a small box, flutters about and whistles — to a great military orchestrion, which, when wound up and set in motion, performs most delightfully, like the full orchestra of an opera, trumpets, cornets, flutes, clarionets, cymbals, drums, and everything else included. One instrument is there, composed of about twenty bugles, constituting a full corps, that would be an elegant acquisition to a cavalry regiment, and might be hauled along on a wagon at dress-parade, in full blast, to the equal delight of both men and horses. There were also some instruments whose sounds can scarcely be distinguished from that of the finest pianos. Altogether, I don't know but what these queer machines afforded me the most perfect concert I ever attended; for I heard here my favorite Miserere from Trovatore, played to perfection, as well as a number of gems from other operas and a brilliant overture. Some of these instruments perform as many as a hundred different pieces, and can easily be adapted for new ones. They may be purchased, but are very costly, some of them being valued at prices as high as ten thousand dollars.

The time of my arrival at Dresden happened to be the week of the so-called Schützenfest of the Vogelwiese, or, Anglicized, Target Festival of the Birdsmeadow. This is a peculiar institution of the Germans, and is associated with the wildest kind and most abandoned enjoyments. Picture to yourself a large, flat field, about twenty acres square, and upon this fancy at least twenty-five separate and distinct companies of "flying horses," where big and little boys and girls can have a circular ride of about five minutes' duration, accompanied by the most bewildering music, for a penny a ride; then there are other similar concerns, composed of small railroad cars, headed by a bogus locomotive, the whole running round in a ring, like a lightning express train, screaming and shrieking with its patent steam-whistle after the most approved style. Next in order are at least a score and a half of different kinds of shows, under canvas tents, the largest of which is the hippodrome, where riding on real horses is done. And then follow successively a number of monkey theatres, where the performance is conducted entirely by apes and intelligent dogs that walk up ladders, and jump through hoops and paper-headed drums; and ponies, that fire off pistols and waltz to the tune of the "Camels are Coming" with wonderful ease and circumspection. Then comes a show with a large and flaming placard, announcing itself as the Great American Institute of Living and Moving Figures. Wondering what new feature of your country's greatness is here exposed to the rude gaze of the plebeian masses, you determine to enter and be surprised. Surprised you are, indeed, upon finding a lot of stupid-looking wax-figures, purporting to represent Napoleons the First and Third, Frederick the Great, Bismarck and Garibaldi, Queen Victoria, and a whole lot of similar Americans, all twisting and nodding their heads and rolling their eyes at you, as if in the very deathstruggle of saying: "Whichever you likes, my dear; you pays your money, and you has your choice." Other tents contain Fat Women, Circassian Beauties, Little Turks, and Big Russians; and one there is with a poor armless creature, who knits stockings with the same members that usually wear them. A long row of shooting-galleries claim our attention next, where a great host of men and boys keep up a sharp, running fire with spring-guns at all manner of targets, for all manner of prizes, from a row of pins to a galvanized watch. At one end of the field the principal company of the occasion shoot mark at a wooden bird, the size of a big rooster, that is perched on the top of a pole at least a hundred feet high, and from this the festival derives its name. Pass we now by yonder long row of booths, where trinkets and toys, cakes and all kinds of drinks are sold; we will arrive at others, where housewifish-looking women bestir themselves in a lively manner with the frying of small, curled-up sausages, and dishing them up with a neat dressing of sour-krout, for scores of hungry ones who stand and sit around, fork in hand, devouring these dainty morsels with a relish that laughs at dyspepsia as at a wild and visionary dream of the doctors. In another part of the field is a pole about twenty-five feet high, the top of which is encircled by a hoop, to which caps, pocket-handkerchiefs, and small blouses are attached; and any boy who can climb up the smoothly polished pole and detach one of these prizes, is entitled to keep it; and many and amusing are the efforts of the boys to climb the pole. Now fancy again, kind reader, all these flying-horses, and circuses, and shows, in full operation, and scattered about the whole field some thirty organ-grinders, all playing at the same time different tunes and within hearing of each other—the scene animated by a crowding, moving, pleasure-seeking, frolicksome, good-natured pepulace of some five thousand or more in number, and you will have a faint idea of the Schützenfest at Dresden.

Seated in a rather elegant equipage—though it was a hired *droschke*—with a spruce-looking driver, we were proceeding one afternoon to this Schützenfest, outside of the city. Another equipage, with a span of beautiful black horses was immediately ahead of us. The street was lined on both sides with crowds of people, who, all along our route, were continually taking off their hats and making all manner of reverential bows as we passed along. Instantly my American friend, who would not be behindhand in courtesy with these very polite people, took off *his* hat and proceeded the rest of the way bareheaded, inclining his body out of the carriage to the right and to the left, kissing his hand to the ladies who were waving handkerchiefs from upper story windows and balconies, and saluting the masses with a countenance beaming with good wishes for their welfare. It was indeed a grand ovation through which we passed, and would have tended, I confess, to disturb our halcyon souls with a little vanity, had we not, at the end of our journey, been apprised of the little circumstance that the carriage which had kept close before us all the way was occupied by the King of Saxony, and that we must have been looked upon as favorite individuals of his retinue. We alighted, however, and so did the King; but he did not approach us with outstretched hands and invite us to dine with him, which relieved my friend, in a measure, for he felt ill at ease at the idea of cultivating the intimacy of kings, as quite unreconcilable with his republican principles. Yet the King looked toward us, too, with something of a quizzical smile, and methought some official, with a handsome star on his left breast, (he was probably a policeman was heard so say: "*Gnädige Majestät, sind nur zwei Amerikaner.*"

Soon after, leaving the King of Saxony to shoot, with a bow-gun, at the bird in the Vogelwiese, at which, it is said, he always takes his turn, we left the fair city of Dresden and proceeded in a steamboat up the river Elbe, through the beautiful and romantic highlands, to Königstein. I cannot concede that the grand and wild magnificence of this scenery loses one particle by comparison with that along the Rhine.

My next point of rest was Prague, in Bohemia, the land of the gypsies. This city, though associated in history with many thrilling events, is otherwise of no great interest to the traveller. It has many large and handsome palaces, and the Hradschin, especially, is an object of no common interest. I remained a day, which was long enough to see pretty much everything of note, and then proceeded, by way of Pardubitz, to Königgrätz, whence I journeyed to Saduwa and all over the last year's battle-field, where the difficulty between Prussia and Austria were so speedily and effectually settled. On the battle-field there are a number of handsome monuments, erected by the Austrians to the memory of their brave dead heroes, though I could not help thinking that the inscriptions on the tablets denoted a rather active exercise of somebody's mythological faculties. Thus, for instance, the following is on nearly every monument: "For the Kaiser and their country they encountered death joyfully," which, considering the compulsory recruiting of European armies, appeared to me as, after all, a pretty strong piece of chiselling, that would not pass for an affidavit under all circumstances.

The Prussians have bought a lot on which many of their dead have been buried. The country all over, from Königgrätz to Sadowa, is dotted with graves, that are indicated by small black crosses. Otherwise there is but little evidence of a great battle having been fought so recently, the fields being in a fine state of cultivation, in which the small spaces occupied by graves alone are kept sacred. The position which the Austrians held at Chlum was as fine a one for a battle as any that can be conceived, and the heroism displayed by the Prussians must have been grand indeed. The country all around Königgrätz is exceedingly picturesque and fertile. The city is strongly fortified with moat and walls.

LETTER XIX.

THE AUSTRIANS.—THEIR PERSONAL POINTS.—THE IMPERIAL VAULTS IN THE CHURCH OF THE CAPUCHINS.—PALACE OF SCHONBRUNN.—UNIVERSITY OF VIENNA.—THE GENERAL HOSPITAL.—ROKITANSKY, THE PATHOLOGIST.—REV. DR. MANN, OF PHILADELPHIA.

VIENNA, *August*, 1867.

I ALLUDED, in my last communication, briefly to my visit to the Königgratz battle-field, and expressed surprise that the Austrians should have been so disastrously routed from a position of such strong natural advantages as that which Benedek and his forces had taken at the commencement of the battle. From what I have since observed in the general character of the good-natured Austrians, I am entirely convinced, that it is their manifest destiny, as it with rare exceptions ever has been, to lose battles, and not to win them. This opinion I have arrived at in no spirit of unkindness or prejudice whatever; for I am, on the contrary, rather prepossessed in their favor. They are such a dear, easy-going, pleasure-seeking, and amazingly civil people, that it is greatly to be wondered at how they ever have the hardihood to fire off a gun at all; and when they do so at their actual fellow beings, it seems to me that it must be with the apologetic reservation of the Quaker soldier, who, driven into battle under dire compunction, said to an enemy who would not go away, "Friend, I am sorry, but thee is standing where I am going to shoot."

Here in Vienna everything moves and is moved in a sort of dreamy languor, as if the people imbibed an infusion of poppy-heads for tea, and smoked opium for breakfast. If a person orders something to eat in a restaurant, he can consider himself very fortunate if he gets it after half an hour's waiting. Or, if he asks for anything in a store, the purchased article undergoes unheard-of evolutions before it changes proprietors, and much time is wasted with complimentary excess. The Bank is a circumlocutory office, and before the teller gets through with you, he moves lazily but smilingly into a half dozen different compartments, coming back from one to ask a civil question; from another, to make a pleasant remark; and from a third, to knock the ashes off his cigar. It is, indeed, marvellous how, in the limited period since the creation of the world, these good citizens of Vienna ever found time to build and absolutely finish so many great and beautiful palaces. For in the number and splendor of its edifices this city is probably second to none other of equal dimensions in Europe.

The nearly finished new opera-house excites the wonder and admiration of all; though a couple of years, it is said, are still necessary for its completion; whereas, if the thing was to be done at New York, a month at the most would suffice. This reminds me that I witnessed a performance the other night of the whole Mythology done up in an operatic play, called Orpheus in the Lower Regions; in which the ancient Jupiter shared my sentiments precisely about this Austrian languor; for, in scolding his children, Venus, Diana, Minerva, and others — all Viennese, of course — he accuses them of being always too late at breakfast, in consequence of which he was obliged to eat his ambrosia cold. Even the trains on the railroads of Austria run slower than in other countries, as if it was feared the engine might feel uncomfortable — they are so very considerate here. It does not appear that the people of Vienna can become passionate or excited; but life seems rather like a sweet dream of sensuality that sweeps in balmy wavelets over every soul, and envelops every physical organization in a mantle of serene content. Here Occident and Orient appear to meet on neutral ground in a kind of holy alliance, — barring the holy, — and a charitable forbearance with each other's frailties is the Alpha and Omega — the first constitutional article of their social deliberations.

In view of the fact that the Austrian people are exceedingly loyal to their imperial guardian, Francis Joseph, and sneeze very dutifully whenever he takes snuff, one would naturally think that the halcyon atmosphere of the public mind would have been ruffled not a little during the past year and better; for a grief happening to the House of Hapsburg is a family grief all over the country; and the defeat at Königgrätz, followed this year by the melancholy death of the Archduchess Matilda, and the still more lamentable fate of Maximilian of Mexico, have been events that certainly tried the sensational capacities of this House with uncommon rudeness. And in reality, too, the people have been for once what they call "*sehr aufgebracht*," especially at the summary proceeding with Maximilian.

Just now Francis Joseph and Napoleon are about having a meeting, for the purpose of condoling with each other, at Salzburg; which event is caricatured in the comic illustrated newspapers of Vienna by a head of Napoleon represented as the nucleus of a comet, followed by a long and streaming tail; and the terror-stricken Salzburgers exclaim: "Behold the comet; this surely portends a war!" for nothing would delight Austria so much as to set France and Prussia by the ears.

As at Paris, the people here are very fond of taking their meals, or-sipping their drinks, in the open air, under pretty pavilions or kiosks, and every hotel has some open ground attached to it for this purpose. There are, however, very large places of this kind for general resort, as Dommayer's Casino at Hietzing, at the Prater, and at the Volksgarten. At either of these places thousands may be seen every afternoon, smoking their cigars and drinking down the nectar of the grapes or barley, and drinking in, also, the delicious strains of soul-stirring music, under the personal direction of the great Strauss himself. Here ladies, in sweet companionship, make time fly swiftly by, or come by themselves to sit under the trees and knit, or chase their busy fingers in the skilful art of some beautiful embroidery. Nor will one of these latter deem it the slightest rudeness if a stranger with polite manners seats himself by her side, and enters into conversation with her. There is absolutely no necessity of securing an introduction first; but frankly and graciously she will probably chat and laugh along with him, as if she were a cousin of the stranger at least, and expected to go to a party with him in the evening. Music of some sort is performed here in these public gardens every day, either by the regimental bands or Strauss' great orchestral corps, and that from five o'clock until nine in the evening. Thus a taste for the divine art is cultivated among the masses, and, as a consequence, almost everybody prefers attending an opera to a drama; in fact, there are hardly any performances on the stage that are not more or less operatic in character. Nor is this to be wondered at; for who would not prefer witnessing a romance performed and expressed through the medium of touching melodies, rather than the unnatural ranting and declamatory violence of the old-fashioned drama? Thus I sat to the opera of the Huguenots a few evenings ago; and the sad story of St. Bartholomew's night was most effectively delineated by those grand and lofty strains, every note of which is full of religious sentiment, and the dulcet love-cadences in a constant though timid struggle with the former, the harmonious timing and blending of all which Meyerbeer has so signally achieved in this great production. And at Dresden I saw the representation of the opera of Rienzi, by Richard Wagner, the second act of which was the grandest musico-spectacular affair I ever beheld on any stage. It depicted one of those joyous festivals with which Rome, in the days of her greatest glory, celebrated all important occasions. There were songs, and processions, and dances, and gladiatorial combats, and the entire scene was dressed up in regal splendor. At least a hundred and fifty persons participated in the performance, and at the back of the spacious stage was a military band, playing in unison with that of the orchestra, and constituting at least eighty musicians in all. How could it have been possible to portray such a festival without the music? Nor was the impression less characteristic that was occasioned by the thrilling accompaniment of the grand finale, when — with a little perversion of history — the last of the tribunes and his sister perish in the flames of their burning palace.

A place of peculiar and solemn interest in Vienna is the vault in the church of the Capuchins, where rest the mortal remains of the Imperial family, from Kaiser Matthias, who died in 1619, to the unfortunate Archduchess Matilda, who was accidentally burned to death some few months ago in her own room, and whose ashes rest in the last sarcophagus that was deposited here. Should Admiral Tegethoff, who has been sent to Mexico for the body of the late Emperor, succeed in obtaining it, that also will be placed into this mausoleum. The vault is very capacious, and contains a great number of sarcophagi, many of which have been produced at enormous expense. That of Maria Theresa, for instance, cost a half million florins, and the one which holds the dust of Maria Louisa, the second wife of Napoleon I., is made of solid silver, and weighs sixteen hundred pounds. Her son, the Duke of Reichstadt, also reposes here. Threading one's way between the individual receptacles of these historic dead, much food there is for earnest meditation over frail mortality — that grim visitor who knows no distinction of persons of high or low degree, but equalizes kings and beggars, and strikes mercilessly home at the vanity of all. Leaving these premises where costly and extravagantly besculptured coffins constitute the very mockery of greatness, I passed into the abode of the living who are destined for, but have not yet reached, this goal of their short career.

The palace of Schönbrunn, the principal residence of the Emperor, is the most gorgeous of any that I have seen — exceeding that of St. Cloud in its internal magnificence. Under the guidance of an official, one may pass, when the family is absent, through all the apartments of the building, save only the chamber of the Empress; that of the Emperor is not withheld from the curious inspection of the visitor. The room is pointed out where the First Napoleon held his receptions, as the conquering hero, in 1809, being the same wherein the young Duke of Reichstadt afterward died. The suite of apartments that are, probably, most brilliantly furnished, are those in which the Sultan was installed a short time ago. A portion of the Palace is still retained in the condition it was in, and with the furniture it contained during the life-time of the great Empress Maria Theresa. Her boudoir was certainly a very charming retreat, of sextagonal sides, walled with mirrors, so that the lady could see her reflection multiplied as infinitely and variously, almost, as the visions of a kaleidoscope.

Then she had another room for private reception, in the centre of which an inlaid portion of the floor constitutes a table that could be caused, by means of some cunning mechanism, to descend into the apartments below, to be there supplied by the domestic myrmidons, and ascend again furnished with good things for the stomach's sake. By this ingenious contrivance, she could avoid the intrusive presence of servants and other household deities; for the number of her retinue — historians say — was great; and if they were half as gossipy as these necessary incumbrances are now-a-days, then this arrangement of the fair Empress was a marvel of utility. The latter clause, I am shocked to say, was the scandalous remark of my American friend.

The University of Vienna is a scholastic institution of the highest merit, the lectures of whose various faculties are attended by an aggregate number of some twenty-five hundred students, and by an equal additional number of honorary hearers. The general hospital is the most capacious asylum of the kind in Europe, and offers unequalled advantages to students of medicine in clinical and pathological studies. I here had the pleasure of forming the acquaintance of the world-renowned pathologist, Professor Rokitansky, and was quite captivated by his generous cordiality. This gentleman, during his valuable professional career, has thus far superintended, personally, the *post-mortem* examination of over fifteen thousand human subjects. His thorough and continued investigations through so many years of all manner of diseased conditions to which human flesh is heir, have so completely familiarized him with morbid and sound structure, and all the manifold distinctions between health and sickness, that before his quick and practised eye men are, as it were, of glass, so ready is he to detect any defectiveness in the human organization. As the skilful watchmaker discovers on a cursory glance the impaired machinery of a chronometer, the small particles of dust or thickened grease, that retard the motion of its wheels; the bent or broken teeth therein; the elongated or contracted lever; the disturbed balance-wheel; the broken main-spring; even so does Doctor Rokitansky take in, with a familiar look, the swollen liver, the enlarged heart, the wasted lungs, and all the cranky parts that disturb in its sublime motion the godlike mechanism of man. He has already distinguished himself so eminently that honors and titles are showered upon him from all sides. Yet he is as plain, single-hearted, and jolly a man as one might wish the whole world to be peopled with. Fortunately, he is still in the very prime and vigor of life; and may continue his usefulness to the human race with many important discoveries; for he is zealous in his labors, lives in the hospital, and is wedded only to science. His professional private duties consist chiefly in consultations, to which he is solicited by other physicians; when he never occupies himself with the treatment, but solely with the matter of establishing a diagnosis of the disease. In this his opinion is law, and respected as such by the entire faculty. If you go to Rokitansky with a sickness that is benignant in its nature and subjective to remedies, he will explain the difficulty and say everything for your encouragement. But if the stealthy fiend is gnawing at your vitals in some terrible or malignant shape, though it may not disturb your body with pain, or your mind with apprehensions, he will tell you that you are going to die, and then — with all the doctors and undertakers in Vienna, your doom is sealed.

The idiomatic modification and dialectic pronunciation of the German language by the masses of the people here are perfectly outrageous; they are as bad as Pennsylvania Dutch, and not very unlike it. My American friend, who understands the Old Keystone lingo to perfection, says he feels quite at home, and is passing himself off for a native Viennian all the time. The other day, however, he was taken aback somewhat, when a fruit-woman in the market-place told him to — "*Schonswoshipschopricosenurzdreikreitzerstick!*"

Much might be written yet of the noteworthy places of this city; but the description could only be similar to those that I have already given of other places. Here is the beautiful St. Stephen's Cathedral with one of the highest steeples in the world, and of a very pure order of Gothic architecture throughout. There are other magnificent churches, galleries of paintings and temples of sculpture; monuments and museums, all of great merit and most interesting associations. Worthy of special mention is the monumental group in the St. Augustin's church, dedicated to the memory of the Archduchess Maria Christina, daughter of Maria Theresa. It was executed by

Canova for the sum of twenty thousand ducats, and is said to be one of the *chefs-d'œuvre* of that distinguished genius.

My visit to Vienna was made doubly agreeable through meeting, on the train hither, with the Rev. Dr. Mann, pastor of the German Lutheran Zion's Church, of Philadelphia, who is here on a visit, expecting to return to America next month. Together we went sight-seeing, exchanging sentiments, and comparing opinions over the various subjects that engaged our attention. And when he was obliged to leave, in another direction from that which I was going, I felt like separating from an old friend, rather than from the casual acquaintance of a few days. For, after all, this travelling and going into ecstacies over the fading glories of the old world is deprived of its greatest charm when there is no one to share the pleasures of it.

LETTER XX.

OVER THE SEMMERING.

VISIT TO A WONDERFUL CAVE AT ADELSBERG.—TRIESTE. THE CHOLERA MORTALITY IN ITALY.—SUPERSTITION AND IGNORANCE OF THE PEOPLE.—VENICE.—FUMIGATION PROCESS ON ENTERING THE CITY.—CURIOSITIES OF THE PLACE.—MILAN.—ITS MAGNIFICENT CATHEDRAL.—THE LAKE OF COMO.—GENOA—ARRIVAL IN FLORENCE.

FLORENCE, *August*, 1867.

LEAVING Vienna for Trieste, I passed over one of the most romantic railroad routes that have thus far been completed; threading its way through and between the Styrian Alps, and over the particular one known as the Semmering, at the highest point of which the road is nearly three thousand feet above the Adriatic Sea. It crosses valleys and rivers over viaducts and bridges to the number of fifteen, and traverses equally as many tunnels; and the scenery along the entire distance of three hundred miles is of the wildest and most picturesque description.

At Adelsberg, a town about fifty miles north of Trieste, I stayed over till the following day, in order to visit under the adjacent mountain the renowned cave, similar to our Mammoth Cave in Kentucky, and which, indeed, presented to my astonished gaze the most wonderful and stupendous eccentricity of nature that I ever beheld. Entering the cave, in company with two English gentlemen and five guides, through a door of iron grating, we passed along a subterranean gangway a distance of a hundred yards or more, when we reached a vast expansion of it, called the Dome, at least a hundred feet high, and the same in width through every direction. Before proceeding farther, I should state, that the entire cave had been illuminated for us, at a reasonable expense, with a great number of lights, amounting in all to over a thousand. We passed along the side of this dome over a corridor or gallery of rock, midway between floor and ceiling, and over two natural bridges, under which a stream of water called the Piuka runs along, and is lost to human ken under the mountain, appearing again in the outer world at a distance from here of about eight miles. This stream, in connection with the section of the cave close by known as the Region of Pluto, fills one's mind with all the dread imagery of a veritable river Styx. What if old Charon should come along with his ugly boat to transport our souls before they were ready; in which dreadful case, never having been honored with funerals, we might have been doomed to wander about in that sepulchral region for a hundred years. (See Lempriere.) As it was, the murmuring sound of this rushing water, coming up from the gloomy depth into the grave-like stillness of these parts, was ominously perplexing to folks of tender nerves. We passed onwards in the windings of this cavernous channel, ascending and descending in its course, and turning angles to the right and left, till we reached another expansion forming a great chamber, known as the Dancing-Hall, which affords comfortable room for a thousand persons. Further on two considerable acclivities of the cave are called the one, the Greater, and the other, the Lesser Mount Calvary; though wherein the analogy consists it is difficult to conceive. In traversing briskly the whole of these subterranean passages, we required precisely two hours' time, from which circumstance some idea may be formed of their capacity. Almost throughout the entire cave the ceiling is studded with innumerable stalactites, large and small, and presenting shapes and figures of every conceivable description; as curtains, hanging in folds of surprising naturalness, appearing like woven texture of alternate white and red-colored stripes — the red being occasioned by the droppings of ferruginous waters — and are perfectly translucent when a light is placed behind them. There are shapes, too, that have an exact similitude to an organ in a church, with all its pipes in view; of pulpits and thrones, and, in short, all manner of eccentric configurations. From the floor of the cave, in numerous places, stalagmites ascend in most grotesque shapes, as of human beings, animals, palm-trees, and cypress. In many instances the stalactites from above, and the opposing stalagmites from below have gradually increased in the direction toward each other, until, ultimately, they united and coalesced, forming solid pillars of Gothic description, resembling, in many instances, the time-faded columns of some old churches and cathedrals, some of them being six feet in diameter, and display an architecture of rare perfection, appearing especially designed to support the vaulted roof of this extensive cavern. When we reflect that all this has been wrought by the gradual deposit and solidification of earthy matter from the droppings of water that take place here, we cannot but be utterly bewildered in contemplating what centuries upon centuries must have elapsed in these wonderful formations.

On Whitmonday of every year great festivities are celebrated in this cave, on which occasion it is illuminated with over five thousand lights; a grand ball is held in the Dancing-Hall mentioned above, with all its accessories of music, banqueting, &c., and is participated in by a great concourse of people that mostly journey hither from Trieste and Vienna.

From Adelsburg the railroad passes over the bleakest, most desolate, God-forsaken country imaginable; but enters a tunnel at length, and emerges suddenly at Trieste in a land where myrtle and olive and fig-trees grow in abundance; where luscious grapes are already ripe, and excite devouring meditations; where the wide expanse of the Adriatic Sea charms the fancy, and seems the very Tethy's lap wherein Phœbus snuffs out his light, and sinks into calm repose.

Here, too, I came at last into a country where no overcoat is necessary; for, with few exceptional days, I was obliged to protect my person with such an article against the inclemency of the weather during the entire summer, which, it is said, was an unusually cold one. But, putting all things together, I am satisfied that the climate of Pennsylvania is very considerably milder than that of Central Europe.

Trieste is an important commercial city, and bears

TRIESTE ON THE ADRIATIC.   285

about the same relation to Austria that Hamburg does to northern Germany. A great deal of traffic by shipping is carried on there; and its population is composed of people from all parts of the globe, Italians being rather in the preponderance. Next follow, in succession, Germans, French, Greeks, Turks, English, and Americans; and the intermingling of all these people of different languages is exceedingly droll. There is a French and a Greek church at Trieste; and the latter being open for service every morning and evening, I took occasion to enter it at one of these times, but cannot say that I was greatly edified; for the worship was all Greek to me, and, unfortunately, only addressed itself to my curious admiration in the light of a sacred pantomime.

It was a beautiful evening; the moon was just full, and the sky as clear and serene as a "pure Italian sky" can possibly be; when, with pleasant anticipations of a moonlight sail, in the true spirit of poetry, over the Adriatic to Venice, I took up my portmanteau, and proceeded to the steamer. There arrived, the officer of the vessel greatly disappointed me with the statement, that all passengers arriving at Venice by sea were obliged to lay fifteen days in quarantine, on account of the cholera which is said to prevail in Trieste, as well as all through Italy. Having neither time nor inclination for such an adventure, I was perforce constrained to reverse my steps, and proceed to the railroad depot; and thence, by the first train, adopt the most practicable way of reaching Venice.

In relation to the subject of cholera, I would state, that it has, beyond doubt, assumed a very grave form, and made fearful ravages, especially in southern Italy. From January to July, as many as 63,376 cases have been reported, of which 32,074 died. The Sicilian provinces have been the most seriously affected, and among the deaths there was that of the Queen-Dowager of Naples. More than half the aggregate cases have proved fatal. Not one of the forty provinces of Italy have been spared, though in some cities, such as Florence, only a few cases have occurred. Besides this, a moral disease, quite as alarming as the physical malady, has been observed throughout Italy, especially in the Calabrias and Sicily, though even the northern provinces are not free from its contagion. This is, the idea that poisonous agencies have been disseminated by malevolent means; and the mind of the suffering population is greatly excited by this horrid apprehension. The soldiers are supposed to be in some mysterious manner connected with the cholera; and a thirst for vengeance is felt by the people, though both officers and men have shown an unremitting zeal and kindness in the care of the suffering and sick. At Mellila, near Syracuse, such was the excitement of the populace, owing to their belief that poison had been administered by agents of the Italian Government, that a large meeting was held in the dead of night in the public cemetery, at which it was resolved, "that all the Carabiniere and Italian agents resident in the place should be killed for spreading the cholera." The plot was fortunately discovered and frustrated by the authorities. At Catania nearly all the shops are closed, and all who had sufficient means have escaped from the city.

Prowling dogs and ravenous mendicants have the place almost entirely to themselves, and the whole active work of life is performed by the soldiers, who too frequently fall victims to their arduous and overstrained labors. They nurse the sick and bury the dead, and, in return for their kindness, meet with scoffs and maledictions. The agitation is indescribable throughout the country, even in the northern portion, and in the polished and enlightened city of Milan itself. Just now the cholera prevails to a considerable extent in Rome, still more at Naples, and fearfully so at Palermo.

I arrived at last, by railroad, at Venice, where I was greatly surprised to find all the passengers driven into a room like a flock of sheep, to be fumigated with chlorine, as a preventative against spreading the cholera. This made matters look a little serious, and persons of constitutional timidity might be frightened into sickness by such a very elaborate caution against it. Besides, the ordeal is excessively annoying, especially to people with tender throats or eyes, to say nothing of the ugly impression it makes upon the sense of smell. We were kept in this chlorinated room about fifteen minutes, during which time all had to expose their luggage to be fumed as well as their persons. It was amusing to observe the different manners in which this fumigation was submitted to. Some groaned, and stuffed handkerchiefs into their mouths; others swore and grumbled knowingly about "such infernal nonsense," "ridiculous farces," "imperious fools," and such things; whilst some, and the more sensible portion, took it all down as a good joke, with much merriment and funny remarks. Since my initiation into the process at Venice, I have been fumigated at every place where I stayed over, at least a dozen times in all, and have come to the conclusion that it is an institution which would not meet with great favor from the travelling public of the United States. I can fancy our ladies, for instance, being obliged to unpack their Saratogas in every station-house, and spread out their wardrobes on extended lines, to be scented with the asphyxiating vapors of chlorine, and become the subject of mutual critical observations about their character of material, the cut of their yokes, and the style and finish of their embroidery. Phew! what a jolly riot! what another War of the Roses there would be! what a refreshing rebellion, after the two years' peace that we have had! though it is doubtful whether all the "hirelings" of the North and South combined could quell it.

To return to Venice. Wonderful place! that seems like the very Noah's ark of cities, which had been built there by unusually cute and perhaps sinful people, in anticipation of another deluge. Just to think of it! A large city resting on a submarine foundation, rearing her capricious head from the blue water as if in coquetry with Neptune, and hoisting her jib-sails, splicing her main braces, and shivering her timbers in derisive scorn of her more land-lubberly sisters; a city wherein residents may be met who have grown gray with years, and have never set foot upon continental soil; where a person may step into the street and take a bath; or fish for sardines with a hook and line out of his chamber-window. Where mothers tie cords around their children's waists by which they support them while they learn to swim in the highways, co-even with their first efforts at walking in the houses. The Venetians are an amphibious people: nobody ever commits suicide by drowning; if they ever attempt it, the cool bath sobers them — produces a reflex action, and they calmly swim back to life again. Indeed, of all the cities that I have visited, none has left a more lasting impression upon my mind than this same curious Venice. I never had been able to realize how thoroughly that beautiful Queen of the Adriatic is immersed in water; and when the train of cars in which I was approaching it was crossing the beautiful bridge, about three miles long or more, (and somewhat in construction like that which spans the Susquehanna at Havre de Grace,) which connects Venice with the land, over the narrowest portion of the lagoon, I first began to comprehend a dim notion of the reality. And when I stepped out of the depot right down into an omnibus gondola, which then shot rapidly through the watery avenues, passing hundreds of other similar boats; turning corners every now and then, and taking the nearest road to a distant point of the city, even as one would through the solid streets of other places; seeing foot-passengers nowhere, and hearing no sound of horse or vehicle; quietness prevailing as you glide noiselessly along over the smooth water, at full noon of the day, — a quietness approaching that of dead midnight in other towns,— then I began to feel as if I had arrived at a city that was floating leisurely about in the sea, independent of all and any thing like the solid foundations of the common earth. Most of the houses are built upon vertical piles that are driven into the ground under the water; and some of the large churches and old palaces are supported by thousands of these piles standing side by side in close proximity, and forming a basis of the most enduring character; for the wood, instead of decaying, is acted on by the salt water exerting a peculiar chemical influence, which, as it were, petrifies it; and thus the oldest foundations are also the strongest of the present day in Venice.

Probably the principal object of interest in this city is the Palace of the Doges, whose senate-halls, chambers of justice (?) Bridge of Sighs, dungeons, and the receptaculi for the letters of those innumerable spies, recall vivid recollections of the history of that strange, cruel, and inquisitorial republic. Passing through the Bridge of Sighs, I could not resist a melancholy tremor in thinking of the many who had passed that way before me with bowed heads, crushed spirits, and hopeless hearts — who knew that no criminal ever crossed this bridge but once, and that then its passage terminated in certain execution. Another object of interest is the Bridge of the Rialto, which is especially curious for containing twenty-four shops, in and around which the busiest traffic takes place. To any one with a keen relish for the ludicrous, this bridge and the scenes around it must needs afford any quantity of amusement. The bustle and turmoil and eternal chattering among the immeasurably comic admixture of people, is enough to fill a body with the very anguish of delight. And as an evidence of the fact to what curious retreats the English language is capable of penetrating, I would mention the circumstance that, while gazing into and admiring the contents of one of the shop-windows on this Bridge of the Rialto, my ears were suddenly greeted with the voice of a mother, jumping her infant child up and down upon her knee, addressing it with the familiar words of the classic and refined passage:

"Dickery, dickery, dock; the mouse ran into the clock;
The clock struck one, and *out* it ran; dickery, dickery, dock!"

Need I add, that this inspired specimen of our beautiful language moved me almost unto tears? I ascertained, on entering the shop to inquire about some Venetian trinkets, that the fond mother was a Jewess who had passed the earlier portion of her life in London.

At one end of the bridge is a column of Egyptian marble, supported by the figure of a kneeling slave, called Gobbo; from which column the proclamations of the Senate, during the time of the Republic, were issued. On it also, it is said, the merchant of Venice, Antonio, was publicly exposed and disgraced, because he "failed in business," by a swindling wild-cat operation;— quite a different story from that which Shakspeare gives of the affair.

All sorts of curious places are pointed out to the stranger; among them the residence, for a time, of Lord Byron; that of Petrarch the poet, who immortalized not only himself, but the Laura whom he loved so dearly; the home wherein Titian, the artist, lived for many years, and died at the advanced age of ninety-nine years, having occupied himself with painting to within a very few years of his death; the palace of the eminent Taglioni, who had come into great possessions because she understood how to dance — certainly her *understanding* had been very useful to her; the house of Lucretia Borgia is also shown; and even — just to think! — the parental residence of Desdemona, the spoony but innocent victim of Othello's jealousy.

The first church (and the one pointed out in my guide-book as that of greatest interest) that I went to see was the St. Giovanni e Paolo, but upon approaching it, observed a great confusion and crowd of people — a hurrying hither and thither with buckets of water — a hydraulic pump in full operation, and, in short, all the evidences of a fire. The interior of the church had been burning, and the fire was just about being subdued; but many valuable relics and paintings, to the estimated amount of twenty million francs, had been destroyed. It is supposed that the church was set on fire by the Dominican friars; and thereby hangs a tale. It seems that ever since the reign of Victor Emanuel over Italy there has been a great war between the Dominican and Capuchin friars on the one side, and the so-called Evangelical priesthood on the other. The king and a great majority of the people support the latter; and recently a decree had been passed depriving the friars of all ecclesiastical rights and privileges; and the day of the fire was that appointed for them to give up the keys of the churches and cloisters heretofore under their charge. The coincidence has occasioned the suspicion alluded to; and up to the present day the friars have been confined in the church under military guard; and will continue to be so (the papers say) until the matter has been properly investigated. What a melancholy picture this bare suspicion presents to the mind! How much of truth there is in Pope's lines:—

> "Aspiring to be gods, the angels fell;
> Aspiring to be angels, men rebel."

How can religion prosper as it should when doctors of divinity are almost as savage, and jealous, and envious, and fault-finding with each other's creeds as doctors of medicine? Will the blessed millennium ever arrive when charity and good feeling shall characterize the human family as it ought to?

Talking about charity reminds me of a species of live stock which enters into the animated nature of Venice that has *no* charity whatever. Allusion is made to the mosquitoes. I have erstwhile encountered some of the distinguished foreigners in other lands, known as the gallinippers of New Jersey; but alongside of their Venetian brethren they might have hung their guilty heads in shame. For these surpass them in the science of phlebotomy so eminently, that henceforth I shall look upon the insertion of a Jerseyite mosquito's frail proboscis with pity for his powerless efforts, and as a pleasant contrast to the fleshing I endured in Venice.

The romance that attaches itself to this place *par*

excellence, is associated chiefly with its aqueous thoroughfares, lined by long borders of lordly mansions — many of them dismantled and unoccupied, decaying relics of the olden time; thoroughfares that are spanned by numerous bridges of every conceivable character and design; of which the one that is composed exclusively of glass, the Ponte Vecchio, the Bridge of the Rialto, and the famous Bridge of Sighs are those most worthy of mention. On these canals the gondolas are the almost universal means of intercourse and transport. They are built in all manner of fashions as to style and elegance and material, though they vary but little in shapes. There are gondola fanciers here as there are horse fanciers elsewhere; and the fancy prices to which some of these gayly mounted (with roofs, against rain and sunshine, similar to carriage-tops) and gorgeously upholstered vessels range is quite in keeping with our prices for blooded horses. Races on the Canal Grande are quite an institution; and the excitement on such occasions runs equally high with that of those on *terra firma*. Every male citizen of Venice understands, of course, how to row a gondola — to be incapable of which would be eminently disgraceful; yet there are some thousands of public gondoliers corresponding to all cab and omnibus drivers in other cities. These are a gallant, genteelly clad, orderly, and well-behaved class of men, that season their occupation with a sprinkling of romance whenever opportunity offers. They are high-toned fellows — proud of their profession, and have a fine sense of honor — evidences of their sterling integrity being of daily occurrence. A short time before my arrival, a woman who kept a small wine-saloon, went to a merchant with something more than a thousand francs to purchase some wines; but not being satisfied with the qualities that were offered her, she returned without buying, but dropped her *porte-monnai* in the gondola before leaving it. After she was gone the gondolier found the money, and on the evening of the next day proceeded to the woman's little shop; whereupon she related to him with tears and lamentation the sad misfortune of her loss; and on his inquiring how she supposed the mishap to have occurred, she replied that she must have dropped it somewhere in the water. The gondolier partook of some refreshment for which he paid; then he restored to the woman her lost money, accompanied by a little sensible advice to take better care of it in the future. Her joy was unbounded; and she instantly offered him a generous dividend from the recovered property; but he would not permit her to reward his honesty with a single centime; yet his self-denial did not extend so far as to reject the kisses and endearments which she lavished upon him in what I was told is the true Italian style.

During one of the wars which Venice waged in the day of her republican glory and military prowess, a carrier-pigeon was intrusted with an important despatch from a general in the field to the authorities at home. The despatch was received just in time to permit reinforcements to be sent to the seat of war, by which the general was enabled to gain a victory on the very heels of a disastrous defeat. Ever since, all pigeons have been held in sacred veneration by the Venetians. There are many thousand of this genus of the feathered tribe in the city, having their living — like true government officials — from the public crib. It is remarkable to witness the accuracy of their instinct, when every afternoon, precisely as the town-clock strikes two, they come flying in flocks from all parts of the city to be fed in the Piazza or St. Mark's Place — which is the principal one of the few public resorts where the people may promenade on a solid bottom.

On this same St. Mark's or Marcus Place I have also heard the finest instrumental music to which it was ever my good fortune to listen. Every evening from eight to ten o'clock, it is the custom of the military band, consisting of about fifty young men of handsome mien, tall and erect stature, magnificently uniformed, to perform at this place for the delight and entertainment of the crowds of impassioned listeners, principally composed of the fashion and beauty of the city, that promenade in this square — which latter is brilliantly illuminated by the numerous gas-lights of the dazzling shop-windows that surround it, and a chandelier lamp-post with many burners that send a bright glare in every direction from its centre. Although the Germans have the reputation of being the best instrumental musicians, yet, to my taste, all that I heard in the Prater of Vienna, or the operas of Munich and Dresden, though eminently grand and sublime, was not equal in delicious sweetness and softness of tonicity to that exquisite discourse of the divine art, which fairly bewildered my senses in this lovely city on the water. I have stood upon one spot, a wrapt listener for two hours, without the least consciousness of the tiresome fact; but felt more, if the truth must be told, as if I was flying rather than standing. The Italian music in itself contains more dreamy poetry and flexibility to my ears than any other; and as it was there rendered, it made the ethereal air tremulous with the very intensity of harmonic sounds.

I cannot omit, in concluding the subject of Venice, to relate my casual observation of one of those melancholy events that wind up the affairs of man all the world over, namely, a funeral. About a mile from the city is situated a small island that is appropriated as a cemetery. As I was scudding along through the Canal Grande, among the many places of interest to be seen there, my attention was arrested by a long procession of gondolas. In the front was one somewhat larger than the rest, which is called a *barke*, and covered with a frame-work draped in black similar to our hearses. Behind it were several gondolas filled with priests, who were chanting, all the while, in a solemn undertone, the evident service of some religious ceremony. These were followed by quite a number of other gondolas filled with silent attendants on the occasion. I had no difficulty in divining that it was a cortege of mourners conveying a fellowbeing to his last resting-place. Noiselessly it glided on over the still waters; and aside from the novelty of its character to my unaccustomed sight, the scene was one fraught with peculiar and earnest impressiveness.

I now crossed the " Italian boot " just about where the straps might be supposed to exist — taking Venice on the Adriatic as one; and Genoa, on the Mediterranean coast, as the other.

The first city that I took a brief look at was Padua, celebrated for its classic university that has sent forth so many learned doctors—not excepting Shakspeare's creation, the fair Portia, whose ingenious argument settled so thoroughly the little matter of old Shylock's bond. Then a glimpse at Verona, whose arena, it is said, will serve to break somewhat the surprise occasioned by the first sight of the Coliseum at Rome. Here, too, one feels an instinctive impulse, as it were, to look for the "tomb of the Capulets," where should repose (if Shakspeare wasn't such a story-teller) the gentle Romeo and Juliet. The tomb is such a familiar scene upon the stage, that one would be able to recognize it at a glance.

Proceeding to the city of Milan, I went over the historic ground and the rivers Tagliamento, Mincio, and Adda—a great portion of that Quadrilateral made memorable by many battles, but especially those of Solferino and Magenta.

Milan is a large, handsome, busy, and apparently very prosperous city; but is distinguished principally —at least in the estimation of all tourists—for the grand Cathedral which it contains; to enter upon a description of which would take much more space than I have at command, and convey no adequate idea in the end. The only way to obtain this is to see the colossal pile of marble itself, which presents in its complicated construction the astounding number of seven thousand distinct statues; to go into its interior and wander through its five great naves and forest of columns of gigantic proportions; and then to ascend its highest pinnacle and look down upon the wilderness of spires, each one surmounted by a statue from the hands of the ablest sculptors. The view from the dome of this Cathedral, of the snow-crowned Alps on the one side, and the rich vegetation on the far-reaching plains of Italy on the other, is one of indescribable beauty and grandeur. Here, too, I witnessed for the first time that the proverbial beauty of an Italian sky is a reality, and no fiction; for viewed from a short distance through the empty spaces of some marble railing that ornaments the top of the Cathedral, it seemed to make windows of these railings, and filled the spaces with apparent glass of a soft azure hue, and the best Bohemian manufacture. The genius who could invent such a color, and such ethereal texture to line the walls and ceilings of our chambers with, would immortalize himself, amass an incalculable fortune, and translate our sublunary dwelling-places into paradisiacal abodes.

From Milan I went to the Lake of Como, and took a steamboat excursion on its water as far as Bellaggio. The numerous villas on its precipitous shores of sloping mountains, and the luxurious vegetation with which these shores are clothed, afford a pleasing prospect to the eye in every direction. My American friend kept a sharp lookout for Claude Melnotte's

> "Palace lifting to eternal summer
> Its marble walls, from out a glossy bower
> Of coolest foliage, musical with birds,
> Whose songs should syllable" the name of Pauline.

There were plenty of such palaces, as well as the "breathless heavens," and "arching vines;" the "orange groves" and "murmurs of low fountains," too, were there; and even the "alabaster lamps" and "music from sweet lutes" were doubtless present in the evening, (I did n't stop to see,) whilst Melnottes and Paulines were sprinkled all over the country in extravagant profusion. At Bellaggio especially, the scenery is quite tropical and lovely in the extreme. There was no spot that I could call my own; but I sheltered myself from the warm sun under somebody else's "vine and fig-tree," and dreamed of Tennyson's beautiful poem — *in a garden*. My next route was by rail to Genoa, through Pavia and Alessandria, over the rivers Ticino and Po; and crossing the Apennine mountains through deep gullies and numerous tunnels, one of which it took the train ten minutes to traverse. To an American the city of Genoa would naturally be interesting from its associations with the discoverer of our country, Christopher Columbus, to whose memory the Genoese appear much more attentive now than they were to him while living; for the monument erected to him of the purest Carrara marble is one of the finest I have seen. The city has all the appearance of a busy, bustling seaport, and, for the rest, is scattered about the mountain sides a great deal worse than Pottsville. It has an old, somewhat slovenly look, and was enveloped, when I was there, in a rather disagreeable odor. In a word, I shall never become a citizen of Genoa.

The dinner that was served at *table d'hôte* the day that I was at Genoa, deserves, methinks, a little more than a passing notice, and shall have it. In the first place, there was Vermicelli soup, into a plateful of which every guest put a tablespoonful of grated Parma cheese. After this was dispatched, we had butter and sardines; then some fried sole, (more fish,) with a slice of lemon. Next, roast veal, with dressing consisting of boiled rice, tomatoes, potatoes, and sourkrout, all on the same dish. This was followed by boiled macaroni, (*not* the kind we buy in the candy-shops,) highly flavored with onions. Then again, roast chicken, cut up in very small pieces, and all covered over with a batter of eggs and a thick sprinkling of young pepper-pods. Next, thin slices of broiled beef all curled up (apparently under the agony of broiling) with a dressing of young lettuce and some more onions. Now followed some kind of pudding, made principally, I think, of macaroni and onions, which was succeeded by a slice of cheese — *not* Parma cheese — and a slice of butter. After this ensued the desert, consisting of sweet cakes, peaches, fresh figs, grapes, watermelons, cantaloupes almonds, and walnuts. During the whole of the meal there had been a plentiful supply of ice-water and wine. I would like to know how it is possible to get the cholera on such living?

Leaving Genoa, I travelled fourteen hours in a *diligence*, all the time in view of the Mediterranean Sea, to Spezzia, and thence per railroad to Leghorn and Pisa. In the latter place I ascended the Leaning Tower, and entered the cathedral, in which, as the most noteworthy thing, may be mentioned the chandelier suspended from the ceiling of the dome, from which Galileo made his first observations of the pendulum in reference to the rotation of the earth. From Pisa two hours of very quick travelling by railroad brought me to Florence, all aglow with expectations, and still more with the temperature of the weather.

LETTER XXI.

LUXURIANT VEGETATION OF ITALY.—THE ITALIAN BEGGARS.—ART.—A VISIT TO THE STUDIO OF HIRAM POWERS.—MY AMERICAN FRIEND'S ADVENTURES.—FROM FLORENCE TO ROME.—A FAIR SNUFFER.—POETICAL EFFUSION OF M. A. F.—THOUGHTS ON THE ETERNAL CITY.—THE CATHEDRALS OF ST. PETER AND ST. PAUL.—HIS HOLINESS, PIUS IX.

ROME, *September*, 1867.

"Kennst du das Land wo die Citronen blühn,
Im dunkeln Laub die Gold-Orangen glühn?"

A JOURNEY through Italy at this season of the year impresses the tourist not only with the triumphs of Art, but also with the abundant generosity of Nature which this land enjoys. Its cereal vegetation does not indeed appear as thrifty as in the greater portion of our own country, and its grass looks strangely sallow and stunted in growth; but the great variety and luxuriousness of its flowers, vines, and, mostly, fruit-bearing trees, afford a panorama of bewildering effect, and such a plentiful harvest of good things to eat, with no apparent labor but the picking of them, that one almost comprehends a natural excuse for the idleness of the Italian people.

There are places where the railroad passes not only through sporadic groves, but whole forests of olive and fig-trees. All around may be seen, scattered about in delightful disorder, peaches, plums, and pears; whilst the blushing apples, pomegranates, and golden-cheeked lemons and oranges peep, half concealed but lovingly, from out their dark-green foliage, or glitter in the sunlight as the train speeds rapidly along. There are great fields of a tall vegetable that resembles sugar-cane, but contains little or no saccharine matter, the leaves of which are used for fodder, and the stalks to support the grape-vines, which grow as natural here as weed, and bend under the weight of their luscious burden. Almonds, hazelnuts, and walnuts abound in great affluence; and I have passed over miles of country where chestnut-trees are as plenty as pine-trees in Schuylkill County, and look far more dangerous with their multitude of bristling burs, than the *nulle me tangeres*, or touch-me-nots, of our hot-house cultivation. The palm, acacia, pine, cypress, myrtle, and pepper are the ornamental trees of the country, and a great variety of the cactus adorn the gardens, some of them attaining a remarkable size. The flowers are so numerous and diversified in hue, that they constitute the natural school for artists in the study of colors.

Thus Italy truly enjoys the blessings of nature to a rare extent; and it is with unfeigned pleasure that I feel enabled to express the conviction, that from the present union of its States, and a judicious rule of Victor Emanuel, a thorough and radical change will take place, that will greatly improve the social condition, and further materially the power and prosperity of the nation. Already, I am told, during the past few years, the cities of Venice, Milan, Florence, and the country generally have brightened up greatly, and manifested an industrial impulse and energy for a long time unknown. The King is generally liked by his subjects, and their admiration for that modern Cincinnatus, Garibaldi, amounts to absolute enthusiasm. With all this, however, there is a great deal in the character of these people deserving of unsparing censure; and whatever improvement is taking place in their moral and social status, is all the more gratifying because there is such wonderful room for it. It is a pity that the Italian people are not possessed of a little more pride—not the pride that clusters around their fine arts; they have plenty of that, the dear knows; but that other quality of pride, which would restrain them somewhat in the practice of their very *vulgar* arts of begging and cheating. They appear to consider themselves lawfully entitled to all the money that anybody brings into the country, and the manner of getting it is a mere matter of talent. Thus at Florence, for instance, on desiring my landlord's bill, I found it fully three times the amount of the usual hotel charges. I had been cautioned against such attempts, and advised to resist them; so I became quite exasperated, and opened on his sensitive Italian ears with such a running fusillade of indignation, such a tirade of abuse, expressed in the horridest, most stupifying American-French he ever listened to, I'll warrant me, in all the days of his life.—*En passant:* it is wonderful how a body can talk French under excitement; probably the language was originally invented for the special accommodation of angry people, or people in love, which, after all, when critically analyzed, amounts to about the same thing, for in both instances it is necessary to be a little beside one's self.—Well, the landlord astonished me with some obsequious twaddle about mistakes, and reduced the bill just *one half*. This circumstance is only mentioned because it illustrates the want of pride above alluded to—in the first place, that the man made such an unscrupulous overcharge; and, in the second place, because he didn't stick to it, like an American would have done after he *had* made it.

Beggars of every description waylay the stranger from all sides, and contribute an annoying constraint upon all his movements, especially in and before the churches, and in all public places. Young boys and girls, and old, palsied women are alike impressive with their demands; while stout, stalwart men desire a pittance for "macaroni" with an imperiousness that makes one almost feel criminally indebted to them, and wonder whether their demand is not backed by a writ of ejection, which they are ready to produce at your first sign of refusal to "poney up." It was not the season during which one might see Florence in its gayest aspect; for the number of strangers in the city was very small, and they, after all, add greatly to the life and attractiveness of all Italian cities. Yet on Sunday afternoon and evening the Lung Arno, its principal street, was quite lively with fashionable turnouts and pedestrian promenaders, whilst the river was motley with many boats, containing, apparently, very happy and troubadourish swains, who made the air vocal with loud songs until late into the night.

Whoever travels in Italy cannot help but unite, in a measure at least, a study of the arts with whatever else may constitute his special motive. Even individuals whose plain understanding does not grasp anything beyond the matter-of-fact realities of life — who have no soul for ideal loveliness, no æsthetical conception of the sublime, — when they come here, they unconsciously, and involuntarily, almost, become admirers of Art. For in Italy, Art is so intimately interwoven with Nature, and so thoroughly associated with the ordinary habitudes of life, as if a knowledge of architecture, painting, and sculpture was a part of the organic law of the land. At every step the creations of human genius arrest the eye; and it is but necessary to breathe, to walk, and to gaze, to become comparative connoisseurs. Every church is a temple of art, every palace an academy of designs, and every public square a colonnade of statues. Next to Rome, Florence is in this respect probably the most replete city in the world; but an adequate description of it comes not within the compass of my letter. Suffice it to say, that it is there where the original of the world-renowned Venus di Medicis, (which, by the way, is in my estimation far inferior to the Capitoline Venus at Rome,) that of Canova, and the Madonna della Seglia may be seen. On this subject I would mildly throw out the opinion, that the hypercritical theory of fanatic artists, namely, that no creation on canvas or in marble, however nude it may appear, can suggest any vulgarity to the perfectly pure-minded spectator, is a bit of enthusiastic fiction; and it is disgraceful that in the boasted refinement of our age the world submits to the public exposure of such works as the Venuses of Titian, or the statues just mentioned, whose very semblance to nature constitutes their objectionable quality.

One of the cheerfullest reminiscences of my sojourn in Europe will ever be my visit to the studio of Hiram Powers, the American sculptor at Florence. He detained me a long time, and was exceedingly obliging, taking me through all his rooms, and conferring, in the running conversation, much useful information on the subject of his beautiful art. Nor was it from any motives of business; for I apprised him at the beginning of our interview that I could make no purchases, and my visit would therefore be an absolute trespass upon his time and kindness. He had in his studio a copy of his Greek Slave, (the price of which is $4000, if any of my readers would like to have it,) another of his statue of California, and was working on a model of a third, to be called the Last of the Tribes. These works are second to no modern productions; but, unfortunately, there is the aforesaid objection to them, of deficiency in the matter of drapery — or, rather, no drapery at all. Mr. Powers was very chatty, and appears to keep himself well posted in the political affairs of our country. He gave his opinion about President Johnson "in phrases not equivocal," and said that one of the greatest trials of his life was that he could not exercise his privilege of the elective franchise.

With a view of going thoroughly into the merits

of this classic city, my American friend signified his desire to have an English guide, to accompany him in the pursuit of knowledge. Presently a little, sharp-featured, wiry-looking old man presented himself before him, with such a spasmodic motion, as if some invisible imp from behind was constantly pricking his flesh with an invisible pin. He had, under his pale, thin, Florentine nose, such a heavy moustache, that the weight of it seemed to pull his head forward, and ever and anon he would jerk it back, like a man constantly catches himself going to sleep in church. He was dressed in a rather shabby-genteel suit of clothes, had a very high, somewhat dented, and faded silk hat under his arm, and an umbrella in his hand.

"Are you the guide I sent for?" said M. A. F.

"Yes, seer," replied he, with a series of contortions that were meant for bows.

"Do you understand English?"

"Yes, seer, I spik Ingliss veree gude."

"Where did you learn it?"

"Oh, seer, I can told you zat I haf lif twentee ye-ars in zee London. You von Signor Americano? Ah, yes, seer — I haf also lif von long time in America. It ees von veree bootiful contree. I haf travel wiz zee lords and zee princes veree much."

"Well," said M. A. F., "you are no great shakes at our good Yankee English, anyhow; but come along and show me what there is to see in this cracked-up town of yours."

So off they started — these two, by force of circumstances, approximated strangers — like twin brothers, in search of useful and ornamental wonders.

After staring their way through the house of Michael Angelo; climbing the Campanile; wandering through the Boboli garden; and then committing to their souls the beauties of the Palazzo Pitti, they came at last to a full pause in the Tribuna of the Uffizi gallery. But oh! the wonders of this famed Tribuna consisted not chiefly in the ravishing Medicean Venus that was standing — apparently shivering with cold — on a pedestal in the middle of this octagonal cabinet; nor in the Madonnas of Raphael or Guido Reni; nor in that seductive masterpiece of the voluptuous Titian. No; not in these. But there sat before an easel the most transcendently beautiful creature that my American friend ever beheld. She was no picture or statue, but a living thing, transforming, with her magic brush, upon the canvas before her, a copy of that simple, honest-looking Adam that was painted by Cranach; and oh! how much more perfect was the copy than the original! It was Adam as he was in his innocence; and he seemed to return the sharp gaze of the fair artiste who was taking his likeness, as though he mistook her for his own gentle Eve, and wondered how she became enveloped in all that covering. The dear, good fellow! had he only stepped down out of that handsome frame, he might have seen Eve similarly situated on the wall behind the door — looking sweetly at, and apparently offering her apple to the young Apollo (in Parian marble) that stood lovingly before her. While my American friend was fast losing his senses over the charms and genius of this Tuscan artiste, he was suddenly brought round again by her saying: "Signor, if you weel, I sell you zis bootifule imitazceone for fiftee francs." Then rising, she walked away from the painting to point out its merits under the best advantages of light and distance — bending her swan-like neck a little to a side, and gazing at her work with a coquettish smile that was quite expressive of a thorough satisfaction. But what ugly limp was that as she walked across the room? and what horrid thump at every alternate step she took? Good heavens! she had a wooden leg! and see, her curls were coming loose! M. A. F. now looked again at the picture that had enchanted him so much, and discovered in the new light that he had been mistaken — it was a mere daub.

"*Non, merci bien,*" said he, "*je n'en reux pas,*" (he always spoke French to these Italians,) and away he went.

The guide now conducted my American friend to the studio of the celebrated Rootho Gordie, known as the greatest Madonna painter of the present century.

Passing through an ante-room, they there found some half dozen or more young ladies, lounging listlessly about the apartment; a few occupied in reading, and the rest in idle prattle.

"Who are these ladies?" inquired M. A. F.

"Zees ladees, seer," said the guide, "are zee môdels for zee arteest."

"But they are all faulty in many respects," returned M. A. F., in a language the models did not understand.

"Yes, seer; but zey all haf von fine traite in particulare, and zat constitute zee môdel."

"Will you please explain yourself?" said M. A. F.

"Wiz pleasure, seer; you see zat ladee wiz zee noble front — zee vat you call zee forehead?"

"Yes; but what good is a fine forehead with a nose like that under it?"

"Pardon, Signor; zee arteest he no want zee nose — he just use zee forehead — and he take zee nose of zat ozzer ladee vat you see by zee window."

"Ah, yes; that one has a fine classic nose, no doubt; but just look at her horrid mouth and shocking bad teeth."

"It ees true; but he get von booteeful mouth and pearlee teeth from zat ladee wiz zee one eye."

"Just so. I begin now to understand you. He takes the best parts of these models; flowing hair here, sparkling eyes there, and splendid bust yonder; ruby lips from one and rosy cheeks from another — combines them all in one painting, and thereby turns out a perfect Madonna."

"Eggzactlee, seer, you compreehend veree well."

They were now ushered into the studio proper, where the great artist was just at work drawing his inspirations from the exquisitely pretty hand of a poor young girl who had a crooked spine.

He received the visitors graciously; and, after showing them successively his entire stock of paintings on hand — mentioning the price of each — he politely requested to know which one or two or half dozen of these incomparable productions the "noble American Signor" desired to purchase.

The noble American Signor wound up this little business matter by purchasing a carte-visite photograph of the noble Rootho Gordie himself, which flattered that gentleman as much as if he had taken a thousand-franc painting. So the noble American Signor and his guide departed.

The next place to be visited was the gallery and studio of the great sculptor, Cutta Figuro. He was giving the delicate finishing touches to the eyes of a Niobe; and as the quick little strokes of the hammer descended on the tiny chisel, the small white crystals flew about as though they might be tears shed by the sorrowful image for the loss of her children.

The famed statuario was so busy at his work, that he did not observe the entrance of his visitors. Yet I suspect that, with all his activity, he was much longer converting this stone into a Niobe, than Jove was in transforming the original Niobe into stone. There was the poor model in plaster, all sprinkled over with geometrical sticks; as if it had been attacked from all sides by a tribe of savage Indians, whose poisoned darts appeared to be quivering in all the prominent points of her body. Or like the martyred Saint Sebastian, who was cruelly pierced through by a thousand arrows. A great many marble and plaster figures were scattered about this workshop — a whole mythology, in short, created from stone, that only wanted the important "breath of life" to set it in motion. Some half dozen sculptor journeymen and 'prentices, with paper caps and white aprons, were at work at the component parts of this mythology; polishing up a Flora here, and chiselling down an Ariadne in a quiet recess yonder; whilst others were shaping at the forms of a laughing Cupid, a jolly Bacchus, and a threatening Jove. They all looked as white as millers, from the dust of marble and gypsum that pervaded the room, and floated around their classic operations.

It was astonishing to see with how much stoicism these laborers worked at their divine trade. Their eyes did not sparkle with the light of inspiration; they did not pause to run their fingers through their hair; nor lay down the tools for a moment to rub their hands with gleeful satisfaction. No; not a bit of it. They plied their mechanism with no more poetry expressed in their looks or action, than may be seen in the poor hod-carrier who delivers the mortar that makes the rich man's palace stick together.

Here, too, the "noble American Signor" was expected to make about a ship-load of purchases; which, however, resolved itself into his becoming the proprietor — for a trifling pecuniary stipend — of a miniature in alabaster of the Leaning Tower of Pisa. This he took in his arms, and carried away in great triumph — visions flitting across his mind of having it standing upon a small table before him, on those future occasions when he should be lecturing to his countrymen about the curiosities of the Old World. But a great misfortune befell this precious trophy of art before even he reached his lodgings. As he was passing through the Lung Arno, he leaned for a moment over the parapet of stone that extends along the river-side, to gaze into the limpid water beneath, and on the numerous little boats that were flitting over its surface. During this interval he placed the alabaster leaning tower by his side upon the wall, and looked as though he was about to deliver a scientific lecture to the fishes, on this curious specimen of architecture, whose deviation from its perpendicular bothered so many learned heads; when the guide, making a sudden turn of his body, incautiously swept it off with the end of the umbrella that stuck out at right angles under his arm—and down with a crash went *that* Leaning Tower of Pisa, breaking into a hundred fragments, which mingled with the pebbles on the river-shore.

Coming from Florence to Rome by railroad, a pretty girl entered my compartment of the car, (the cars in Italy are divided by lateral partitions to about one-third their height; over which the occupants of one division can converse with those of the others — there being four to every car,) and immediately commenced a conversation with me. But on my giving her to understand that her language was too much for my comprehension, she said: "*Aha! si, si, Signor*," and turned her remarks to some ladies and gentlemen who occupied the next compartment. She was apparently about eighteen years of age; had long, flowing, raven ringlets; large and animated black eyes; a rich and beautiful complexion; a faultless figure; and was altogether charming to behold. She was splendidly attired, and to all appearance of genteel family. Her conversation with our neighbors became animated, and they seemed to take quite a fancy to each other. Presently she produced a snuff-box from her pocket and took a pinch; then passed the box around, and everybody took a pinch of snuff, as if it

M. A. F. WRITES BAD VERSES.

was the most natural thing in the world to do so. Looking upon this process as upon the going around of the peace-pipe among the Indians, I silently took a pinch of snuff also, and almost sneezed my head off as the consequence. By-and-by the young lady curtsied an excuse to me, and deliberately climbed over the partition into the next division, (exposing a pair of ingeniously worked garters,) where she could continue her conversation with more comfort, and which was interspersed with frequent requisitions on the snuff-box. As we approached Rome, however, the fair snuffer, with many other passengers, had disappeared, and the train became very much depopulated, so that every man almost possessed an entire compartment to himself, in which he could march from side to side, as we rushed along — like a wild beast in his cage. Indeed, my American friend carried out this idea in a letter which he wrote home, and which — there being no secrets between us — I was permitted to read. He sometimes writes verses, and on this occasion went on as follows: —

"The next coupé contained two growling men,
Like royal Bengal tigers in a pen,—
An Arab and a Greek I think they were,
And the adjoining one a Russian bear.
A long, giraffish-looking Mussulman,
Who was a Con-stan-ti-no-pol-i-tan,
Subsided in his stall with wondrous ease,
Next to a pair of chattering Portu*geese*.
My friend — 't would doubtless be conjectured soon —
Was still distinguished as 'that same old coon.'
And, thus proceeding, you may clearly see,
We constitute a true menagerie;
Just like Dan Rice's caravan, that still

Exhibits every year on Prison Hill;
Because, where'er our devious ways we thread,
The elephant is sure to be ahead.
With a keen relish of our vigorous chase,
He ambles ponderously from place to place;
Ascends a mountain now, and now a steeple,
And then comes down to mingle with the people;
Takes a great interest in the affairs of man,
And even strays into the Vatican.
Heigho! I'm weary of this latitude,
Where foul, malarious influences brood;
Where both the weather and the trees we scan
Suggest the comfort of a palm-leaf fan;
Where burning insects on a body *prey*,
In the most impious, sacrilegious way.
My comrade — in all kindness — is a fool,
To take the matter of this heat so cool.
Should fell disease, or even death betide,
It really would appear like suicide;
For 't was at foolish hardihood's behest,
And not the courage of a manly breast,
That thus we wandered forth in dubious ways,
To broil beneath an equatorial blaze,
At Leghorn, and at pestilential Rome —
I wish to goodness we had stayed at home!"

. . . .

"I read no more; but gently pulled his ear,
And bade him laugh away his *choleraic* fear.
'What! with such whimpering phrases would you rend
The heart-strings of your trans-Atlantic friend?
Distract her prospect of approaching joy?
Cheer up, and be a *man* again, my *boy!*'"

If my American friend does not soon recover from the cholera mania, I shall send him home. There is no danger in being here at all. I never felt more comfortable in my life than during my week's residence in this city. Even now there is a heavy shower, and it is thundering and lightning in a way that I never have seen equalled. This will purify the atmosphere, and make Rome as healthy as any place in the world.

To be in Rome—the Eternal City—the City upon Seven Hills—the city of Consuls and Emperors and Tribunes—the city of the Pope—is a privilege even now, in these days of railroads and unlimited locomotion, that is not vouchsafed to every man; and I feel that it is one of the great turning-points of my life—especially as it is to be the end of my journey, whence my course will be directed homeward once more.

Oh, Rollin and Gibbons, how you crowd yourselves upon one's brain at the sight of all these ruins! How you rush upon the memory here with a suddenness that becomes painful, after the long years of undisturbed quietness! The Forum, with its rostrum and temples to the heathen gods, where the plebeians gathered, where Cicero declaimed, and where Marc Anthony wailed over the body of the slain Cæsar; the remnants of the temples of Vesta and Venus and Mars, and of the habitations of Titus, Tiberius, and Nero; the gigantic fragment of the Coliseum, that has stood a score of centuries and more—where thousands of spectators gloated over combats between men and the wild beasts of the forest; and where, under the cruel Nero, the adherents of the Christian faith suffered the most frightful martyrdom—oh, who can gaze on these footprints of the past history, and not feel that men's use of the intelligence which distinguishes them from the brute creation has been a wonderful, unaccountable, and mysterious one!

The Capitoline Hill, the Tarpeian Rock, and the old dungeons wherein Paul and Peter were once confined, and the associates of Jugurtha and Cataline ended their lives; the Triumphal Arches of Titus and Constantine; the Augustus Forum; the Trajan Column, and hundreds of wasting ruins that are here, how they excite the wonder and quicken the recollection of the beholder! In fact, nearly the whole of Rome has such an antiquated appearance, that it seems the peculiar pride of all its inhabitants, that nothing should look new.

What shall I say of the great dome of St. Peter? It often happens that, from much reading and hearsay, people form such extravagant conceptions of certain great objects, as the Niagara Falls, the Ocean, the Alps, or a structure like this of St. Peter's, that when they at length obtain a view of them they are disappointed. But any conception that I had formed of this great edifice fell far short of the reality that I beheld. I have been in the habit of telling European people that I had seen no structure yet in this country equal to the Capitol at Washington; but that speech may no longer be repeated, now that I have seen St. Peter's. Some idea of the capacity of its enormous cupola may be conceived when it is stated, that from one of its inside galleries one may gaze at some angels in Mosaic on the opposite wall, and they appear of the size of a small infant; but when I walked around to that side and measured the foot of one of these angels, it was the length of my fore-arm from the elbow to the points of the fingers. This cupola was designed by Michael Angelo, and it certainly is the proudest monument that ever man erected to the perpetuation of his own name and glory. In entering the copper ball upon its summit (which appears no larger than a cocoa-nut from the earth's surface outside), I was obliged to squeeze myself through an opening scarcely large enough to admit my body, yet the interior of the ball has sufficient capacity for a dozen men. It is said that the present Emperor of Russia took breakfast in it with two friends on the occasion of his ascending the dome. The roof of the building outside of the dome is almost flat, and as large as a good-sized square in a city—say Franklin Square, in Philadelphia. It is paved and cemented like a street, and, with its many buildings and turrets, presents the appearance of a small town.

What St. Peter's is in comparison with other monuments of architecture, the Vatican Palace is in respect to other museums. For, as a general *receptaculum* for all manner of art specimens and relics of antiquity, it far excels the other museums of Europe that I have seen, not excepting the Louvre, of Paris. In the Sixtine Chapel I was quite disappointed with Michael Angelo's renowned painting of the Last Judgment. In fact, all his paintings and statues are extravagantly overdrawn, and easily distinguishable from all others by their excessive muscularity. He gives all his figures a gladiatorial appearance, and seems to make no allowance for any cutaneous covering. His statue of David, at Florence, and his Moses, in one of the churches in Rome, are undoubtedly his two finest productions, wherein his favorite display of anatomical knowledge is not so ill-timed as in some others — his Jesus, for instance, which is entirely overdone in this respect. I do not mean to undervalue the great talents and genius of that wonderful man; but feel convinced that among his manifold capacities of painting, sculpture, and architecture, the latter was decidedly his forte. In the Sixtus Chapel there is a frightfully graphic painting of the terrible St. Bartholomew's Massacre at Paris, which one of the Popes had the bad taste to honor and commemorate in this way. The St. Stephen's Church is distinguished chiefly for its capacious rotunda, and for its many paintings in fresco, that delineate, in a vivid manner, the various and repulsive means by which the early Christians suffered martyrdom in the reign of Nero. I visited the Holy Chapel, in which is the staircase said to be the same which Christ ascended when he was tried before Pontius Pilate. They are marble steps covered with wood (to secure their preservation), and no person is allowed to ascend or descend them except on bended knees. During my short stay there one Friday afternoon, the number of genuflexed pilgrims upon these steps was not less than fifty at the lowest calculation.

Next to St. Peter's, the most imposing church edifice in Rome is St. Paul's, situated about two miles outside of the city, and halfway between the city and a place where it is said St. Paul was killed. This pile of marble of the rarest qualities has already cost an aggregate of some *twenty million dollars*, and is not finished yet. Its great beauty and richness is more apparent in the interior than its exterior would indicate, which constitute its principal points of difference from the cathedrals of Milan and Cologne. It is built on the pure Corinthian style of architecture, and presents a harmony of parts that gratifies the eye, and fills the soul with insatiate admiration. While I was strolling about in its interior, among its forest of columns, admiring its ceiling of incomparable beauty, my attention was suddenly arrested by a great excitement among the numerous custodians and officials within and around the edifice. They were hastening hither and thither, calling to each other in Italian, which I did not understand, and apparently putting certain things in order for an unusual occasion. Then there was an influx of a stream of people, some thirty in number, which was followed by the tramp of horses outside, and the sound of a rolling carriage. Directly, several officers in cavalry uniform entered, followed by two gentlemen attired in priestly robes, and then came his Holiness, Pius IX., the Pope of Rome, after whom followed a small number of other officers and priests. Then nearly everybody in the church fell upon their knees, while he passed them, bestowing his blessing alike upon all, and entered one of the side chapels, where, kneeling before an altar, he engaged in prayer for about ten minutes, then returned into and walked around the body of the church, examining some new paintings that had been recently finished. During this promenade he was followed about by the people, who had by this time increased to a large number, and whose imploring looks he occasionally rewarded with his blessing and a slight inclination of the head. Whenever he stood still a moment they would crowd forward, and, the ladies especially, frequently fell upon their knees before him, and endeavored to kiss his feet. He was attired in a white merino robe, closed nearly to the throat, and over this he wore a cape of the same material, that just covered his shoulders. His waist was girdled by a white satin belt; his head covered by a small white cap, that was hardly distinguishable from his smooth gray hairs; his feet were encased in red morocco shoes, over the instep of which was a gilt cross.

He left the church, entered a handsomely gilt chariot, drawn by four magnificent black horses, and was soon on his way back to the city, followed by a mounted guard of gayly decorated soldiers. He has an extremely fresh and vigorous appearance for his age, and his face wears a cheerful and benevolent aspect. He is, I am told, kind-hearted and generous, and the people are devotedly attached to him.

LETTER XXII.

*THE APPIAN WAY.— THE CARACALL BATHS.— THE CATA-
COMBS.—CIRCUS MAXENTIUS.— CHOLERA.— THE DIET OF
THE ROMANS.— VISIT TO THE POPE'S RESIDENCE.— THE
PANTHEON.—RAPHAEL.—ADIEU TO ROME.—EN ROUTE TO
PARIS.—OVER THE MT. CENIS PASS.*

ROME, *September*, 1867.

ONE of the most replete associations with Roman historic memoranda is afforded by a drive along the Appian Way; and the first object that arrests the attention, outside of the present city limits, is the fragmentary remnant of the palace of Cæsar. Sombre and desolate, its broken arches and spectral corridors excite a feeling of awe; and, although owls build nests in the angles and niches of its crumbling walls, and no sign of magnificence clusters around the imperial pile of rubbish, there is still presented in the colossal proportions of the ruin, an evidence of its former grandeur.

After this, the next subject to explore is that which once constituted the celebrated Caracall Baths — for the Romans were as ablutionary then as they are absolutionary now ; — in other words, they have turned their attention from physical to spiritual cleanliness; and while the latter habit is a very good one, it is greatly to be regretted that they have adopted it at such a large expense of the former. This relic of the

Roman baths is, next to the Coliseum, the largest ruin of the ancient city. It is entirely roofless, and many of its compartments have been filled up by the material of the walls and ceilings that have tumbled down, to the height of ten feet and more. Some of its chambers, however, are still quite recognizable, even to the handsome mosaic floors, inlaid with small square stones of different kinds and colors. From the vast debris hereabouts have been dug, at various times until quite recently, many of the finest statuary and other relics that adorn the museums of the Lateran, the Capitol, and the Vatican. Even now men are still digging as ardently as Colorado goldsearchers, and ponderous pieces of corniced marble, with headless trunks of gods and demigods, may be seen protruding half-way from the rubbish; whilst here and there are strewn about all manner of heads that are difficult to define, whether they belonged to Jupiters or Centaurs.

We next came to an old and shabby-looking house, which is built, however, over a subterranean vault that constitutes the tomb of Scipio. There can be no doubt of it; for the names of numerous members of the family are engraved upon respective tablets, whose originality and genuineness are not disputed, and inspire confidence with reference to the record of the great warrior. It is not a tomb like that of Napoleon in the Invalides; yet the dust which it encloses was once as quick and fiery and warlike as that of the great Predestinarian. From this place it is not a great way to the church of St. Sebastian, under which is one of the entrances to the famous labyrinth of

Catacombs. These subterranean passages, with longitudinal niches in the sides, where the mortal remains of the first Christians were shelved away by thousands, are so long and serpentine in their course, that they encircle and bisect the city in various directions, and may be followed for miles to terminate at length in an outlet upon the sea. Occasionally these passages widen into chamber-like spaces, where the persecuted flock who worshipped the true and living God, held their timid gatherings for prayer and communion, far from the knowledge and observation of their Pagan enemies. Yet even here they were sometimes followed and massacred in great numbers. Guided by a monk, each of us holding a lighted candle, I wandered about in these dark, chilly, and awe-inspiring excavations upward of half an hour, and felt all the solemnity of groping through the narrow streets of a city of the dead — even such whose resurrection has already transpired, and whose empty dwelling-places returned the sound of human voice, as one might expect in the fearful silence of chaos. With something of constraint in respiration and all the functions of vitality, I emerged from this dread region, thankful to behold God's heavenly light and breathe earth's balmy atmosphere once more.

How different is the place where next we pause! It is the Circus Maxentius, that was built in the early part of the Christian era, is nearly fifteen hundred feet long, and over two hundred wide. Its walls are still in a pretty well-preserved condition; and at the end nearest the Via Appia are two round towers, the lower portion of which constituted the compartments of the slaves; whilst the top was for the trumpeters who sounded the charge for the charioteers who engaged in the races. The long parallelogram of walls is still very high; and the several galleries of its interior must have afforded capacity for a concourse of many thousand spectators. From here this "Queen of Roads," as it is called, is bordered on both sides with many antiquated tombs as far as Albano, some six or eight miles distant from Rome.

On my way back, as I was approaching the suburbs of the city, a poor victim of the cholera, enclosed in a plain, unpainted coffin, was carried by four uncouth, hard-featured men in shirt-sleeves, to his last home. Not that it makes much difference to one's body after death how it is disposed of; but this looked rather unceremonious, I must confess;—and, if it was a man that was thus carried away, I could not help hoping that he had no wife and children in America. My panic-stricken guide almost fainted with terror, and snuffed at his camphor-bottle with a vehemence that was ridiculous to behold. These Romans are very timid. One would scarcely suppose that they are the people whose ancestors used to throw themselves upon their swords at the slightest misfortune — or run one another through at the least provocation. Come to think, however, their feeling of self-preservation always over-balanced that of forbearance in sacrificing each other; and I believe that the Brutuses, Virginiuses, and Horatiis have not all died out — there being plenty who would probably immolate a sovereign, a daughter, or a sister, to appease the cholera; but would save their own lives if any amount of camphor on earth could do it.

The truth is, these people help to superinduce the prevalence of cholera by their excessive fear of it. Besides which, the great majority of them live squalid, in illy ventilated houses, and upon a diet almost exclusively vegetable. But, worst of all, their bodies are subjected to excessive carbonization by being over-taxed with labor under the noonday sun. It is among these, of the lower, and among the intemperate of the richer classes, that the cholera finds its victims. The decomposition of vegetable matter on low and marshy surfaces, and the prevalence of the Sirocco winds may do their share toward engendering cholera; but I am satisfied that every human being who gets it, contains within himself a morbid susceptibility, occasioned by a low state of the nerve forces; or by an irrational want of attention to hygienic laws. I have found, too, that cases are pronounced to be cholera that are not, in fact, anything of the kind. This dread malady has to father all sudden attacks of illness or death, though they may be occasioned by violent engorgements of any of the important organs. In hot seasons and climates, diseases of all kinds are generally more severe in their attacks, and more rapid in their progress than in the reverse circumstances. I visited, one day, the hospital that is exclusively appropriated for cholera patients at Rome, and saw several cases that I had no doubt were but violent congestions of the liver. To be sure, to die from the one is just as disagreeable as from the other; but then, the indiscriminate crowding of all manner of deaths under the black shadow of one tyrannical cause, is calculated to spread terror among the ignorant; and none other than evil consequences can result from it. When I returned to my hotel from the hospital, as above related, the landlord — who had already been informed of my heinous offence — ordered me out of the house, with permission to return only after I should have fumigated myself thoroughly with chlorine. So I went to a place where clouds of this vapor were curling upward from a vessel, and had myself done brown. After which, like a naughty boy who has just been spanked, I trotted, wiping my eyes, into my room. Ah, me! I have read Ik Marvel's delightful nonsense about a beautiful black-eyed Italian girl, inspired by the dying embers of a wood fire, or the spiral wreaths of smoke from his cigar. But, let him stand over a pot of *this* incense for fifteen minutes, until he can scarcely identify himself from a big chunk of cured — not sugar-cured — Cincinnati bacon, and *then* write about his "angelic creature," if he can — I defy him.

Allusion has been made to the diet of the people hereabouts; and I desire not to leave that statement imperfectly expressed, by omitting to say that the national regimen (though not entirely to the exclusion of other things) is composed largely of macaroni and onions. For the latter, some people substitute garlic, because, they say, *there is no taste in an onion*. I went with my guide into a restaurant frequented by the masses, and told him to order me a real Roman dinner; for I make it a point to find out the different *tastes* of people as I travel. What my dinner was composed of I have not the eloquence to describe; but during the disturbed sleep of the night that followed it, I had a vision — lo, an apotheosis! My American friend was ascending heavenward, wrapt in the drapery of an aromatic cloud. With him was an Italian poetess — a Signorita Piccolonioni. Above the twain, suspended by a golden thread from the index-finger of an angel, dangled, in provoking oscillations, a savory esculent, yclept an onion. With outstretched arms and tearful eyes they struggled, the one to get, the other *not* to get, the pungent bulb. 'Twas not the first lachrymose effusion at the sight of such an object. Suddenly, the golden thread separated; the angel dissolved, like a lump of sugar in a cup of hot tea; and the vegetable disappeared behind the larynx of the Italian songstress. The same vision — tableau number two: an Arcadian bower, festooned with pendent vines, loaded with a luxurious multitude of Isabella grapes. Within, in mealy ripeness, under the softening rays of the silver moon, sat my American friend by the side of the poetic Italienne. He had evidently become reconciled to her mode of living, and was breathing an atmosphere of pure delight. Many pleasant things had he, doubtless, said to her; for she answered him *a la* Pauline: "As the humming-bird banquets upon the sugary petals of buckwheat-blossoms and honeysuckles, even so do I, oh, my Columbian orator, drink in the sweet libations of your flattering phrases."

It was daybreak; and I awoke with a thick film upon my eyes, and an atmosphere in the room that you might have colored Easter eggs with. Relating the curious dream to my American friend, he replied: "Believe me, there is much poetry and inspiration in an Italian bill of fare. This is the land, my dear fellow, the glorious land, where you may 'find tongues in trees, books in the running brooks, sermons in stones, and '—— onions everywhere."

It would not do to leave Rome without paying a visit to the Pope's residence, for one is naturally curious to know how his Holiness fares in this "valley of tears," and whether he ekes out a miserable existence by "the sweat of his brow," or graciously leaves it to other people who are willing and thankful to sweat for him. I therefore wended my ways to the Quirinal Palace, and was permitted to pass through all of its gorgeous apartments, bedroom, dining-room, throne-room, audience and ante-chambers, galleries and libraries, all of which were furnished in the most elegant and elaborate style. Among the rest there is a billiard-room; and on the ceiling, directly over the table, is one of the finest paintings I have ever seen, representing Julius Cæsar dictating in four different languages to as many amanuenses, one of them being a female. His Holiness, it is said, is very fond of playing billiards, and is quite an adept in that exciting game of angularities.

Of all the architectural relics of ancient origin, that which still exists in its entirety, and in a comparatively good state of preservation, is the Pantheon, though many of the original statues and architectural embellishments, that, under the vicissitudes of time and dynasties, were obliterated or transported, have been replaced by the less classic productions of modern times. Yet the rotunda, unparalleled in point of capacity, with its mighty colonnade, presents to the beholder an example of man's constructive genius that overwhelms him with awe and admiration. Under one of the altars is the grave of Raphael, with the inscription on a tablet: " Born 6th April, 1483. Died 6th April, 1520," and on the wall, over the head of the grave, the epigrammatic lines by Cardinal Bembo: —

" Ille hic est Raphael, timuit quo suspite vinci
Rerum magna parens, et moriente mori."

I had just seen his sublime painting of the Transfiguration, that is preserved in the gallery of the Vatican; and could not help thinking that the homage which many generations of men have already bestowed upon his exalted genius, and the high and honored distinction which his mortal remains have received, in being enshrined in this illustrious monument, have been all, and perhaps more, than his most ambitious fancies could have dared to prophesy. Yet they were well deserved; for never was human intellect more godlike in its creative glory, than was that of Raphael; and his productions as far transcend all others in their almost living perfection, as the bright light of a noonday sun transcends the pale and sickly lustre of the moon.

The time has come to leave Rome, and begin the backward journey, which, God willing, will terminate at home. Again, I inquired whether it was not possible to sail from Civita Vecchia to Leghorn, or Genoa, or Marseilles, without being subjected to the unpleasant constraints of quarantine. I was told that it was not. I would be obliged to abide in the Lazaretto at least four days at either of those places. So no alternative was left but to proceed again by railroad to Leghorn, along the coast of the Mediterranean; thence to Bologna, &c. As we passed through the portals of the city, my American friend moistened the corner of his handkerchief with a tear that had been trembling on his eyelashes, and expressed his adieus in the following pathetic terms:—"Good-bye, Rome! You are an old town, and pretty badly wrinkled; but then you have nursed some ugly fellows in your time, and I am not surprised at your deep-drawn furrows and marks of desolation. I have much respect for your venerable age, but cannot say that I am filled with grief at leaving you, though your severe temperament, and quiet sombre aspect, would make you almost as desirable to dwell in as good old Orwigsburg. You have survived the ravages of time and adversity so reasonably well in the past, that I feel confident you will still be able to take care of yourself without my aid in the future. Preserve yourself well, old Town; for to get up another like you would involve the expenditure of more time, and money, and ingenuity, than the world can afford just now. You are like a photographer's negative, and many impressions have been taken from you; but if an earthquake or some similar accident should befall you,—though it is hard to say what a similar accident would be,—you would be *ruined* worse than you are now, and could never be reproduced. Therefore, take care of yourself, old Negative, and beware of the earthquakes and Garibaldis! Take care of your seven hills; of your Tiber River and many fountains; of your big church, your Pantheon and Coliseum; of your Vestal and other temples — your Trajan and other forums — your Tarpeian and other rocks; and oh, take care of the numerous relics of your *Pagan ninnies*. It is not very likely that we will ever meet again, old Town; but cheer up! there will be many an other stripling of the future, quite as zealous to spend his money and open his verdant eyes to have a look at you. And when the oblivious shades shall hide me from the memory of man, the prestige of your antiquity will still rejuvenate itself with every year in universal *greenness* for all time to come. Old Town, farewell." * * * *

PARIS, *September*, 1867.

As before mentioned, I was obliged to return to Paris by railway; and the route that I took was replete with interest and novelty to such a degree, that I do not now regret the necessity that spoiled my previous plans. From Florence to Bologna the road passed over and through the Apennine mountains, the grade most of the way being about one in thirty; and although the distance is not greater than that from Pottsville to Philadelphia, the road passes through *forty-seven* tunnels, scarcely any of which is shorter than the one at Port Clinton, on the Philadelphia and Reading road. Near the top of the road are several viaducts, spanning deep and wide gorges. From these the beautiful plains of Tuscany, with

Florence in the distance, and Pistoja with innumerable surrounding villages, all garlanded with vines, olives, mulberries, and magnolias in the near ground, form a prospect of the rarest and most exceeding loveliness. From Bologna I passed through a long section of the district of Lombardy, and arrived at Turin near midnight, where I remained until midnight of the following day.

Turin is a large city, having over two hundred thousand inhabitants, and is decidedly the most modernized, in point of architectural appearances, of all the cities in Italy. It has scarcely any traces of an old-fashioned character, its streets being laid out in such precise rectangular directions, and its houses having such a bran-new appearance, surrounding in several places such handsome public squares, that the first sight of the place occasions an agreeable surprise.

From Turin to Susa is but an hour's ride by railroad; and here begins the ascent over the Mt. Cenis Pass over the Alps. There were in all, when I passed over, seven diligences full of passengers, each containing about fourteen persons, and was drawn by two horses and *ten mules*. I took a seat in what is called the "imperial," right back of the driver, where a body has the best chance for breathing fresh air and viewing the scenery. Every team of horses and mules had six drivers — making twenty-one in the whole cavalcade; and it was amusing to hear these screaming at the poor animals, and calling them all by some name or other of the heathen gods; the Plutos and Cerberuses being the greatest in number; though occasionally they would yell out Juno and

Minerva, that would make the echoes ring among the crags of those snow-capped mountains. Running parallel nearly all the way with the stage-road, a railroad has been constructed; the engineers of which, I believe, are Americans. This railroad has a third rail in the middle of the track, which is clasped between two lateral wheels of the engine, that only roll in a forward, but not in a backward, motion. These wheels, by an easy controllable mechanism, can be made to clutch the rail so tightly that the impetus of the car's motion can be spragged off at will. I could not have an opportunity to observe their exact construction, but am told that it is very ingenious — and the running of these cars is going to be quite safe. Successful trial-trips have already been made, though in some places the road is, I really believe, almost as steep as that famous road which ascends Mount Pisgah, near Mauch Chunk, in Pennsylvania. Yet this railway is only to be a temporary one, until the great tunnel shall be completed. The speed at which they propose running over this track is twelve miles an hour, which will be a great improvement on the old mode of stage-coach travelling. The openings of the tunnel I have seen. This herculean undertaking was begun some twenty years ago, and will take five years more to complete it. It is estimated that, when finished, a railroad train will require half an hour's time to traverse it.

At St. Michel, on the Savoy side of the mountain, the passengers, myself among the rest, who had been pretty thoroughly shaken by our ten hours' ride in the diligences, entered a train of cars that were in waiting, and left about an hour after our arrival, the most of us for Paris. Presently the night closed over us, and the pearly jewelry of heaven sparkled in the deep-blue firmament, while the monotonous warblings of the katydids was heard above the puffing of our express engine, as we rushed and rumbled rapidly along over the curiously named "sleepers." There were some sleepers inside the cars, too; and as they generally subsided and collapsed into a state of somnolence, they afforded an interesting study to the anatomical mind, as to the various shapes, positions, and attitudes that the human figure is capable of assuming. Then turning our attention again from these upon the outside world, and the lovely constellation overhead, it was pleasant to see that we were moving regularly in the direction of the Dipper and North Star; for — it was a little warm down there in Rome, after all.

LETTER XXIII.

DEATH OF PROFESSOR WATTS.—DOCTORS TROUSSEAU, VELPEAU, AND NELATON.—A SPELL OF SICKNESS.—THE FASHIONS OF PARIS.—THE OPERA SEASON.—A MUSICAL ANECDOTE.—AMERICAN FRIEND IN TROUBLE.

PARIS, *Sept mb r*, 1867.

A SHORT time ago I had the sad privilege of attending the funeral service of Professor Robert Watts, of New York. He had been declining for many years with pulmonary consumption, and had come to Europe, in company with some of his friends, with a last, desperate hope of recruiting his health somewhat thereby; but shortly after his arrival in Paris he died. To me this circumstance was peculiarly impressive; for he was one of the members of my Alma Mater; and when, fifteen years ago, I was listening to his able lectures on anatomy, in the College of Physicians and Surgeons of New York, how little did I anticipate one day to assist at his obsequies, and that, too, in the city of Paris! Two of his associate professors, Doctors Dalton and Sands, were here, as also Professor Pancoast of Philadelphia, and quite a number of other American physicians. It was a solemn service indeed to those who understood its import; for there was a gathering of gentlemen in a foreign land, wishing, as it were, the soul of their brother and countryman God speed to that "bourne whence no traveller returns;" and though all the members of the family of the departed spirit were not present, yet the bowed heads and moistened eyes of all these sympathizing friends bespoke a mourning that was not of the surface only. The mortal remains of the deceased are to be conveyed, I am told, at an early day, by steamer, to America.

Since my departure from Paris in May last, death has also stricken the two great luminaries of the medical and surgical professions of this city, in the persons of Doctors Trousseau and Velpeau. The latter, though over fourscore years of age, had worked in his profession, and given counsel to the sick of the hospitals almost to the day of his death. But a few months ago I listened to his clinical discourse, and saw him execute an operation of the most delicate description on an affected eye. He was entirely a self-made man; and his success in life affords a graphic illustration of the results that may be expected from industry and perseverance when combined with talent. His education in youth simply amounted to this, that he was taught to read, and coming across an old doctor-book one day, which belonged to his father, who was a blacksmith in a country village, he read and re-read it until he almost knew its entire contents by memory. Then he commenced doctoring horses; and being successful, his opinions were soon consulted at the bedside of his suffering fellow-beings — and this was the beginning of his medical career. On one occasion, especially, the prompt though heroic exercise of a good sound judgment brought him under the notice of a celebrated physician, who thereupon took an interest in him, seeing the natural bent of his genius, and pointed out to him the possibility of acquiring a proper medical education. And now, being put upon the right track, and taught how to proceed, he applied himself day and night to study. Such diligence and persistency had never been surpassed. He lived and slept in the hospitals, and grew in knowledge and capabilities until, eventually, he attained and held, during many years, an eminence in his profession second to no other man's in France.

The great remaining light in the medical world of Paris now is Dr. Nelaton, who achieved such great renown a few years ago by curing Garibaldi; and since, recently, the Prince Imperial recovered from hip-disease under his treatment, honors and wealth have been lavished upon him so profusely that he has grown too independent to continue his duties in the hospitals and lecture-room. Instances of this kind are very rare; but I should judge from it, that doctors ought not to be paid too well — as they are apt to become spoiled by it.

I managed to become the victim of a right smart spell of sickness myself since my return to Paris; nor would I mention the circumstance, but that it brought me in communication with one of the medical institutions of this city in quite a different relation from any that I expected, or — I may modestly add — desired. My progress from Rome hither had been too uninterruptedly fatiguing; and it was not long before a congestion of the liver manifested itself, followed by a kind of break-bone fever. Finding I was going to be sick pretty seriously, I had myself conveyed to a sanitary establishment, called Maison de Santé, which should combine the comforts of a hotel with all the advantages and appurtenances of a hospital. Mind, I say, it *should* have these advantages; but let it not for a moment be understood that it *has* them. In the first place, the charge is eight francs, or a dollar and sixty cents, a day; for which amount one can obtain excellent pension or boarding almost everywhere, but here the sanitary character of the institution enables them to keep the boarders down to the very minimum of low diet. In the administration of medicines they are Allopathic, but in the matter of food the doses are exceedingly Homœopathic. The medicaments employed are generally of the cheap kind, as salts, castor-oil, ipecac, and all other things that keep a tight rein on the appetite; but at one time the doctor was seized with the extravagant idea of prescribing quinine for me. To this, however, I objected, appealing to his forbearance with all the pathos in my nature. "It really isn't worth while wasting such valuable medicine on my case," said I. "It is certainly good, excellent, *very* excellent — to *sell*, but hardly good enough to *take*. Oblige me by keeping it in your bottle; it will look so much nicer than in my stomach. Place it upon the shelf there, and let me gaze upon its snowy flakes — perhaps that will answer the purpose just as well. But oh, don't make matters worse by mixing it with the gall and bitterness of my existence! Let us trust to the '*Vis Medicatrix naturæ*,' and you will soon see how well-founded will be our faith." Well, we trusted, and I recovered, after the expense of an extravagant amount of patience on my part, seasoned well with the yellow lucre that contains the impression of his Imperial Majesty's likeness; for the officials of the Maison de Santé were not above bribery, and every crumb of the staff of life was almost worth its weight in silver.

Now, I suppose there are those among my readers, and the most amiable portion too, who would be right glad to know all about the fashions of Paris. Well, I will do what I can toward conveying an idea, with the premonitory caution, however, that all expectations must be limited; for my talent does not run in that direction. In the first place, Crinoline— that imperious and impudent fellow who has embraced the whole female creation these many years— is really in the decline; and the figure of the preferred sex, that has been a problematical mystery all this while, is beginning to assume shadowy outlines and proportions not quite so funnel-shaped as of yore. It is remarkable how reluctantly this habit is relinquished by the fair wearers. Like pretty house-birds, they have fluttered in their steel cages so long, that when they were opened, they have made little sorties into the outer world occasionally, but still to return to the accustomed restraint of these narrow domiciles in the end. At length, however, all affection for the cages seems to have waned away, and they are now hung aside upon the nails of attic joists, for the peculiar carnival of spiders and grand-daddy longlegs. The most positive proof that crinolines are among the things of the past is the fact, that they are not exposed for sale any longer — except in very out-of-the-way shops, frequented by the *demi-monde;* and there, I suspect, they are placed more for ornament (!) than with any hopes of selling them.

As to colors, it would puzzle the most astute observer to decipher which is the most prevalent. A walk through the Boulevard des Italiens, or the Champs Elysées, fairly bewilders a body with the multiplicity of hues. One seems to be jostling one's way through a grand confusion of broken rainbows, that perch on the heads of ladies, encircle their necks, hang negligently over their shoulders, twine around their waists, and droop in dazzling folds over their entire persons. In the article of dresses, however, I have observed a distinction of shade, and that most *recherché* at present is a kind of bright reddish-brown, —"chocolate color" is the name they give it here,— though in other countries it is known by the popular name of Bismarck. It is not that the greatest number wear this color, but certainly the grandest ladies do — those who drive out in splendid equipages, and live in magnificent residences,—points of observation not to be despised by a man who is trying to discover the fashions. The dresses are generally gored (I don't know whether I have spelled the word rightly — wonder if Webster does?) and short, which, in connection with the absence of crinoline, reduces the amount of material necessary to develop a "divine creature" to about half the quantity that was formerly used. What shall I say about bonnets? Not that there is any especial innovation upon the size and shape of those I have last seen in America — they could not well be smaller, that the dear knows; and for their size they could not well have any different shape. What a variety there is in the manner of trimming them! and, after all, in *that* lieth the secret of a "love of a bonnet." The proper arrangement and harmonious blending of materials and colors, so as to call forth the most charming effects, is the great art of this part of a lady's toilet. How frequently does a bonnet receive credit for setting off a head, when all the while it is the head that glorifies the bonnet. I have seen waving feathers, flowers, and ears of grain bend forward over a bewitching face like little Prometheuses stealing fire from the light of pretty eyes; but if the light of those pretty eyes did not exist, there would be no fire to steal. I cannot, of course, enter into a description of the different patterns of coats, sacks, sleeves, &c., but take it for granted that Mr. Godey has all these properly and brilliantly illustrated and explained in his Lady's Book. Or if he has basely and maliciously failed in giving the latest and most stylish cuts, then I am sure that Madam Demorest has not; and you need only refer to these works upon the fashions in order to be perfectly *au fait*, just as you would look up the definition of a word in the latest dictionary. Cashmere shawls, Alençon and Brussels point laces, diamonds, and Neapolitan corals are the great accessories that make up the attractiveness of a Parisian belle; the coral especially is very extensively worn, and as to the *point d'Alençon*, the high price to which this lace with invisible seams ranges, point out at once the *distingue* and wealthy character of the happy creatures who are privileged to wear it. A robe of this lace at the Paris Exposition was valued at the enormous sum of forty thousand dollars in gold.

As a curious fact I may state, that the latest style

of jewelry of every description is in the shape of a horse-shoe; thus you have little gold horse-shoes hanging from ladies' ears, uniting the collars around their throats, embellishing their wrists and fingers, and clasping the belts around their waists. They are ugly-looking things,— the trinkets, not the ladies,— and I cannot conceive by what eccentricity of fashion they ever came in vogue.

It is presumable from one's every-day observation, that every lady of distinction considers it an imperative necessity to take a little dog along with her whithersoever she goes, but especially when out walking of an afternoon. These precious pets are generally led (when not carried like infants in arms) by pink ribbons, and sometimes they are so numerous that they become a great annoyance to other people. The other day I inadvertently stepped upon the tail of one; and it was not so much the yelping of the little cur, as the horrified look of his proprietress, that made me feel as if I had committed a murder. She picked him up soothingly, and pressed him like a baby to her breast, where, apparently conscious of the warm maidenly sympathy he excited, the snarling brute whined and rolled his watery eyes about, and looked for all the world as sick as any canine sickness possibly could be. I offered to take his fair mistress to the dog-market, to buy her another; but she passed on with a scowl that I hope never to see duplicated on any female countenance again — or I shall certainly go crazy with remorse.

The opera season has now fairly commenced, and M'lle Adelina Patti was rapturously received on her *rentree* at the Italiens. She played Amina in La Somnambula ; and divinely did she sing, charmingly did she act. If the choicest bouquets that the flower-market of the Madeleine can produce can attest how much *la diva* is admired, then could there be no doubt of it. Whether it be that her voice has gained in mellowness and sonorousness by repose since last spring, or whether it be that absence makes the heart grow fonder, certain it is that the audience was enraptured with her.

It is interesting to stroll through the lobbies and saloons during the intervals of the play, and study the people and dresses that there exhibit themselves ; for people visit the opera in their most gorgeous array, whilst hardly any attention to dress is paid at the theatres. There is a curious little old lady here, who, I am told, visits the opera night after night from the beginning of the season to the end. She is taciturn and reserved, but two or three times during the progress of the piece, she has a *cafe noir* brought to her which she sips at leisure. At the termination of the performance, a footman in livery receives her at the door of her box, and takes her off — nobody knows where, and nobody knows who she is.

In brilliant contrast to this may be cited the instance of a very beautiful girl, radiant with youth and health, who is also here a nightly visitor with her "protector." She electrifies the lobbyites every evening with a new and gorgeous toilette. When I saw her she was attired in Bismarck satin inlaid with maize lozenges, and a splendid *parure* of coral set in dead gold. She appears passionately, feverishly fond of music, and seems scarcely to breathe during the performance; but during the intervals she recovers herself with ices and other refreshments. Whoever liquidates her financial obligations has, I should think, an expensive luxury on his hands, and must feel as if he had been presented with a white elephant or the Great Eastern.

I saw a little musical anecdote in one of the French papers the other day, worthy of being repeated here. The *dramatis personæ* of the story are Meyerbeer, Jenny Lind, and Viardot. Meyerbeer had been asked, whom he considered the most accomplished vocalist of the day; to which he replied: "When perfection of vocal facility has been attained by any two artists, it is very difficult to judge between them." Then he mentioned, that at one of the concerts he conducted, Lind and Viardot were to sing together his duet of "La Mere Grande." At the rehearsal, nothing was said about a cadenza, and none was tried. During the evening, he asked the ladies what they intended doing; and they replied, that they had not determined. The moment arrived for the duet to be performed, and they had evidently settled nothing. It was sung, however, with immense effect, being constantly interrupted by applause. At the pause for the cadenza, Meyerbeer raised his baton, and waited to hear what the fair vocalists would do. Viardot led off with a series of the most elaborate runs and *fioriture* -- her *cadenza* was a composition of itself. When she had concluded, to the amazement of Meyerbeer, Lind repeated every note of the entire cadenza that Viardot had sung, without a fault or the slightest hesitation. "This, to my mind," added the great composer, "was a most remarkable instance of the complete perfection of vocal facility which both of these singers have attained."

My American friend is in trouble. He has just been the recipient of a budget of letters from home, the writers of which, knowing that he is about to return to his native shores, all desire him to "do a small favor" for them; and "won't you be kind enough to bring" this, that, and the other "little matter" "along for me?" is the burden of their writing. One requests a set of jewelry, another a velvet coat, another a silk dress, another a lot of books, catalogues of the Exposition, and flute diagrams; another, some yarn of a certain kind; another, English lace for dress trimming; quite a number want meerschaum pipes; and one, a Newfoundland dog! "Now," said M. A. F., apparently greatly perplexed, "how am I to smuggle all these things in? for my correspondents seem to be unanimous in the opinion that I am not above smuggling. Just imagine an interview with the New York Custom Officer something as follows:

Officer, with the open trunk before him, "Well, sir, what does a gentleman want with a lady's velvet coat in his trunk?"

"Why, Mr. Officer, that is my *robe de chambre*, the latest style worn in Paris."

"But how about all this silk, eh?"

"Why, that is a handkerchief, sir."

"What! nonsense, a handkerchief fifteen yards long!"

"Yes, sir, I always use a handkerchief very long — especially when I have a cold; besides, I am very sensitive to the changes in the weather, and sometimes wrap this around me like a Scotch Highlander does his scarf, to keep me warm."

"Humph!" grunts the officer; "but how about this yarn?"

"Why, the sailors spun it for me, sir."

"Come now, you're a rum one, ain't you, to think of coming such a fib over me—when did they do it? tell me that."

"Between watches, sir, and when they were not busy tattooing blue ships and anchors and sweethearts on each other's arms."

"Pshaw! who ever heard tell of such a thing before?"

"Why, sir, permit me to say that you are sadly uninformed; if you will read Marryatt and other nautical philosophers, you will find it there recorded that sailors do spin yarn sometimes."

"But," quoth the Officer, "what explanation have you for this black lace trimming?"

"A very simple one, sir. You see I belong to the Order of the Knights of Babylon, and this trimming is a part of the regalia—every member being obliged to festoon himself with it from head to foot."

"Indeed! I never heard of that Order before."

"Ah, sir, it is evident that you never travelled in Europe, or you would know that the Babylonic knighthood there is a great institution."

The Officer scratches his head, as if in doubt what next to say or do, when he espies a lot of pipes in the bottom of the trunk. "Oho! what about these?" quoth he?

"These pipes? Why sir, I took them with me to

Europe for presents to my friends; but finding that my numerous German friends all had meerschaum pipes, I brought these back with me again."

"Well, what do you propose doing with this new gun?"

"That, sir, is for my own sporting purposes."

"Has it ever been used?"

"Yes, sir; I have been hunting with it."

"Where?"

"In the forest of Fontainebleau."

"What was you hunting?"

"Anything I could find in general, but principally, my way out of the woods."

"How about this jewelry?"

"Oh, sir, that is all galvanized trash — I will sell it to you for half a dollar."

"There," said my American friend, slapping me on the shoulder, as he closed up this long prospective dialogue with a custom-officer, "how do you think I will manage it, eh, my boy?"

I replied, that I thought he would do admirably; but expressed myself a little shocked (for I was always a conscientious tariff man, and went in strong for protection to home industry) at the cool effrontery that he proposed to assume in this transaction between himself and his country.

"Why," said he, "don't you see that my friends all expect it of me? They make no conscientious scruples about the matter; then why should I? Do you think," he continued, after a thoughtful pause, "that I will have any difficulty in persuading the captain of the steamer to stop at the coast of Newfoundland till I get that dog?"

LETTER XXIV.

*THRILLING INCIDENT OF PARISIAN LIFE.—A QUERY.—ANEC-
DOTE.— REMINISCENCES OF THE FIRST NAPOLEON.—
CEMETERY OF PERE LA CHAISE.—MANUFACTORY OF THE
GOBELIN TAPESTRY.—HOTEL DE VILLE.—JARDIN D'AC-
CLIMATATION.— BIRDS, BEASTS, AND FISHES THEREIN.*

PARIS, *October*, 1867.

HERE is one of the thrilling incidents of Parisian life. The other day a very young girl, with something in her arms that she carried with great care and tenderness, was gambolling merrily to and fro upon the Bridge of Jena; when suddenly, by some unhappy inadvertency, she dropped her precious charge over the railing of the bridge, and it fell with a faint splash into the river Seine. "Oh, the baby! the baby!" she screamed with wild and frantic bursts, "Oh, the dear baby! will nobody save my baby?" Among the many pedestrians who were passing over the bridge at the time was my American friend — a young and noble-looking fellow; heroism stamped upon every feature of his countenance; firmness and intrepidity settled in every glance of his eye. Without a moment's hesitation — without divesting himself of a single article of clothing, he leaped into the river — which was quite deep at the place — and swam with herculean exertion after the lost object, that was bobbing up and down in the water. At length he approached it; caught it tenderly around the waist, and raised it in the air to discover that it was — *a doll baby!* Pitching it back into the middle of the river, he made for the nearest shore; shook himself like a poodle, pulled up his coat-collar, and his hat down over his eyes, then hurried away under the eaves of the houses to avoid being carried home on the shoulders of the admiring crowd.

Indeed, I often wonder where the French novelists get the material for their books from — at least the tragic parts: they must have astonishing imaginations, for there appears nothing in real life to assist them; or if there is, it is kept out of the newspapers with exceeding care.

By means of the journals, during my travels on the continent, I have been more or less cognizant of the news of this city now for the past six months; and, I believe, during all that time there has not been a single fire, murder, robbery, abduction, elopement, or any other interesting event to afford characters that one might work into the chapters of a story — as they are worked into the tapestries at the Gobelins — with much twisting, and sorting, and tying of knots. To take the single matter of fires alone, and consider that in New York and Philadelphia hardly a night passes by without giving the gallant firemen an opportunity to rescue interesting maidens from the fourth-story windows of burning houses, whilst nothing of the kind is ever heard of here, though the city is larger than either of those just named, affords strange subject for surprise. Now, this thing is important — the contrast is too great to be lightly passed over — let us reflect! Can it be that there is no safety in a republican form of government? Is it because men individually cannot generally govern themselves, that they cannot do so collectively? Does democracy promote murder, robbery, and arson? Is it hopelessly identified with bribery and public plunder? If so, then let us get an emperor as soon as possible — perhaps Napoleon can send us one like he did the Mexicans. In alluding to the almost total absence here of those criminal exploits that are so frequently woven into rhyme and romance, I had forgotten a half-military anecdote that is just now in circulation. It is this: General Cluseret, returning home late one evening, was attacked by an armed brigand. So that, after all, it would seem that such events do take place sometimes. The great strength of the General rendered him indifferent to any approach of the kind, however; and he seized the ruffian by the throat and threatened to strangle him. On examining the captive more closely, Cluseret recognized him as a personage with whom he had already had dealings. "Why, you rascal, you are the same man who robbed my tent in Algeria of five hundred francs in gold!"

"Ah, General, but if you knew the circumstances. They had written to me from Europe that my poor mother was dangerously ill, and I wanted to send her some assistance. But I entreat you, General, have some pity on me; give me my liberty this time, and I swear to pass the rest of my life in repentance, after I shall have repaid you the sum I stole from you."

The General granted the prayer, let the fellow go, and thought no more about the matter. A long time afterward he received a box containing five hundred francs and the following letter: "This restitution, General, proves to you that a kind action is not always unappreciated, even by the poor outlawed brigand. To procure this sum, that I engaged myself to return to you, I have been obliged to beat out the brains of two men; to force three secretaries; and commit burglary on three inhabited country-houses. You see, General, that a benefit is never thrown away."

The other day I had curiosity enough to hunt up the different residences that the young Napoleon Bonaparte occupied, from his first arrival in Paris up to the 18th Brumaire, and the establishment of the Consular government. I had always been an ardent admirer of that great military hero and imperial parvenu. Sir Walter Scott suffered greatly, in my estimation, for the prejudicial life that he wrote of this unequalled chief, that seemed an impossible act from, and could almost make me weep tears of penitence for, the author of the "Waverly Novels," "Marmion," and "The Lady of the Lake." Well do I remember when Abbott's "Life of Napoleon" first appeared in "Harper's Monthly Magazine;" how long, for a season, appeared to me the intervals between those periodicals; and when they arrived, with how much ecstasy I pored over the partial, undoubtedly, yet perfectly just record of that wonderful life. This life passed again in panoramic review before my mind's eye, as the different homes of the great chieftain came before me, though some of them, and the neighborhoods wherein they are located, have, under the more peaceful reign of the almost equally great nephew, undergone many changes. The first of these was the *École Militaire*, where he was admitted from the military school of Brienne in October, 1784, and occupied a small room in the upper story of the establishment. Did he dream sometimes, while dwelling in these humble quarters, of the fame he was destined to acquire by the armies he would lead in battle? of the mutations in the affairs of France that would dethrone and decapitate the king whose loyal subject he professed to be, and make him — the occupant of that small chamber — the imperial sovereign of that bloodstained nation? No, he did not; for it was impossible that the wildest fancy should conjecture the events that could only bring about a change like that. He next lived in the house No. 5, *Quai de Conti*, in a small garret; then in *Hotel de Metz, rue du Mail*. Bonaparte being then a captain of artillery, was ordered to Paris to answer for some strong political opinions he had expressed. He probably little thought then what a shape his opinions would take ere long, and how they would mould the destinies of kings and nations. In 1794, he lived in the *Hotel des Droits de l'Homme* — he was then general of artillery. His friendship for Talma, which continued unabated to his death, commenced in this house, to which the great actor resorted to give lessons in declamation to "la citoyenne Petit," afterward Mme. Talma. Probably this was the most halcyon and undisturbed period of his life, when the quiet pursuit of pleasures arising from the associations of friendship conveyed that serene repose to which his speculative and ever restless mind was naturally a stranger. The next house he occupied was No. 19, *Rue de la Michodiere;* here he was without employment, and in very straitened circumstances. Was there no broker in all Paris that would advance a few thousand on the prospect of Napoleon's future? Bah! brokers are as stupid as other people, and could not see the dead certainty that would repay them with interest never heard of in financial annals before. Then, when in disgrace, he removed to the *Hotel Mirabeau,* where he occupied himself in visiting the members of the National Convention to solicit employment. In this hotel he slept on the eve of the 13th Vendemiaire, of that memorable day on which, having obtained the command of the troops through the favor of Barras, he defeated "the sections," and opened his way to the appointment of " General-in-chief of the Army of Italy." It was here that his successes had their beginning; and the star of his destiny, that had thus far but flickered coquettishly between light and darkness, darting forth occasionally a fitful flash, to be hidden again behind a great cloud of political obscurity, now burst forth in all the glory of its transcendent effulgence. He next occupied the *Hotel de la Colonnade,* where his marriage with Josephine was celebrated; after which he removed to No. 60, *Rue Chautereine.* That marriage with Josephine! had he but remained faithful to the sacred duty it imposed upon him, and clung, under all circumstances, to the chaste and amiable companion she had ever been to him, perhaps the morale thereof would have exerted a different influence on nations and himself, and the fate that overclouded his latter days might have been averted. He now assumed command of the Army of Italy, and returned hither again the following year, 1797, in great pomp and triumph. Here he received his appointment to the command of the expedition to Egypt; and from this hotel emanated those intrigues which led to the 18th Brumaire and his dictatorship.

The far-famed cemetery of Père La Chaise, situated on the slope of a hill to the north-east of Paris, affords a large field for a day's ramble among the many great names of the past, that are tableted over the ashes that once answered to them, quick with all the passions and agitations of life. Heroism, poetry, art, science, and genius of every description are represented in this garden of death for many generations of the past. Let us step lightly over this consecrated soil; for lo! we are gazing on the shrine that contains the once loving hearts of the gentle Eloise and Abelard. How we reverence their immortal love! and how the beautiful lines come uppermost in our minds,—

"Death, only death can break the lasting chain;
And here, even then, shall my cold dust remain;
Here all its frailties, all its flames resign,
And wait till 'tis no sin to mix with thine."

Here lies the dust of the satirical Rabelais, and of the exalted and classical Corneille and Racine; and yonder, in the Jews' Quarter, that of their most faithful interpreter, the tragedienne Rachel. There, a little farther up the acclivity, repose, in close proximity, the genial Moliere and the fabulistic La

Fontaine. How well and proper it is that their dust should lie so close together; for, I am sure, their lucid spirits commingle happily in the other world. Here lies the lyrical poet Beranger, and Judith Frère, whom he immortalized in song under the name of Lizette. Here, too, reposes all that is left of Bellini, whose sweet, melodious music has charmed the world wherever it is known. "Hear me, Norma!" with all its plaintive and fascinating eloquence, occurred to my soul as I stood over this grave; and the air around me seemed to vibrate with the spiritual warblings of "La Sonnambula," and swell up at last into the grand and soul-stirring liberty duet of "I Puritani." The grave of the eminent surgeon Dupuytren has an honored place in this honorable midst, not far from that of Napoleon's great army surgeon, Baron Larrey. And here one may read in quick succession the illustrious names of those gallant heroes, Kellerman, Macdonald, Masséna, Davoust, and many others. Of all the graves here situated, there was none the sight of which filled me with a sadder emotion than that of the ill-fated Marshal Ney. No monument or pompous inscription marks the spot where he lies; but the ground is laid out as a small garden, and the iron railing that surrounds it is mantled with ivy.

When, after the disastrous defeat at Waterloo, Ney was captured in the house of his kinsman, near Aurillac, he might have escaped from his captors by telling them a falsehood, or misdirecting them; and even from the gensdarmes while they were refreshing themselves at a roadside inn on their way to Paris; but he was too proud that he should stoop so low to save a life that he had risked so often where glory led the way. And when, a short time afterward, he was led to the place of execution, he refused to be blindfolded, and said to the soldiers who were to shoot him: "Soldiers, I have confronted death on five hundred battle-fields — too often to be afraid of it now. Aim at my heart, that I may die without unnecessary pain."

The number and costliness of the monuments of Père La Chaise, and the illustrious names it contains, will doubtless save it from the fate with which the other cemeteries of Paris are menaced, in consequence of the extension of the capital to the fortifications. Some of the monuments, of large dimensions and elegant architecture, represent temples, sepulchral chapels, mausoleums, pyramids, and obelisks; others cippi, altars, urns, &c.; most of them are enclosed with iron railings, and adorned with flowers and shrubs; and retired seats are provided for the convenience and accommodation of kindred and friends. A subterranean canal, which in olden time conveyed water to the Maison de Mont Louis, then situated here, still exists, and partly furnishes a supply to keep the plants and herbage in verdure.

Allusion has been made in this letter to the Gobelin tapestry. Let us now make a brief visit to the establishment where this tapestry and carpet are manufactured. The place and its artistical productions derive their names from two brothers, Gobelins, who were very expert dyers of wool in the fifteenth century. The establishment has been for many years, since the time of Louis XIV., owned and conducted by the government. Nothing is sold that is manufactured here, but retained in the Imperial family. The carpets and tapestries are of the most elaborate character and of indescribable beauty — it being almost impossible to distinguish them from the paintings of the ablest artists. Years of labor are sometimes spent upon a single piece of this workmanship.

The visitor will pass through five rooms, filled with rich specimens from the reigns of Francis I., Louis XIV., and Louis XV., besides many modern examples. Among the latter are copies of the Emperor and Empress, from the full-length portraits by Winterhalter, both executed in about four years; another from the Transfiguration by Raphael, which took six years; and of Juno, Ceres, and Venus, by the same master, which required four years to complete.

Next follow the work-rooms, six in number, containing twenty-five looms, where the operatives may be seen at their employment. In the tapestry work, which is called *tissu*, the warp is placed vertically, and the workman stands at the back of the canvas on which he is engaged, with the model behind him, to which he occasionally refers, in order to adjust the color of his woollen or silken thread to that part of the picture he is copying. The carpet work is called *velours*. Here the workman stands on the right side, with the model over his head. The carpets manufactured here are considered far superior to the Persian, for the evenness of their surface, the firmness and the strength of their texture. The colors and designs are perfect. Some of them are as long as ten years in process of manufacture, and cost from sixty thousand to a hundred and fifty thousand francs; and even at these high prices the skilful workmen are very inadequately paid. Connected with the manufactory is an establishment for dyeing wool, directed by able chemists, where an infinite variety of shades, many unknown in the trade, are produced. The closeness with which the painter's art is here imitated, cannot but excite the visitor's astonishment and admiration.

One of the most magnificent palaces of Paris, especially in its interior, is the Hotel de Ville, or City Hall, which has either survived the ravages of revolutionary spoliation remarkably well, or been most gorgeously renovated since. It is memorably associated with the war of the Fronde, and still more with the Revolution of 1789. It was from one of the windows of this building that the unfortunate Louis XVI. harangued the infuriated populace with the cap of liberty on his head; and from the same window, the noble General Lafayette presented Louis Philippe to the people in 1830. In one of the rooms of this palace Robespierre held his council, and once attempted to destroy himself. From one of its staircases, Lamartine most bravely exposed his life in 1848, by declaring to the enraged mob that so long as he lived, the red flag should not be the flag of France. We will pass by the Throne Room, many grand saloons, courts, and state departments, and stop for a moment to admire the *Grande Gallerie des Fêtes*, which is the saloon generally appropriated for occasions of great ceremonies, court balls, and receptions.

This hall is immense in proportions, and is separated from two others by two transverse arcades, the gilt cupolas of which support the orchestras; and one's first entrance into it has a magical effect. The spectator is bewildered with a profusion of decorations of every kind that baffles description. The Corinthian columns, with their gilt bases and capitals; the delicate sculpture and gilding of the compartments of the ceiling; the coves, painted by Lehman, representing Man exercising his activity and talent over Nature, Science, and Art, illustrated by a hundred and eighty full-sized figures, in fifty-six groups; the rich chandeliers and costly furniture — all these form a unique *ensemble* of taste and art. Communicating with this *Salle*, by open arches in the coves of the ceiling, is a gallery decorated with equal minuteness, where, on festive nights, the guests may witness the brilliant scene without mixing with the dancers below. Three doors lead into the *Salle des Caryatides*, which is a splendid Corinthian refreshment-room, the ceiling of which, painted in perspective, is supported by fourteen graceful caryatides. Two Ionic passages with elegant seats, communicate with the staircase, thus procuring a free circulation of air, and lead to the almost paradisiacal court or garden. Let the reader picture to himself this beautiful hall, illumed with floods of light, streaming from hundreds of tapers, arranged in graceful symmetry around, clustered in cornucopias held by cupids, or crowning the lustres depending from the ceiling; elegant fountains playing under the arch which supports the stairs, and forming miniature cascades, which, rushing through the artificial channels left between the costly flowers thickly planted around, find their way into the grottos beneath, where lovely genii are seen sporting in the cool waters, or peeping from behind the evergreens; — let him imagine this scene ingeniously diversified in the other gorgeous apartments, the whole enlivened by all the wealth, beauty, and fashion the capital can muster, and he will come to the conviction that the fairy dreams of the Arabian Nights may fall far short of the reality

One of the pleasant resorts in the neighborhood of Paris is the *Jardin D'Acclimatation*, which contains a large and curious variety of animated and vegetable nature. Unlike the garden of Plants, however, this establishment only harbors such animals of foreign origin as are fit to be domesticated; so that the visitor would in vain seek the lion, tiger, and hyena, which are here replaced by the hemione, tapir, Chinese pig, kangaroo, llama, besides various kinds of sheep, goats, stags, antelopes, gazelles, &c. The grounds comprise an area of thirty-three acres, beautifully laid out in walks encircling the pens or enclosures where the quadrupeds are kept, with picturesque little pavilions or cots containing the stables. They are intersected by a streamlet, dotted with islands, and spanned by rustic bridges. Here various aquatic plants are grown, while other rare specimens of vegetation abound on the surrounding grass-plots, such as the Spanish and California firs, the Japanese *Spiria Argentea*, the Chinese plum-tree, &c. Proceeding along the enclosures which skirt the rivulets, swarming with various kinds of fish, besides ducks, geese, and swans from Canada, Patagonia, the Sandwich Islands, Egypt, and other parts of the world, presenting a scene of agreeable animation, we arrive at the Aquarium, which is the chief attraction of the place, and beats the aquariums that of late years have become so very fashionable as ornaments in American parlors, graphically speaking, "all to pieces." Of the fourteen compartments which compose it, the first four are devoted to fresh-water fish, such as trout, salmon, eels, carp, &c. The habits of these finny occupants may here be accurately watched; whether to admire their almost transparent bodies, or to follow their motions upward, to dart at some fly, or downward, to rest themselves upon the sand. The three next compartments are chiefly tenanted by various kinds of sea-anemones, some of extraordinary beauty, attached here and there to the rocks with which the compartments are lined. Among these there are also sea hedge-hogs, starfish, &c., quite as sluggish as the anemones. The remaining places are occupied by zoöphytes, crustacea, molusks, &c.

Not far from the Aquarium there is an elevated artificial rock for the gazelles, pierced with a grotto, from the crevices of which a good view may be had of the surrounding scenery. Then there is a semicircular amphitheatre, with many-wired enclosures for poultry; and further on a vast Aviary, consisting of sixteen wired cages, each provided with a little fountain and shrubs, and tenanted by peacocks, pheasants, doves, and other gallinaceous tribes. It is amusing to see the keepers, after sunset, coaxing the birds into their respective roosting-places, an operation not always unattended with difficulty. The number of eggs laid here by the fowls is immense, and the sale of them produces an aggregate sum of ten thousand francs per annum. The last object of importance here is a silk-worm nursery, where important experiments have been made for the acclimatization of the Chinese and Japanese silk-worms, said to be hardier races than that of Europe, so subject to epidemics.

LETTER XXV.

THE RAILROAD DEPOTS OF EUROPE. — DEPARTURE FROM PARIS. — CROSSING THE CHANNEL. — SEA-SICKNESS. — CALAIS. — ARRIVAL AT LONDON. -- COMFORTABLE ONCE MORE. — THE TOWER. — ST. PAUL'S. — UNDERGROUND AND OVER-HEAD RAILROADS. — WESTMINSTER ABBEY. — LONDON AND PARIS. — HOSPITALS. — LIVERPOOL. — VOYAGE HOME. — AN INCIDENT. — M. A. F.'S " POME."

NEW YORK, *November*, 1867.

ONE of the most striking features of Europe, and one that impresses the stranger from America very favorably, too, is embodied in the magnificent railroad depots that the traveller encounters everywhere, in small unimportant towns as well as in great and commercial cities. They are perfect palaces to all appearance, exceeding generally in capacity any that we can boast of in the United States, except, perhaps, the famous depot at Chicago. Many of them are built of marble, most tastefully designed and embellished with many appropriate statues and bas-reliefs. And of these, perhaps none is more beautiful and costly, nor more perfect in style, dimensions, and arrangement, in whole and in detail, than the Northern Depot of Paris. It was in this edifice of imperial splendor that I bade farewell to the gay city, and was glad to enter — still weak and delicate from my recent sickness — the comfortable car that was to carry me to the brink of the continent, previous to crossing over into England. Only a few minutes, and Paris was behind us.

"Tell me, Charley," said my American friend, "can things go on as usual there, when we are absent? can all those gay and festive people still continue to be jolly after we have gone? will they ever be able to discuss their absinthe and their *café noir*, and make their horrible grimaces when we shall be no longer in their midst?"

I nodded that I thought they would, and away we sped.

It was the express train, and in about five hours delivered us safely at Calais. A short time previously, at Arras, the passengers were given five minutes time to gulp down a hasty dinner; but few availed themselves of the generous opportunity; for everybody seemed to have certain unmentionable misgivings about the effect that the crossing of the channel would have on these dinners if indulged in. One of the few, however, who knuckled down to the wants of the inner man was the subscriber; nor did he violate the laws of digestion by dispatching his dinner in the five minutes allotted by a railroad company, who evidently knew nothing about physiology. He carried the half of a cold chicken, a small bottle of claret, and a good honest chunk of bread with him into the car; then, with his handkerchief spread across his knees for a table-cloth, he was prepared to enjoy his meal leisurely, while the train moved on. An envious-looking Englishman in the opposite corner, who was watching this process, and saw the clean-picked chicken-bones pass one by one out of the coach-window, at length remarked:

"I am afraid, sir, that old Neptune will exact a heavy tribute from you, by-and-by."

"Are you, sir? Well, possibly he may; but I have just recovered from a spell of sickness, and am in the enjoyment of such a royal appetite that I would consider it sinful not to respond to it with the most obedient homage; and if the angry sea-god chooses to make me pay up roundly, I will have at least the satisfaction of knowing that the ugly feeling he occasions was preceded by a right thoroughly contented stomach."

As the toll which the sea exacts from uninitiated landsmen is only one of surplus gall, and I had none to spare, he knocked in vain at the portals; for my *portal* circulation was in excellent *humor*, and I was left in undisturbed possession of my dinner at Arras; whilst of the two hundred passengers on board, some hundred and fifty or more — my mistrusting English companion among the rest — with sallow skins and jaded, melancholy looks, paid up their dues to the relentless tax-collector, whose insignia of power is the awful trident. Indeed, the sight of all those sick people, with that display of tin basins that had been dealt out by the stewards, like cards in a game of whist, with a settled consciousness that there is no danger in the malady, was — to one who was not sick himself — about as droll and miserably ludicrous as any that can be conceived.

However, we were only two hours crossing the channel, and when we were standing on the white cliffs of Dover, it was gratifying to see how all the recently distressed faces brightened up again in the clear October atmosphere that floated about our heads like gaseous wine, strengthening the weakest of us almost instantly into vigorous vitality. We did not stand there long. There was a train of cars in waiting for us, and soon there was a general scramble for good accommodations and first-class corner-seats. It was quite a novelty to hear the guides and conductors sing out in English, "London, sir? will you go to Charing Cross, or Cannon Street Station, sir?" Even the passengers, who but an hour ago appeared to be French people, now chattered lively in the English language, as though they had thrown up all their French into the bosom of the ocean, and imbibed a healthy English vocabulary with the first whiff of air that rushed into their lungs on a solid bottom.

Soon we were rattling along, with almost lightning speed, by the pretty villages, beautiful roadside cottages, and famous hop-fields of the county of Kent; and arrived, at seven o'clock in the evening — twelve hours from the time of our departure at Paris — in the great metropolis of the world, London. The train had entered the city some distance before I was aware of it; for it was moving along on the elevated tracks, from which we had to look downward to see the roofs of the buildings; and I wondered for a while — it being in the dusk of the evening — what the countless little stacks and steeples of bricks signified, among which we seemed to be threading our serpentine course, when I was suddenly apprised of the fact that they were the chimneys of houses. We crossed and re-crossed the Thames twice, over two of the handsome and efficient bridges that span that river, and then glided slowly into the sombre enclosure of the Charing Cross Depot. Here I was detained but a brief period by the courteous custom officer, and then proceeded, in a Hansom cab, driven by a "coachy" perched high up at the back of the vehicle, to the quiet comforts of Morley's Hotel, in Trafalgar Square.

How pleasant it was to be installed once more in a cosy room, furnished with carpet — such a rare occurrence on the continent — and warmed (it was near the middle of October, and rather chilly out-of-doors) by a cheerful grate-fire all aglow with burning bituminous coal. And how gratifying it was to listen to the English questions relative to one's personal and alimentary requirements, propounded by genteel clerks and polite, sprucely dressed waiters! I don't believe that I ever enjoyed a meal in my life like that first supper in London. What a savory joint of beef was there, and what a luscious leg of mutton! and then the mealy and nutritious potatoes; the pearly wheaten bread, and sweet, delicious butter; the great mountain of old English cheese that graced the centre of the table, by the side of a small forest of celery in a towering cut-glass goblet! What! Dainty morsels of these viands, discussed at leisure, over a cloth as white as driven snow, and moistened under the gates of the palate by frequent libations from a mug of Allsop's beer — now, by the powers! if I were skilled in Epicurean lore, or had at my command the honeyed phraseology of Miss Leslie's cook-book, methinks I could grow eloquent on the subject, and delight my readers with inspired periods.

Of London, what shall I briefly say of the vast picture of a partly stationary and partly moving body of art that it presents, with its Tunnel, under the bed of a large river, and its railroads, now underground among the foundations of the houses, and now, as before mentioned, in the air among their chimneys? There is the grim-looking Tower, sombre and solid and ancient to gaze upon, almost shrouded under the clustering patchwork of historic memories, that cling to us more from the writings of the great Shakspeare than from either Hume or Macaulay.

There is the towering St. Paul's, cleaving and transpiercing the smoky atmosphere, till the gilded ball that crowns its steeple, fades away in the high distance, and becomes inscrutable to human eye, except on very exceptional clear days, of which I did not happen to experience any. Yet I have been on the highest outside gallery of its cupola, and gazed down upon the vast sea of houses, but dimly and imperfectly visible through the thick volume of fog and smoke that was between us, and saw the Thames like a gray and milky stream winding its course lazily along between the high palaces and royal governmental edifices that adorn a large portion of its shores. Then I have entered its interior Whispering Gallery, satisfied myself of its astonishing acoustic properties, and gazed down upon the people who were wandering about in the great nave of the cathedral, and looked like Lilliputian babies with precocious propensities for walking. Down below the building, among the consecrated vaults and proudly enshrined ashes of the great dead have I also strayed; where the sarcophagi of Wellington and Lord Nelson stand out in royal conspicuousness above the rest, teaching the same lesson there that we may learn in our own cemeteries, in comparing the costly monuments they contain with the plain tomb-stones that tell the simple record of more humble graves, that there is in reality such a thing as a mockery of aristocracy preserved by the living even among the dead.

Then there is Westminster Abbey, in the beautiful perfection of its Gothic architecture, with its remains of the great Queen Bess, Henry the Eighth, Mary Queen of Scots, and hundreds of others whose deeds and writings have preserved their names in the recollections of men for generations and generations to come.

I cannot describe the feeling that possessed me in view of these reminiscences which called up the great record of the past, in the instructive and momentous history of England, any more than I could depict the emotions that were called forth in migrating through the avenues of this great city, crowded with the present living. How queer it appeared to me, to see, painted on boards fastened to the actual corners of streets, the familiar names of the Strand, Fleet Street, Temple Bar, Cheapside, Lincoln's Inn Fields, Piccadilly, Paternoster Row, Bow Street, Regent Street, and hundreds of others that figure so conspicuously in all the novels that we have read time and again, and that make Dickens and Bulwer and Reynolds and Reade such very smart writers and cute observers of human nature, in our opinions.

Altogether, I was agreeably surprised with London, and found it a much pleasanter place than I had formed any idea of from my previous readings. Its streets were not nearly so narrow nor so muddy as I had been taught to believe — though my sojourn there was at an unfavorable season. It appears at once very and strikingly dissimilar from Paris in this, that, although it has many costly and magnificent public and private structures, some of which, like St. Paul's and Westminster Abbey, are unequalled in Paris, yet it does not indicate any general architectural ambition in the people who have built this city. Whilst Paris has pervading all through it an outward appearance of show and beauty,—which appearance Napoleon is constantly engaged in magnifying from year to year,— London, on the contrary, indicates a more general arrangement for business purposes and practical utility. And although there is nothing in the way of popular amusements and facilities for fun and frolic that may not be participated in London, yet there is something of periodicity observed in the indulgence of these things; whereas, the Parisians are governed by no set times, but a general seeking after pleasure seems to be the order of the whole day, and, apparently, the whole night too. In London you will see crowds of carts and omnibuses and cabs jammed up in the streets, and your ears be constantly greeted with the technical phraseology of teamsters and hack-drivers; the doors of public buildings are constantly swinging on their hinges; men are hurrying back and forth, hither and thither, in a quick, nervous, agitated gait, with business written on every feature, and indicated by every movement of their bodies — just as it is in New York; whilst in Paris, you never see a blockade of vehicles; the people never appear to be in a hurry, and there is comparatively little confusion, even in their great market-houses, during the busiest hours of the day.

There is nothing in connection with my tour that I regret so much, as that I was not enabled to remain a month at least in the city of London. It has so many excellent hospitals, so many charitable and noble public institutions to which I would have liked dearly to devote more than a passing glimpse, that the necessary brevity of my stay there was a great loss to me. One thing is sure, that, whatever England's faults may have been, there is no nation on the earth more philanthropic, and more active in the grand work of progressive civilization, nor more crowded with different societies whose ruling creed is charity and benevolence to all men, than she. And I am not ashamed to say, that my feeling toward the British Government, in lieu of the little that I have witnessed during my brief stay among its people, is much kindlier than it was before. Perhaps the very fact that I had been travelling during six months in lands and among people where nothing but German, French, and Italian sounds greeted my untrained ears, was enough to make me cherish a hearty attachment for a nation whose people first approached me with the pleasant and familiar language of my own country. I regretted especially that I was not privileged to devote more time and attention to the clinical service in the wards of the widely celebrated Guy's and Bartholomew's hospitals; but the limited observations that I did make in these noble institutions filled me with respect and admiration, for the exceedingly kind and humane bearing that is maintained by all the attendants upon the afflicted occupants; and by the very sensible and practical nature of the medical treatment that is there carried out. And while I listened in one of the amphitheatres to an instructive lecture by the distinguished Professor

Paget, in which he dwelt mainly on the advanced medical and surgical treatment of the present day, I could not but cherish a lively gratitude for his unbiassed candor. He frankly admitted, that the world was indebted, in a great measure, for our improved medical resources at the bed-side, to the rapid advances of Homœopathy. He did not use the hackneyed excuse, that there are cycles in disease which often require great deviations in treatment; and that, although in the maladies of to-day blood-letting may not be appropriate, yet that should be no reason why fifty years ago such treatment was uncalled for. He stated that he had not bled a patient in five years, nor had that sanguinary measure been resorted to with any of the numerous inmates of Guy's Hospital during a period of at least six months.

From London to Liverpool, a distance of two hundred and four miles, I passed by railroad in five and a half hours, and I think it was the fastest travelling I ever did in my life. We made but four or five stoppages on the road, and then only long enough to supply the exhausted engine with water.

The morning after my arrival at Liverpool, while in the breakfast-room of the Washington Hotel, (it almost seemed like home to be in a hotel called after that name,) I suddenly espied, among the guests seated at the numerous tables, Mr. and Mrs. B. Bannan, of Pottsville. It was quite a curious coincident, that after having accidentally kept clear of each other during the several months that we both were exploring Europe, we should at length, purely by accident, again meet on the very day of our departure from the

Old World, to find that we had unwittingly secured berths on the same steamer.

At noon of the 16th October we glided down the Mersey, on board the reputed fast steamer City of Paris, of the Inman line. After a rough voyage, during the first week of which we encountered many gales and head-winds, we arrived at length at New York on our fourteenth day out from Liverpool. Nothing occurred on board the ship during our passage across the Atlantic to distinguish it from any similar event, except, perhaps, the very trifling circumstance of a birth of twins among the steerage passengers, which my American friend considered of sufficient importance to commemorate with the following lines : —

> Down, underneath the hatches, in a gloomy steerage hold,
>   Where the sea against their cradle made an ever-wailing noise;
> Where no sunshine ever chased away the dank and loitering cold,
>   Two tiny little babes were born, two rosy Irish boys.
>
> A moment, and the billowy spot on which they had their birth
>   Could not be recognized again 'mid all the waste around;
> For them no blessed fatherland on all the wide, wide earth —
>   No fixed and cherished natal-place can evermore be found.
>
> And hark! the ocean sings to them a mournful lullaby;
>   It roars the smallness of the world into their feeble ears;
> Drowns, with its moaning surge and splash, their new-awakened cry.
>   The Ocean is their country, and the fishes their compeers.
>
> Rocked on the bosom of the sea, their Irish mother weeps
>   To see her own caressing cares thus early cut in twain.
> Her jealous heart, by day and night, its faithful vigils keeps;
>   Her soothing voice and cradling arms would tire the mighty main.
>
> Who knows but in a future day these native sailor-twins
>   May devastate a nation's forts, and raise another's joys —
> Two other Nelsons, in respect to all but Nelson's sins —
>   These on the surging broad Atlantic, free-born Irish boys.

LETTER XXVI.

REVIEW OF MY TRIP.—EUROPEAN MANNERS, CUSTOMS, POLITICS, &c.

POTTSVILLE, *November*, 1867.

IN a comparative allusion to the general topographical character of the two countries, especially with reference to their agricultural capacities, I would state, that nowhere in Europe have I seen land so rich in its productiveness as is the major part of our American soil. To say nothing of the vast plains in the Far West, where the pristine forces of the ground have never been drained by any cultured vegetation, or of the reeking fatness that throws such abundant harvests from the fields of Missouri and Illinois—we need go no farther than our own rich soil of the Lebanon Valley, or the beautiful district that is bisected by the East Pennsylvania Railroad, to challenge, for the abundance of their fertility, the choicest lands of Europe.

Of England it must be said, that it exceeds in its agricultural loveliness anything that is presented by the Continent. Intending no disparagement of the fertile plains of Normandy, in Italy, or the romantic, joyous, vine-clad slopes of Tuscany, abounding with mulberry and olive trees, all garlanded with the creeping vines of luscious grapes, or the flowery environs of Milan, Bologna, Pistoja, Florence, Genoa, Spezzia, and Rome, there is nevertheless such a rich, deep-green, healthful, vigorous growth that characterizes what little I have seen of England with exceeding excellence, carries rapture to every observant eye, and touches the heart with all the poetry of Nature.

In the county of Kent there is an especial beauty and freshness that captivate the senses with a delicious charm, and give evidence, not only of the natural resources that lie tranquilly dormant within the soil, but of the industry and scientific economy that make the best possible uses of the land. The gentle roll and undulation of its surface, just enough to break up the monotony of a tiresome flatness, clothed in a mellow and deep-tinted verdure, intersected by numerous hedges, whose bewildering entanglement affords an apt illustration of the general perplexity of all human affairs, dotted all over with multifarious trees, like the big and little spots that beautify the leopard; the copious and irregular sprinkling of snug and cosy-looking cottages, festooned with ivies and honeysuckles, and surrounded with collateral granaries, haystacks, dairies, and spring-houses; animated with sleek, happy-looking kine, sportive sheep, proud and imperious gobblers in a fluttering dominion of barn-yard fowls; the timid hare frisking spasmodically along the hedges, the shy squirrel, tumbling and rolling and leaping from branch to branch of the old royal-oak tree that stands by the side of the barn; pussy with her playful kittens having a frolicsome time on the greensward in front of the house, and Carlo, the faithful dog, basking dreamily under the genial rays of the sun on the back porch; while the flowers all around make the air redolent with an aroma of delicious sweetness,—all these constitute of the country districts, and rural life in England, a subject to which no words, nor the divine brush of Rosa Bonheur can contribute any adequate degree of justice.

Of Italy it has been said that it is the garden of Europe; but though it abounds in a variety of luscious fruits and vegetation that make it ornate and picturesque, there appears to be, nevertheless, a want of force and stamina in the soil that keeps the various grains and grasses down to a dwarfish relation with those of many other countries. In France and the south of Germany, when Nature is arrayed in her bridal vestment of summer, the appearance that she presents is luxurious in the extreme.

In northern Germany the ground is more gravelly, stony, in many places—as the district wherein Berlin is situated—very sandy, and not nearly so replete with spontaneous fertility as in the countries before mentioned. Still, by dint of industry, and the application of science, very excellent crops of grain and such fruits as are incident to the colder portions of the temperate zone, as plums, apples, pears, and cherries, are very generally harvested. Thus Nature has favored Europe with much of her sublimity; and though it has no lakes that equal those situated in the north-west of our own country, no rivers like the Mississippi and its tributaries, no cataract of water like that of Niagara, no plains and prairies, abounding with those other ornaments—luxurious eccentricities of Nature—the Indians and the buffaloes, like those of our Far West,—yet there are mountains and other scenery as wild and picturesque and majestic as any of our own continent; and its smaller lakes and rivers, as well as its old towns encircled with dilapidated crumbling walls, are associated with the sacredness of historic lore and traditionary legends, so as to attach more or less interest to almost every fragment of their construction.

As I was almost constantly on the great thoroughfares of travel, resting at the different important places only long enough to observe their most interesting features, and stopping, with a very few exceptions, at the hotels, which are pretty much alike all over the Continent, it will be readily seen, that my opportunities for social intercourse and observation of life among the masses were extremely limited. Nevertheless, without insinuating myself into the sanctity of their domestic affairs, I have seen enough to be well assured, that the people all over Europe are exceedingly sociable, comparatively happy, and universally cordial and good-natured.

In this latter respect, however, I beg leave to except Paris; for, although the Parisians appear to be possessed of great courtesy and kindness, yet I make bold to assert, that it is only so long as these qualities do not interfere with the smallest fraction of their own selfish interests. Their world-famed politeness is only a superficial glossing over of their true characters — a studied and artistic accomplishment of the brain, that has about as much to do with genuine good-will and generosity of heart, as the coat of varnish has with the uncouth knots and roughness of a pine board which it covers and disguises. They are about the most heartless people in the world, capable of no act of charity, except under the high pressure of the law. This extreme selfishness is, after all, the nucleus of their "Equality" philosophy and revolutionizing spirit, whose only alternative to the pursuit of extravagant pleasure appears to be an unconquerable thirst for blood. It is eminently necessary, therefore, that they should be kept under the iron rule of despotism; and Napoleon deserves great credit for the very effectual manner in which he does it. All the excellent qualities that characterize France, and especially Paris, all its royal splendor and magnificence, all its order and regularity, all prosperity in business, owe their continued existence to the great fiat of the law, carried out by the ever vigilant *sergeants de ville*, who are the intermediate vassals between the people and the great power at their head, that bends and moulds them to his will. I write advisedly of Paris; for I have been sick in its ungracious, inhospitable midst, and know that every smile costs a franc, and every apparently kind action a whole fistful of them.

How different is it in Vienna! There the people are affable and generous to a fault. You stop any one in the street, and ask him the direction to such or such a place, and though it be a mile off, he will insist upon going with you to the very spot that you are in search of. They say the most absurd things to each other without getting angry, and nothing can upset them in their irresistible flow of good humor. They are a mutual contribution society of little affectionate attentions to each other, such as one meets with nowhere else. I met an Austrian officer one day at Geneva; and ere we had been an hour acquainted, upon finding out that I would shortly visit Vienna, he insisted upon it that I should occupy his quarters, and make use of his servant during my stay in that city; "for," said he, "you might as well; the fellow has nothing to do, and the rooms are vacant. I would fain do my humble share toward extending to you the hospitality of the city." Indeed, I do not wonder that these good-hearted Austrians make such indifferent soldiers; the wonder is, how they could ever be induced to use the keen-edged steel and swift-winged bullets in deadly warfare against their fellow-beings at all. Even then they will be sinned against much more than sinning, and allow themselves to be cut up and slaughtered to the admiration of their enemies, and as martyred sacrifices to their social constitutions. It is amusing to listen to the good-humored way in which these people talk about their defeat at Königsgrätz; they "nothing extenuate nor set down aught in malice." Nothing can be equal to their ingenuous candor, unless it be that with which we Northern people of our own country have always admitted the disastrous defeat at Bull Run.

Then, there is Munich; another place where the citizens are as good-natured as the day is long. It is true, they are a little heavy from drinking too much beer; heavy in almost everything but music — and I am not sure but they are a little ponderous in that; for it is generally of that intensely classical style which none but a thorough-bred Teuton can understand. When on the subject of music, or seated behind their beer, the Munichians are like the rebels were — in this that they want to be let alone. Their great musical genius is Richard Wagner, the composer of Tannhäuser, Lohengrin, and Rienzi, and for whom their admiration amounts to positive frenzy. Whenever any of his operas are performed, the usual prices of admission are doubled; and the rush is so great that in order to obtain seats it is necessary to secure them days in advance. Yet from the history that was told me of a portion of his career, it would seem that he is a most unscrupulous scoundrel, this same Wagner of Munich. Having taken part in the revolutionary troubles of 1848, he was proscribed by the government, and was, on one occasion, at the point of being arrested in the theatre of Dresden, when his friend, Franz Liszt, the great pianist, who was musical director of the orchestra, apprised him of his danger, and secretly conveyed him from the theatre to his own house; after which he sent him, with a letter of introduction, to one of Liszt's friends at Zürich, in Switzerland. This kindness on the part of Liszt, and the hospitality he received from the gentleman at Zürich, he rewarded by imposing financially on the generosity of the latter, and, in the end, basely seducing his wife.

Oh, but to see these people of Munich drink beer! Staid, and dignified, and stiff-backed they sit at tables, with the capacious pots by their sides, and guzzle it down as if it was an inspiration from the gods, and every quart of it was worth a volume of the soundest dogmatism that was ever put on record. Yet it never seems to muddle their brains in the least, either. In connection with this subject I may say, that all over Germany — in fact, all over Europe — I saw but one intoxicated individual, during the whole time I was there, and that one was a sailor in Wapping, of the city of London. I do not pretend to say, that there is not considerable drunkenness in Europe, but if there is, I did not see it. People undoubtedly drink a goodly quantity of wine throughout the day, and always with their meals, as well as brandy with their café, but the latter is only imbibed from small glasses (which, I am told, are called " poney glasses " here), in which it is measured out to the drinker. Were any one to pour out for himself " four fingers' full," in a tumbler, as it is too often the case with us, it would be looked upon as a suicidal proceeding. Such a thing as " going on a spree," I confidently believe, is not known in Germany; and, in this respect at least, we in America have much to learn from the more rigid moderation in such things of the people of the Old World. As a matter of curiosity be it also said, that I did not observe a single person to chew tobacco; an inordinate quantity is undoubtedly smoked, in pipes and in the form of cigars, and a good deal is also stuffed up the nostrils in the form of snuff; but the chewing of it, with its accompanying filthy habit of spitting, is a very rare occurrence. Whilst stopping at one of the really fine hotels in Switzerland, a German gentleman seeing a spittoon placed by the side of a fluted column in one of the halls, not knowing what it was for, and being possessed of an inquiring mind, called the attention of a waiter to the pretty and still cleanly article of queensware, and said,

"Why do you have that handsome dish standing on the floor? That is no place for it; wherefore do you not remove it?"

"Oh, yes," said the waiter, with a perfectly sober mien, "that is an article that we keep there *for the Americans to spit in.*"

Another very important matter that forced itself upon my attention was the good behavior of the youth all over Europe, but especially in Germany. The children are not nearly so boisterous, fast, and progressive in all sorts of worldly matters as in our own country. Demonstrations of rudeness from them are nowhere to be seen; but politeness, and a due share of respect for all grown-up persons characterizes their conduct at all times.

Politically, the various peoples of Europe have, in truth, very little to say; they have only to come up to the requirements of the various sovereign wills that fate has placed over their heads, and that is all. Indeed, I cannot but wonder how a revolution on such a grand scale as France has several times been visited by, was at all possible, except by a weak army only partially under the control of the government, or through the spirit of dissension entering its rank and file. At present the armies of the different nations of the continent of Europe are so enormous in numbers, and kept under such perfect subjection, that all the governments may be looked upon as so many systems of purely military despotism. A great deal has been written recently by long-headed philosophers about an approaching millennium, when, it is hoped, all the great powers of Europe will unite in a general disarmament. Poor, short-sighted philosophers! Do they not see that the great armies are maintained not so much to wage war against a foreign foe, as to keep down in abject discipline the otherwise furious spirit of domestic revolution? With all despotic nations the armies, if they would sustain themselves, must always be increased in proportion to the increasing danger from the outraged and oppressed people. Small armies are only possible to republics. Thus, then, the people of Europe have little participation in political matters. Their free discussion is prohibited in the newspapers, and no opinions of any kind that do not strictly accord with the powers that be, either in public assemblages or in private intercourse, are permitted to be uttered.

To all persons who purpose travelling through Europe, too much stress cannot be laid on the importance and propriety of making themselves familiar with at least one of the continental languages; and of these the most important is the French, which is understood by almost all business people in Italy, and, to a large extent — especially on railroads and in the hotels — in Germany. It is extremely annoying and unsatisfactory to be sojourning among a people with whom one can have no verbal communication. Although it is possible to get along by means of interpreters and guides, who are always to be had; yet, to be dependent entirely upon these, constitutes one's enjoyment a very lame affair, besides being attended with considerable extra expense, as one is sure to be subjected to all sorts of inexplicable extortions from every direction.

LETTER XXVII.

CONCLUDING LETTER, BY MY AMERICAN FRIEND.

United States of America, a. d. 1867,
And of their Independence the 91*st year.*

MY friend has had *his* say in the preceding twenty-six letters, and I am afraid that he has inflicted therein a vast amount of wishy-washy stuff upon the dear, good-natured American public. As I take exceptions to these letters *in toto*, in sum and in substance, in whole and in detail, from beginning to end, as contrary to my loyal American feelings, I, therefore, claim it as my just right to be heard also. I am, like Elihu, the friend of Job, almost bursting to express my opinions, and "sink or swim, live or die, survive or perish," whether or no, come what come may, I am bound to let 'em rip.

In the first place, going across the Atlantic is a humbug; there is n't a particle of sense in it; it is worse than folly—it is madness. I paid an enormous big price to go in a nuisance of a French steamer, with a tempting bill of fare, and the wine thrown in for nothing. They know very well that nobody but sailors could eat anything if they would, and nobody but Frenchmen would drink their wine if they could; for, drawn ever so mildly, it is as sour as crab-apple vinegar. I did n't eat a dollar's worth all the time I was on board. Was sick all the way—sick! sick is n't the word; if there had been a prospect of a decent burial, I would have committed suicide; but there wasn't, and so I remained alive, to spite my enemies and the sharks.

Pah! I shall never be able to get the smell of bilge-water out of my nostrils; for my berth was near the rudder, and whenever the poop was struck by a heavy sea, the sulphuretted hydrogen, or whatever the abominable gas might be, would swell up like a whiff from the infernal regions. Goodness! to be laid up on a narrow shelf, with a tin pan fastened to the rim of it, for unmentionable purposes; with a tight bandage around your stomach, another around your head, the shelf twisting and grinding and rocking from side to side, and head to foot alternately — goodness! I say, where's the poetry, or comfort, or fun, or anything else but misery in crossing the sea. "But hold," says my friend, "you're going ashore again some day; you're not to float upon the mighty main forever." No; not if the court knows herself — and she thinks she do.

Hurrah! Land ho! Just look at all the people rushing for the sides and taffrail of the ship, peering through their double-barrelled spy-glasses, to get a glimpse of the promised land. Look at the bright smile that lights up their faces once more; listen to their shout of joy, will you? See how they go down stairs into the various cells of this floating dungeon, to pack up their fixings, strap down their trunks, and presently appear again on deck with new silk hats on their heads, and their best go-to-meeting clothes on their backs. Ha, ha, ha! I see that I'm not the only one that is anxious to get off the shaky foundation of this crazy ship. Steady there! look sharp, boys, when you go down that ladder, for its bottom end touches an empire. Well, what if it does? Hurrah for the President of the United States, anyhow! Hurrah for George Washington! Hurrah for General Jackson! Hurrah for the great and glorious Fourth of July!

Hallo there, you man on the wharf, with the brass coat and blue buttons — I mean the blue coat and brass buttons — how's a fellow going to get his things off that ship? "*Je ne comprend pas, monsieur.*" Oh, you be blowed! why don't you talk English like a gentleman and a scholar, and stop *parleyvooing* in that horrid style to your republican cousins across the ocean, and your betters?

The customs officer wants to know whether you have any cigars or tobacco, as if you was a smuggler from Cuba; you answer with a whopper, and say — *Non, monsieur,* like a perfect lamb of innocence, and pride yourself on your wonderful French pronunciation. Now you are fairly in for it, and the skinning begins; at least such was the case with myself; and the man that takes in the stranger approached me from every direction; — I found out that France was full of "poor boys," which was the definition I gave for a long time to the word *pour boire,* that was in everybody's mouth. By dint of these extorted bribes a man manages, from the time he opens his eyes in the morning to his going to sleep at night, to get rid of about as much small change as would buy shooting-crackers for a large family of patriotic boys on Independence Day.

Now being once more on *terra firma*, though it still seemed a little more *see-sawy* than before I entered that plaguey steamer, why, Richard was (without exaggerating the matter) himself again, and was, moreover, possessed of an enormous appetite, for the days of his fasting had been twelve in number. Accordingly, one of the first sights of the Old World that I familiarized myself with was the interior of an eating-house. I gave one of the satellites to understand that I was hungry and wanted something to eat. This I did in bad English; for whenever a body wants a foreigner to understand our sublime language, his first impulse, whereby he hopes to simplify the matter, is to mutilate the sentences and pronounce the words as execrably as possible. I found out, after a long and laborious conversation, in which any quantity of pantomime, shrugs, and grimaces were brought to bear upon my unsophisticated perceptions, that about the only substantial dish they were then supplied with was a *ragout de veau*, or stewed veal. Now the French, I have since learned, are a great people to serve up these *ragouts* — a form in which almost any kind of meat is most mysteriously disguised. Again, I found that in Paris an immense number of kid gloves are constantly manufactured; but the kid is purely an Irish idiom, for the skins that the gloves are made of are of the domestic animals better known as rats, not kids. These skins are so readily converted into the finest kind of coverings for human hands, all that is necessary is to stretch them, tan them, cut them across the middle, and double the four legs over for fingers, and the tail for a thumb; and, when finished, you have the very best of Jouvin's gloves — of all sizes, too, from those fitting the hand of a tiny little Miss, to that of a grenadier officer on dress parade. Sweet reader, can you draw the inference between the *ragouts* and "kid" gloves? As to myself, I cannot help associating the savory, highly seasoned French stews, with the dainty meats that once filled out these skins before they were gloves.

Oh, what boots the doubtful character of the *ragouts*, or the fricasseed fish that have been kissed by the perfume from the sewers, or the hundred nasty kinds of cheese, when they may be washed down by the delicious nectarine juices, or the bottled nepenthe of fragrant cognac? So says the enthusiastic tippler. Come, now; that is all a hoax; steady your nerves, my dear bamboozled friend, while I let you into the secret.

Behold, then! it is evening, and in the brilliant lustre that is shed upon the Boulevard des Italiens from the thousands of gas-lights, it is enough to make your eyes squint to keep the run of the two opposing currents of good-looking people who flit by you. You seat yourself among a crowd under one of the numerous awnings. You leisurely light a cigar, and smoke like the rest. Presently a *garçon* appears, and you order brandy and water — for you hate the sight, smell, and taste of their black coffee. In a few minutes the brandy stands before you in a graduated decanter, whose transverse marks denote the number of taken drinks as surely as the chalk record behind the closet-door of a country tavern. There is nothing amiss about the first drink, and you take the second to make sure of its quality; then you become absorbed in interest over the incidents of the moving scene before you, and, quite oblivious of your actions, one *petit verre* follows the other, until late at night, when, on rising to go home, you suddenly realize that you are drunk.

Now this is nothing more nor less than what will happen to you if you drink the same amount of Old Bourbon whiskey; and until French brandies can be drank with impunity without being followed by intoxication, I contend that they are not a jot better than the distilled liquors of our own country—no, not a jot.

As to the wines over which a large portion of my fellow-beings go into such foolish ecstasy, I abominate them all; they are either too sweet or too sour, too white or too red, too weak or too strong, too cheap or too dear; they split your head with pain, and your feet with gout, sour your temper and stomach both, and play the deuce with your feelings generally — they don't half come up to the currant and gooseberry wines of our own Pennsylvania manufacture.

The great and crowning bore to which every American is subjected when he visits the Old World, is the everlasting sight-seeing and rhapsodies he is expected to indulge in over the played-out relics of the dark ages. I walked in the great museums of art through gallery after gallery, and stared at the stupid designs and dingy, jaundiced-looking paintings, until my eyes and neck pained me to distraction, and my legs trembled with fatigue. And I venture to submit, that if the great army of men and women who utter their stereotyped admiration, or scribble it, nodding over the midnight lamp, into their diaries, were to be compensated with money, (as in the honest pursuit of a professional calling,) for the labor they incur daily, the pay they would demand would be a good substantial one, I warrant me, though all the rapturous feelings to be enjoyed were thrown in to boot. In sober truth, now, what is there in all the greasy daubs that decorate those "classic" walls, that can at all compare with the modern productions of photography, whose counterfeit resemblance of any given object is impressed by the bright god of day himself, and by those stubborn laws of nature that never deviate from a fixed precision? As to the painted mythological allegories that we pretend to gloat over, what in common sense is there, in all their heathenish fanciful discrepancies, that can possibly reward us for the trouble?

I have always had a more charitable feeling for the sculptor's art. There really is great skill and ingenuity in the creation of a correct and beautiful image of any kind from a block of marble. It is purely of art, requiring accurate manipulation of eye, muscle, and nerve to produce, that cannot be eclipsed by any mysterious, inscrutable laws of chemistry. It has a tangible shape, body, and outlines, and is altogether a much pleasanter object than the flat deception on a piece of canvas, which, unlike the sculptured figure, admits of no close investigation. But then, dear me, we have plenty of that sort of productions to admire in our own country; we have only to ramble through the multifarious and sylvan avenues of Greenwood, on Long Island, or Laurel Hill, at Philadelphia, and the prospect of every variety of chiselled marble that there expands itself before the vision should satisfy, methinks, the most Canovian mind. Besides, the ramble is associated with a lesson in morality; for it is well to see here what we may come to when we die.

Of all the stupid employments wherein tourists do engage, the most sublime stupidity selects that of exploring the tumble-down ruins of old castles built by our semi-barbarous ancestors. To climb up all manner of precipitous slopes, from the verge of rivers and lakes, over endless zigzag roads, to where

> "The eagle and the stork
> On cliffs and cedar-tops their eyries build,"

just to see how strong and comfortless and unapproachable those people could rear their uncouth homes, is a pleasure far beyond my dull perceptions; and I am thankful that such architectural folly was never perpetrated in America. It is much more agreeable to dwell upon the points of beauty, style, comfort, and the environs of our own Fifth Avenue and Broad Street mansions. Those European medieval dungeons, with horrid historic associations, and baronial halls are enough to give a body the ague or the rheumatism; it is sufficient that, in my youthful days, I have read the stories of their dark traditions, crouched near the flickering light of the fagots on the hearth, and I can well deny myself the pretended satisfaction of loitering among their goblin ruins.

Then there is the ascent of the customary number of Alpine peaks, the Rhigi, the St. Gothard, the Tête Noir, perhaps even Mont Blanc; oh, Jupiter! to what extremities men's folly leads them! How my friend would trudge on, with chamois-hunter's staff, and provision-pouch slung across his shoulders, working himself all aglow with bodily exercise and poetic fervor. Like that famous body of belligerents, he "first marched up the hill, and then marched down again." He had seen the sun rise and set — as if it was not possible to see that from the low purlieus of ordinary habitation; had taken snow in his hand during the hot summer months on those mountain tops, and examined it as if it was a Yorick's skull; had looked down into the misty clouds below him, and saw nothing; but, oh, how jaded and fagged out he was in the evening, when he went to bed! I was very intimate with him, and knew his secret thoughts upon the subject.

"Charley, my boy," said I, " why do you persist in tiring yourself out, body and *sole*, in climbing up these horrid mountains?"

"Why, my dear friend," said he, "there is a gigantic elephant on every mountain-top, and you know that, however inaccessible the animal may seem, I could never deny myself the inspection of him, wherever it is at all possible."

They have some grand churches in Europe, it is true; and I have run the risk of breaking my neck in going up many of their steeples; for it requires little less than the agility of a circus-actor to ascend some of them.

It is mournful to behold what base and impious purposes these churches too often serve. I have seen rencontres of nearly every description, of love, jealousy, and hatred, take place in the dark shadows of their marble columns; and have observed mysterious love-signs pass between spruce young clerks and pretty dark-eyed maidens, while the latter were on their knees, and mechanically muttering a *Pater Noster;* I have noticed dirty and importunate beggars and skulking thieves pollute, with their unholy presence, these consecrated naves; have witnessed the exchange of money for bartered goods in quiet nooks and private altars, between the worshippers of Mammon and the filthy lucre. Indeed, Rome, ostensibly the central city of Christianity, with all its churches, to the number of all the days in the year, has probably more unbelievers at heart in it than any other city of an equal population in the world.

I protest, finally, against the railroad system of Europe. Their little, suffocating boxes of cars, wherein half the passengers are obliged to ride backwards are a nuisance. You are suffering from bronchitis, or sore eyes, or a weak chest, or have an idiosyncratic horror of tobacco; when, presently, one of your fellow-passengers lights a cigar and smokes it. This is a signal for all the rest; cigars of every quality, sooty pipes, tobacco, tinder-boxes, and matches are brought to bear upon your nerves, and directly the volume of smoke in the coach becomes so thick and dense that you cannot see the man who sits beside you. Without seeing him, however, you beg him to be kind enough to open the window; to which he replies, with a grunt between the whiffs, that he could not think of it, for fear of taking cold. Almost strangling with the fumes of nicotin, you make a rush at the door, with the desperate intent of throwing yourself out; though your speed is thirty-five miles an hour, you have resolved to take your chances thus in a pure atmosphere, rather than perish in this poisonous exhalation; but the door resists — it is locked from without, and you are a prisoner. With a piercing shriek you fall back into your seat again, and pass over the remainder of the journey in convulsive agony. Such is the penalty of travelling in the railroad cars of Europe.

In sober earnest, now, let me say, in answer to the question that has been asked me by numerous friends, "Did you see any place in Europe that you liked better than America?" No, I did not. Much there was to admire in the path of my travels; the yearning wish that I confess to have felt for years has been gratified; and I cannot say but that it was entirely satisfactory. But I never loved America more than when I was away from its blessed shores; and I never cherished it so dearly as I will hereafter, as long as I live. The magnitude of the ocean, and the serener charms of the Adriatic and Mediterranean seas; the legendary and noble rivers — the Thames, the Rhine, the Danube and the Po; the picturesque beauties of the Swiss lakes, and the grandeur of its towering, snow-capped mountains; the historic interest of Venice and Rome; and the fascinations of London, Paris, Berlin, and Vienna, have all exerted their various and peculiar influences over me. But all the time I was never forsaken by an uncomfortable sensation — the consciousness that I was continually suffered to wander under the heavy shadow of despotism, whose dark and lowering wings extended outward over my fellow-beings in every direction, even unto the borders of the mighty sea. And when my truant feet touched once more the fixed foundation of our mother earth, at the city of New York, under the beautiful and redeemed banner of the Great Republic, I assure you, kind reader, that the contact sent a thrill of joy through every nerve, and filled my every vein and artery with rejuvenated life.

God bless our glorious country! and grant that it may ever be in the future a terror to despots and tyrants, and continue what, with divine grace, it always has been in the past — a refuge for the oppressed and persecuted spirits of every nation — " the Land of the Free, and the Home of the Brave."

THE END.

www.ingramcontent.com/pod-product-compliance
Lightning Source LLC
Chambersburg PA
CBHW030349230426
43664CB00007BB/585